Larsen, Leif.
Learning microsoft
cognitive services : use
2018.
33305243788985
sa   05/29/19

rosoft

rvices

Third Edition

Use Cognitive Services APIs to add AI capabilities to
your applications

Leif Larsen

BIRMINGHAM - MUMBAI

Learning Microsoft Cognitive Services
Third Edition

Copyright © 2018 Packt Publishing

All rights reserved. No part of this book may be reproduced, stored in a retrieval system, or transmitted in any form or by any means, without the prior written permission of the publisher, except in the case of brief quotations embedded in critical articles or reviews.

Every effort has been made in the preparation of this book to ensure the accuracy of the information presented. However, the information contained in this book is sold without warranty, either express or implied. Neither the author, nor Packt Publishing or its dealers and distributors, will be held liable for any damages caused or alleged to have been caused directly or indirectly by this book.

Packt Publishing has endeavored to provide trademark information about all of the companies and products mentioned in this book by the appropriate use of capitals. However, Packt Publishing cannot guarantee the accuracy of this information.

Commissioning Editor: Pavan Ramchandani
Acquisition Editor: Chaitanya Nair
Content Development Editors: Rohit Kumar Singh
Technical Editor: Ketan Kamble
Copy Editor: Safis Editing
Project Coordinator: Vaidehi Sawant
Proofreader: Safis Editing
Indexers: Aishwarya Gangawane
Graphics: Alishon Mendonsa
Production Coordinator: Shantanu Zagade

First published: October 2016
Second edition: October 2017
Third edition: September 2018

Production reference: 1250918

Published by Packt Publishing Ltd.
Livery Place
35 Livery Street
Birmingham B3 2PB, UK.

ISBN 978-1-78980-061-6

www.packtpub.com

`mapt.io`

Mapt is an online digital library that gives you full access to over 5,000 books and videos, as well as industry leading tools to help you plan your personal development and advance your career. For more information, please visit our website.

Why subscribe?

- Spend less time learning and more time coding with practical eBooks and Videos from over 4,000 industry professionals

- Learn better with Skill Plans built especially for you

- Get a free eBook or video every month

- Mapt is fully searchable

- Copy and paste, print, and bookmark content

PacktPub.com

Did you know that Packt offers eBook versions of every book published, with PDF and ePub files available? You can upgrade to the eBook version at `www.PacktPub.com` and as a print book customer, you are entitled to a discount on the eBook copy. Get in touch with us at `service@packtpub.com` for more details.

At `www.PacktPub.com`, you can also read a collection of free technical articles, sign up for a range of free newsletters, and receive exclusive discounts and offers on Packt books and eBooks.

Contributors

About the author

Leif Larsen is a software engineer based in Norway. After earning a degree in computer engineering, he went on to work with the design and configuration of industrial control systems, for the most part, in the oil and gas industry. Over the last few years, he has worked as a developer, developing and maintaining geographical information systems, working with .NET technology. Today, he is working with a start-up, developing a brand new SaaS product. In his spare time, he develops mobile apps and explores new technologies to keep up with the high-paced tech world.

You can find out more about him by checking out his blog, "Leif Larsen", and following him on Twitter (@leif_larsen) and LinkedIn (lhlarsen).

Acknowledgments

Writing a book requires a lot of work from a team of people. I would like to give a huge thanks to the team at Packt Publishing, who have helped make this book a reality. Specifically, I would like to thank Rohit Kumar Singh and Pavan Ramchandani, for excellent guidance and feedback for each chapter, and Denim Pinto and Chaitanya Nair, for proposing the book and guiding me through the start. I also need to direct a thanks to Abhishek Kumar for providing good technical feedback.

Also, I would like to say thanks to my friends and colleagues who have been supportive and patient when I have not been able to give them as much time as they deserve.

Thanks to my mom and my dad for always supporting me.

Thanks to my sister, Susanne, and my friend, Steffen, for providing me with ideas from the start, and images where needed.

I need to thank John Sonmez for his great work, without which, I probably would not have got the chance to write this book.

Finally, I want to thank my girlfriend, Christin, for her amazing support and patience through the writing process.

About the reviewer

Abhishek Kumar is a Microsoft Azure MVP and has worked with multiple clients worldwide on modern integration strategies and solutions. He started his career in India with Tata Consultancy Services, before taking up multiple roles as consultant at Cognizant Technology Services and Robert Bosch GmbH.

He has published several articles on modern integration strategy over the Web and Microsoft TechNet wiki. His areas of interest include technologies such as Logic Apps, API Apps, Azure Functions, Cognitive Services, PowerBI, and Microsoft BizTalk Server.

His Twitter username is `@Abhishekcskumar`.

I would like to thank the people close to my heart, my mom, dad, and elder bothers, Suyasham and Anket, for the their continuous support in all phases of life.

Packt is Searching for Authors Like You

If you're interested in becoming an author for Packt, please visit `authors.packtpub.com` and apply today. We have worked with thousands of developers and tech professionals, just like you, to help them share their insight with the global tech community. You can make a general application, apply for a specific hot topic that we are recruiting an author for, or submit your own idea.

Table of Contents

Preface

Artificial intelligence and machine learning are complex topics, and adding such features to applications has historically required a lot of processing power, not to mention tremendous amounts of learning. The introduction of Microsoft Cognitive Services gives developers the possibility to add these features with ease. It allows us to make smarter and more human-like applications.

This book aims to teach you how to utilize the APIs from Microsoft Cognitive Services. You will learn what each API has to offer and how you can add it to your application. You will see what the different API calls expect in terms of input data and what you can expect in return. Most of the APIs in this book are covered with both theory and practical examples.

This book has been written to help you get started. It focuses on showing how to use Microsoft Cognitive Services, keeping current best practices in mind. It is not intended to show advanced use cases, but to give you a starting point to start playing with the APIs yourself.

Who this book is for

This book is for .NET developers with some programming experience. It is assumed that you know how to do basic programming tasks as well as how to navigate in Visual Studio. No prior knowledge of artificial intelligence or machine learning is required to follow this book.

It is beneficial, but not required, to understand how web requests work.

What this book covers

Chapter 1, Getting Started with Microsoft Cognitive Services, introduces Microsoft Cognitive Services by describing what it offers and providing some basic examples.

Chapter 2, Analyzing Images to Recognize a Face, covers most of the image APIs, introducing face recognition and identification, image analysis, optical character recognition, and more.

Chapter 3, Analyzing Videos, introduces the Video Indexer API.

Chapter 4, Letting Applications Understand Commands, goes deep into setting up the **Language Understanding Intelligent Service (LUIS)** to allow your application to understand the end users' intentions.

Chapter 5, Speaking with Your Application, dives into different speech APIs, covering text-to-speech and speech-to-text conversions, speaker recognition and identification, and recognizing custom speaking styles and environments.

Chapter 6, Understanding Text, covers a different way to analyze text, utilizing powerful linguistic analysis tools and much more.

Chapter 7, Building Recommendation Systems for Businesses, covers the Recommendation API.

Chapter 8, Querying Structured Data in a Natural Way, deals with the exploration of academic papers and journals. Through this chapter, we look into how to use the Academic API and set up a similar service ourselves.

Chapter 9, Adding Specialized Search, takes a deep dive into the different search APIs from Bing. This includes news, web, image, and video search as well as auto suggestions.

Chapter 10, Connecting the Pieces, ties several APIs together and concludes the book by looking at some natural steps from here.

Appendix A, LUIS Entities, presents a complete list of all pre-built LUIS entities.

Appendix B, License Information, presents relevant license information for all third-party libraries used in the example code.

To get the most out of this book

- To follow the examples in this book, you will need Visual Studio 2015 Community Edition or later. You will also need a working internet connection and a subscription to Microsoft Azure; a trial subscriptions is OK too.

- To get the full experience of the examples, you should have access to a web camera and have speakers and a microphone connected to the computer; however, neither is mandatory.

Download the example code files

You can download the example code files for this book from your account at http://www.packtpub.com. If you purchased this book elsewhere, you can visit http://www.packtpub.com/support and register to have the files emailed directly to you.

You can download the code files by following these steps:

1. Log in or register at http://www.packtpub.com.
2. Select the **SUPPORT** tab.
3. Click on **Code Downloads & Errata**.
4. Enter the name of the book in the **Search** box and follow the on-screen instructions.

Once the file is downloaded, please make sure that you unzip or extract the folder using the latest version of:

- WinRAR / 7-Zip for Windows
- Zipeg / iZip / UnRarX for Mac
- 7-Zip / PeaZip for Linux

The code bundle for the book is also hosted on GitHub at https://github.com/PacktPublishing/Learning-Microsoft-Cognitive-Services-Third-Edition. We also have other code bundles from our rich catalog of books and videos available at https://github.com/PacktPublishing/. Check them out!

Download the color images

We also provide a PDF file that has color images of the screenshots/diagrams used in this book. You can download it here: `https://www.packtpub.com/sites/default/files/downloads/9781789800616_ColorImages.pdf`.

Conventions used

There are a number of text conventions used throughout this book.

`CodeInText`: Indicates code words in text, database table names, folder names, filenames, file extensions, pathnames, dummy URLs, user input, and Twitter handles. For example; "This can be achieved when we put some content into the `DelegateCommand.cs` file."

A block of code is set as follows:

```
private string _filePath;
private IFaceServiceClient _faceServiceClient;
```

When we wish to draw your attention to a particular part of a code block, the relevant lines or items are set in bold:

```
private string _filePath;
private IFaceServiceClient _faceServiceClient;
```

Bold: Indicates a new term, an important word, or words that you see on the screen, for example, in menus or dialog boxes, also appear in the text like this. For example: "Open Visual Studio and select **File | New | Project**."

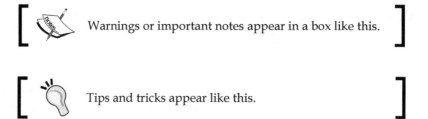

Warnings or important notes appear in a box like this.

Tips and tricks appear like this.

Get in touch

Feedback from our readers is always welcome.

General feedback: Email `feedback@packtpub.com`, and mention the book's title in the subject of your message. If you have questions about any aspect of this book, please email us at `questions@packtpub.com`.

Errata: Although we have taken every care to ensure the accuracy of our content, mistakes do happen. If you have found a mistake in this book we would be grateful if you would report this to us. Please visit, http://www.packtpub.com/submit-errata, selecting your book, clicking on the Errata Submission Form link, and entering the details.

Piracy: If you come across any illegal copies of our works in any form on the Internet, we would be grateful if you would provide us with the location address or website name. Please contact us at copyright@packtpub.com with a link to the material.

If you are interested in becoming an author: If there is a topic that you have expertise in and you are interested in either writing or contributing to a book, please visit http://authors.packtpub.com.

Reviews

Please leave a review. Once you have read and used this book, why not leave a review on the site that you purchased it from? Potential readers can then see and use your unbiased opinion to make purchase decisions, we at Packt can understand what you think about our products, and our authors can see your feedback on their book. Thank you!

For more information about Packt, please visit packtpub.com.

1
Getting Started with Microsoft Cognitive Services

You have just started on the road to learning about Microsoft Cognitive Services. This chapter will serve as a gentle introduction to the services that it offers. The end goal is to understand a bit more about what these Cognitive Services APIs can do for you. By the end of this chapter, we will have created an easy-to-use project template. You will have learned how to detect faces in images and have the number of faces spoken back to you.

Throughout this chapter, we will cover the following topics:

- Applications that already use Microsoft Cognitive Services
- Creating a template project
- Detecting faces in images using a Face API
- Discovering what Microsoft Cognitive Services can offer
- Doing text-to-speech conversion using the Bing Speech API

Cognitive Services in action for fun and life-changing purposes

The best way to introduce Microsoft Cognitive Services is to see how it can be used in action. Microsoft (as well as other companies) has created a lot of example applications to show off its capabilities. Several may be seen as silly, such as the How-Old.net (`http://how-old.net/`) image analysis and the *what if I were that person* application. These applications have generated quite some buzz, and they show off some of the APIs in a good way.

The one demonstration that is truly inspiring, though, is the one featuring a visually impaired person. Talking computers inspired him to create an application to allow blind and visually impaired people to understand what is going on around them. The application has been built upon Microsoft Cognitive Services. It gives us a good idea of how these APIs can be used to change the world, for the better. Before moving on, head over to `https://www.youtube.com/watch?v=R2mC-NUAmMk` and take a peek into the world of Microsoft Cognitive Services.

Setting up the boilerplate code

Before we start diving into the action, we will go through some initial setup. More to the point, we will set up some boilerplate code that we will utilize throughout this book.

To get started, you will need to install a version of Visual Studio, preferably Visual Studio 2015 or later. The Community Edition will work fine for this purpose. You do not need anything more than what the default installation offers.

 You can find Visual Studio 2017 at `https://www.microsoft.com/en-us/download/details.aspx?id=48146`.

Throughout this book, we will utilize the different APIs to build a smart-house application. The application will be created to see how a futuristic house might appear. If you have seen the Iron Man movies, you can think of the application as resembling Jarvis, in some ways.

In addition, we will be making smaller sample applications using the Cognitive Services APIs. Doing so will allow us to look at each API, even those that did not make it to the final application.

What's common with all the applications that we will build is that they will be **Windows Presentation Foundation (WPF)** applications. This is fairly well known, and allows us to build applications using the **Model-View-ViewModel (MVVM)** pattern. One of the advantages of taking this road is that we will be able to see the API usage quite clearly. It also separates code so that you can bring the API logic to other applications with ease.

The following steps describe the process of creating a new WPF project:

1. Open Visual Studio and select **File | New | Project**.

2. In the dialog, select the **WPF Application** option from **Templates | Visual C#**, as shown in the following screenshot:

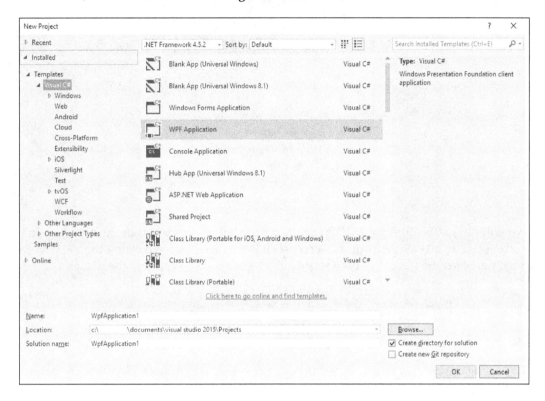

3. Delete the `MainWindow.xaml` file and create the files and folders that are shown in the following screenshot:

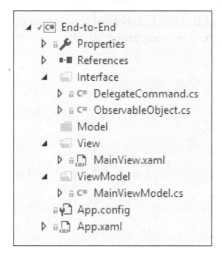

We will not go through the MVVM pattern in detail, as this is out of the scope of this book. The key takeaway from the screenshot is that we have separated the `View` from what becomes the logic. We then rely on the `ViewModel` to connect the pieces.

 If you want to learn more about MVVM, I recommend reading `http://www.codeproject.com/Articles/100175/Model-View-ViewModel-MVVM-Explained`.

To be able to run this, however, we do need to set up our project. Go through the following steps:

1. Open the `App.xaml` file and make sure the `StartupUri` is set to the correct `View`, as shown in the following code (class name and namespace may vary based on the name of your application):

```
<Application x:Class="Chapter1.App"
xmlns="http://schemas.microsoft.com/winfx/2006/xaml/
presentation"
xmlns:x = "http://schemas.microsoft.com/winfx/2006/xaml"
xmlns:local="clr-namespace:Chapter1"

StartupUri="View/MainView.xaml">
```

2. Open the `MainViewModel.cs` file and make it inherit from the `ObservableObject` class.

3. Open the `MainView.xaml` file and add the `MainViewModel` file as
   `DataContext` to it, as shown in the following code (namespace and class
   names may vary based on the name of your application):

```
<Window x:Class="Chapter1.View.MainView"

        xmlns="http://schemas.microsoft.com/
winfx/2006/xaml/presentation"
        xmlns:x="http://schemas.microsoft.com/winfx/2006/xaml"
        xmlns:d="http://schemas.microsoft.com/
expression/blend/2008"
        xmlns:mc="http://schemas.openxmlformats.org/markup-
compatibility/2006"
        xmlns:local="clr-namespace:Chapter1.View"
        xmlns:viewmodel="clr-namespace:Chapter1.ViewModel"
mc:Ignorable="d"
        Title="Chapter 1" Height="300" Width="300">
        <Window.DataContext>
            <viewmodel:MainViewModel />
        </Window.DataContext>
```

Following this, we need to fill in the content of the `ObservableObject.cs` file. We
start off by having it inherit from the `INotifyPropertyChanged` class as follows:

```
public class ObservableObject : INotifyPropertyChanged
```

This is a rather small class, which should contain the following:

```
public event PropertyChangedEventHandlerPropertyChanged;
protected void RaisePropertyChangedEvent(string propertyName)
{
    PropertyChanged?.Invoke(this, new PropertyChangedEventArgs
(propertyName));
}
```

We declare a property changed event and create a function to raise the event.
This will allow the **user interface** (**UI**) to update its values when a given
property has changed.

We also need to be able to execute actions when buttons are clicked. This can be
achieved when we put some content into the `DelegateCommand.cs` file. Start by
making the class inherit the `ICommand` class, and declare the following two variables:

```
public class DelegateCommand : ICommand
{
    private readonly Predicate<object> _canExecute;
    private readonly Action<object> _execute;
```

The two variables we have created will be set in the constructor. As you will notice, you are not required to add the _canExecute parameter, and you will see why in a bit:

```
public DelegateCommand(Action<object> execute,
Predicate<object> canExecute = null)
    {
        _execute = execute;
        _canExecute = canExecute;
    }
```

To complete the class, we add two public functions and one public event, as follows:

```
public bool CanExecute(object parameter)
{
    if (_canExecute == null) return true;
    return _canExecute(parameter);
}

public void Execute(object parameter)
{
    _execute(parameter);
}

public event EventHandlerCanExecuteChanged
{
    add
    {
        CommandManager.RequerySuggested += value;
    }
    remove
    {
        CommandManager.RequerySuggested -= value;
    }
}
}
```

The functions declared will return the corresponding predicate, or action, declared in the constructor. This will be something we declare in our ViewModel instances, which, in turn, will be something that executes an action or tells the application that it can or cannot execute an action. If a button is in a state where it is disabled (that is, when the CanExecute function returns false) and the state of the CanExecute function changes, the event that is declared will let the button know.

With that in place, you should be able to compile and run the application, so go on and try that. You will notice that the application does not actually do anything or present any data yet, but we have an excellent starting point.

Before we do anything else with the code, we are going to export the project as a template using the following steps. This is so that we do not have to redo all these steps for each small sample project we create:

1. Replace the namespace names with substitute parameters:

2. 1. In all the `.cs` files, replace the namespace name with `$safeprojectname$`

3. In all the `.xaml` files, replace the project name with `$safeprojectname$` where applicable (typically the class name and namespace declarations)

4. Navigate to **File | Export Template**. This will open the **Export Template** wizard, as shown in the following screenshot:

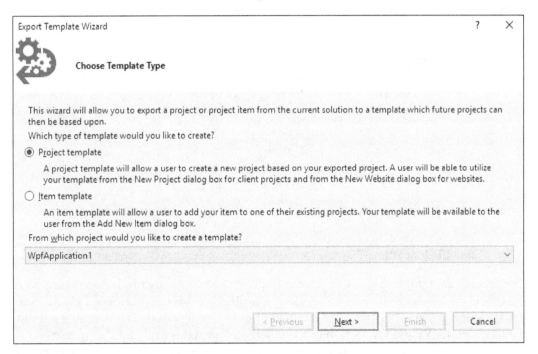

5. Click on the **Project Template** button. Select the project we just created and click on the **Next** button.

6. Just leave the icon and preview image empty. Enter a recognizable name and description. Click on the **Finish** button:

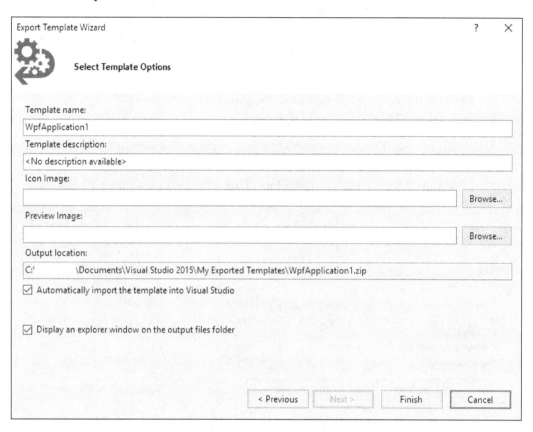

7. The template is now exported to a `.zip` file and stored in the specified location.

By default, the template will be imported into Visual Studio again. We are going to test that it works immediately by creating a project for this chapter. So go ahead and create a new project, selecting the template that we just created. The template should be listed in the **Visual C#** section of the installed templates list. Call the project `Chapter1`, or something else, if you prefer. Make sure it compiles and that you are able to run it before we move to the next step.

Detecting faces with the Face API

With the newly created project, we will now try our first API, the Face API. We will not be doing a whole lot, but we will still see how simple it is to detect faces in images.

The steps we need to go through in order to do this are as follows:

1. Register for a Face API preview subscription at Microsoft Azure
2. Add the necessary **NuGet** packages to our project
3. Add a UI to the application
4. Detect faces on command

Head over to `https://portal.azure.com` to start the process of registering for a free subscription to the Face API. You will be taken to a login page. Log on with your Microsoft account; if you do not have one, then register for one.

Once logged in, you will need to add a new resource by clicking on **+ New** on the right-hand menu. Search for **Face API** and select the first entry, as shown in the following screenshot:

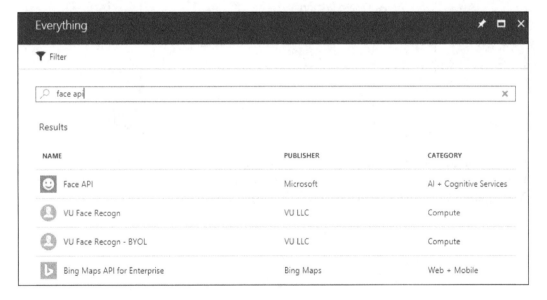

Enter a name and select the subscription, location, and pricing tier. At the time of writing, there are two pricing options, one free and one paid, as shown in the following screenshot:

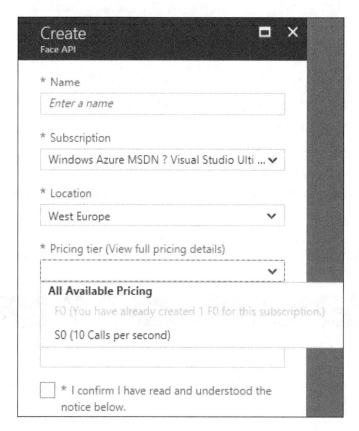

Once created, you can go into the newly created resource. You will need one of the two available API keys. These can be found in the **Keys** option of the **Resource Management** menu, as shown in the following screenshot:

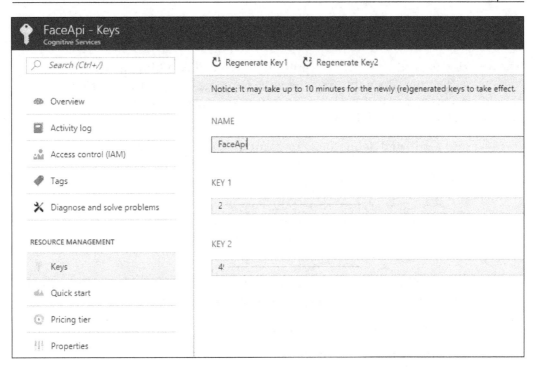

Some of the APIs that we will cover have their own NuGet packages created. Whenever this is the case, we will utilize those packages to do the operations we want to perform. A common feature of all APIs is that they are REST APIs, which means that in practice you can use them with whichever language you want. For those APIs that do not have their own NuGet package, we call the APIs directly through HTTP.

A NuGet package does exist for the Face API we are using now, so we need to add that to our project. Head over to the **NuGet Package Manager** option for the project we created earlier. In the **Browse** tab, search for the `Microsoft.ProjectOxford.Face` package and install the package from Microsoft, as shown in the following screenshot:

As you will notice, another package will also be installed. This is the `Newtonsoft.Json` package, which is required by the Face API.

The next step is to add a UI to our application. We will be adding this in the `MainView.xaml` file. Open this file where the template code that we created earlier should be. This means that we have `DataContext`, and can make bindings for our elements, which we will define now.

First, we add a grid and define some rows for the grid, as follows:

```
<Grid>
    <Grid.RowDefinitions>
        <RowDefinition Height="*" />
        <RowDefinition Height="20" />
        <RowDefinition Height="30" />
    </Grid.RowDefinitions>
```

Three rows are defined. The first is a row where we will have an image, the second is a line for the status message, and the last is where we will place some buttons.

Next, we add our `image` element, as follows:

```
<Image x:Name="FaceImage" Stretch="Uniform" Source=
    "{Binding ImageSource}" Grid.Row="0" />
```

We have given it a unique name. By setting the `Stretch` parameter to `Uniform`, we ensure that the image keeps its aspect ratio. Further on, we place this element in the first row. Last, we bind the image source to a `BitmapImage` in the `ViewModel`, which we will look at in a bit.

The next row will contain a text block with some status text. The `Text` property will be bound to a string property in the `ViewModel`, as follows:

```
<TextBlockx:Name="StatusTextBlock" Text=
    "{Binding StatusText}" Grid.Row="1" />
```

The last row will contain one button to browse for an image and one button to be able to detect faces. The `command` properties of both buttons will be bound to the `DelegateCommand` properties in the `ViewModel`, as follows:

```
<Button x:Name = "BrowseButton"
        Content = "Browse" Height="20" Width="140"
        HorizontalAlignment = "Left"
        Command="{Binding BrowseButtonCommand}"
        Margin="5, 0, 0, 5"Grid.Row="2" />
```

```
<Button x:Name="DetectFaceButton"
        Content="Detect face" Height="20" Width="140"
        HorizontalAlignment="Right"
        Command="{Binding DetectFaceCommand}"
        Margin="0, 0, 5, 5"Grid.Row="2"/>
```

With the `View` in place, make sure that the code compiles and runs it. This should present you with the following UI:

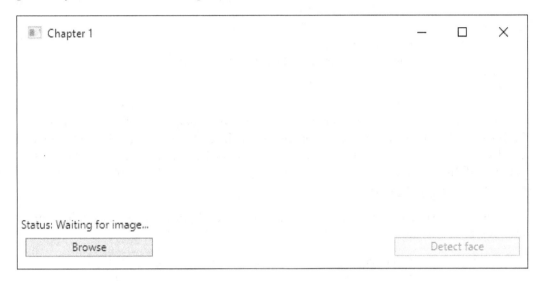

The last part of the process is to create the binding properties in our `ViewModel` and make the buttons execute something. Open the `MainViewModel.cs` file. The class should already inherit from the `ObservableObject` class. First, we define two variables as follows:

```
private string _filePath;
private IFaceServiceClient _faceServiceClient;
```

The `string` variable will hold the path to our image, while the `IFaceServiceClient` variable is to interface the Face API. Next, we define two properties, as follows:

```
private BitmapImage _imageSource;
public BitmapImageImageSource
{
    get { return _imageSource; }
    set
    {
        _imageSource = value;
```

```
                    RaisePropertyChangedEvent("ImageSource");
            }
        }

        private string _statusText;
        public string StatusText
        {
            get { return _statusText; }
            set
            {
                _statusText = value;
                RaisePropertyChangedEvent("StatusText");
            }
        }
```

What we have here is a property for the `BitmapImage`, mapped to the `Image` element in the `View`. We also have a `string` property for the status text, mapped to the text block element in the `View`. As you may also notice, when either of the properties is set, we call the `RaisePropertyChangedEvent` event. This will ensure that the UI updates when either property has new values.

Next, we define our two `DelegateCommand` objects and perform some initialization through the constructor, as follows:

```
        public ICommandBrowseButtonCommand { get; private set; }
        public ICommandDetectFaceCommand { get; private set; }

        public MainViewModel()
        {
            StatusText = "Status: Waiting for image...";

            _faceServiceClient = new FaceServiceClient("YOUR_API_KEY_
HERE", "ROOT_URI);

            BrowseButtonCommand = new DelegateCommand(Browse);
            DetectFaceCommand = new DelegateCommand(DetectFace,
CanDetectFace);
        }
```

The properties for the commands are `public` to get, but `private` to set. This means that we can only set them from within the `ViewModel`. In our constructor, we start off by setting the status text. Next, we create an object of the Face API, which needs to be created with the API key we got earlier. In addition, it needs to specify the root URI, pointing at the location of the service. It can, for instance, be `https://westeurope.api.cognitive.microsoft.com/face/v1.0` if the service is located in west Europe.

If the service is located in the west US, you would replace `westeurope` with `westus`. The root URI can be found in the following place in Azure Portal:

At last, we create the `DelegateCommand` constructor for our command properties. Note how the `browse` command does not specify a predicate. This means that it will always be possible to click on the corresponding button. To make this compile, we need to create the functions specified in the `DelegateCommand` constructors: the `Browse`, `DetectFace`, and `CanDetectFace` functions.

We start the `Browse` function by creating an `OpenFileDialog` object. This dialog is assigned a filter for JPEG images, and, in turn, it is opened, as shown in the following code. When the dialog is closed, we check the result. If the dialog was canceled, we simply stop further execution:

```
private void Browse(object obj)
{
    var openDialog = new Microsoft.Win32.OpenFileDialog();
    openDialog.Filter = "JPEG Image(*.jpg)|*.jpg";
    bool? result = openDialog.ShowDialog();

    if (!(bool)result) return;
```

With the dialog closed, we grab the filename of the file selected and create a new URI from it, as shown in the following code:

```
_filePath = openDialog.FileName;
Uri fileUri = new Uri(_filePath);
```

With the newly created URI, we want to create a new `BitmapImage`. We specify it so that it uses no cache, and we set the URI source of the URI that we created, as shown in the following code:

```
BitmapImage image = new BitmapImage(fileUri);

image.CacheOption = BitmapCacheOption.None;
image.UriSource = fileUri;
```

The last step we take is to assign the bitmap image to our `BitmapImage` property so that the image is shown in the UI. We also update the status text to let the user know that the image has been loaded, as shown in the following code:

```
    ImageSource = image;
    StatusText = "Status: Image loaded...";
}
```

The `CanDetectFace` function checks whether or not the `DetectFacesButton` button should be enabled. In this case, it checks whether our image property actually has a URI. If it does by extension, then that means that we have an image and we should be able to detect faces, as shown in the following code:

```
    private boolCanDetectFace(object obj)
    {
        return !string.IsNullOrEmpty(ImageSource?.UriSource.
ToString());
    }
```

Our `DetectFace` method calls an `async` method to upload and detect faces. The return value contains an array of the `FaceRectangles` variable. This array contains the rectangle area for all face positions in the given image. We will look into the function that we are going to call in a bit.

After the call has finished executing, we print a line containing the number of faces to the debug console window, as follows:

```
    private async void DetectFace(object obj)
    {
        FaceRectangle[] faceRects = await UploadAndDetectFacesAsync();

        string textToSpeak = "No faces detected";

        if (faceRects.Length == 1)
            textToSpeak = "1 face detected";
        else if (faceRects.Length> 1)
            textToSpeak = $"{faceRects.Length} faces detected";

        Debug.WriteLine(textToSpeak);
    }
```

In the `UploadAndDetectFacesAsync` function, we create a `Stream` from the image, as shown in the following code. This stream will be used as input for the actual call to the Face API service:

```
private async Task<FaceRectangle[]>UploadAndDetectFacesAsync()
{
    StatusText = "Status: Detecting faces...";

    try
    {
        using (Stream imageFileStream = File.OpenRead(_filePath))
```

The following line is the actual call to the detection endpoint for the Face API:

```
Face[] faces = await _faceServiceClient.
DetectAsync(imageFileStream, true, true, new List<FaceAttributeType>()
{ FaceAttributeType.Age });
```

The first parameter is the file stream that we created in the previous step. The rest of the parameters are all optional. The second parameter should be `true` if you want to get a face ID. The next parameter specifies whether you want to receive face landmarks or not. The last parameter takes a list of facial attributes that you may want to receive. In our case, we want the `age` parameter to be returned, so we need to specify that.

The return type of this function call is an array of faces, with all the parameters that you have specified, as shown in the following code:

```
        List<double> ages = faces.Select(face =>face.
FaceAttributes.Age).ToList();
        FaceRectangle[] faceRects = faces.Select(face =>face.
FaceRectangle).ToArray();

        StatusText = "Status: Finished detecting faces...";

        foreach(var age in ages) {
            Console.WriteLine(age);
        }
        return faceRects;
    }
}
```

The first line iterates over all faces and retrieves the approximate age of all faces. This is later printed to the debug console window, in the foreach loop.

The second line iterates over all faces and retrieves the face rectangle, with the rectangular location of all faces. This is the data that we return to the calling function.

Add a catch clause to finish the method. Where an exception is thrown in our API call, we catch that. We want to show the error message and return an empty FaceRectangle array.

With that code in place, you should now be able to run the full example. The end result will look like the following screenshot:

The result debug console window will print the following text:

```
1 face detected
23,7
```

An overview of different APIs

Now that you have seen a basic example of how to detect faces, it is time to learn a bit about what else Cognitive Services can do for you. When using Cognitive Services, you have 21 different APIs to hand. These are, in turn, separated into five top-level domains depending on what they do. These domains are vision, speech, language, knowledge, and search. We will learn more about them in the following sections.

Vision

APIs under the **vision** flags allow your apps to understand images and video content. They allow you to retrieve information about faces, feelings, and other visual content. You can stabilize videos and recognize celebrities. You can read text in images and generate thumbnails from videos and images.

There are four APIs contained in the vision domain, which we will look at now.

Computer vision

Using the **computer vision** API, you can retrieve actionable information from images. This means that you can identify content (such as image format, image size, colors, faces, and more). You can detect whether or not an image is adult/racy. This API can recognize text in images and extract it to machine-readable words. It can detect celebrities from a variety of areas. Lastly, it can generate storage-efficient thumbnails with smart-cropping functionality.

We will look into computer vision in *Chapter 2, Analyzing Images to Recognize a Face*.

Face

We have already seen a very basic example of what the Face API can do. The rest of the API revolves around the detection, identification, organization, and tagging of faces in photos. As well as face detection, you can also see how likely it is that two faces belong to the same person. You can identify faces and also find similar-looking faces. We can also use the API to recognize emotions in images.

We will dive further into the Face API in *Chapter 2, Analyzing Images to Recognize a Face*.

Video indexer

Using the **video indexer** API, you can start indexing videos immediately upon upload. This means that you can get video insights without using experts or custom code. Content discovery can be improved, utilizing the powerful artificial intelligence of this API. This allows you to make your content more discoverable.

The video indexer API will be covered in greater detail in *Chapter 3, Analyzing Videos.*

Content moderator

The **content moderator** API utilizes machine learning to automatically moderate content. It can detect potentially offensive and unwanted images, videos, and text for over 100 languages. In addition, it allows you to review detected material to improve the service.

The content moderator will be covered in *Chapter 2, Analyzing Images to Recognize a Face.*

Custom vision service

The **custom vision service** allows you to upload your own labeled images to a vision service. This means that you can add images that are specific to your domain to allow recognition using the computer vision API.

The custom vision service will be covered in more detail in *Chapter 2, Analyzing Images to Recognize a Face.*

Speech

Adding one of the Speech APIs allows your application to hear and speak to your users. The APIs can filter noise and identify speakers. Based on the recognized intent, they can drive further actions in your application.

The speech domain contains three APIs that are outlined in the following sections.

Bing Speech

Adding the **Bing Speech** API to your application allows you to convert speech to text and vice versa. You can convert spoken audio to text either by utilizing a microphone or other sources in real time or by converting audio from files. The API also offers speech intent recognition, which is trained by the **Language Understanding Intelligent Service** (**LUIS**) to understand the intent.

Speaker recognition

The **speaker recognition** API gives your application the ability to know who is talking. By using this API, you can verify that the person that is speaking is who they claim to be. You can also determine who an unknown speaker is based on a group of selected speakers.

Translator speech API

The **translator speech** API is a cloud-based automatic translation service for spoken audio. Using this API, you can add end-to-end translation across web apps, mobile apps, and desktop applications. Depending on your use cases, it can provide you with partial translations, full translations, and transcripts of the translations.

We will cover all speech-related APIs in *Chapter 5, Speak with Your Application*.

Language

APIs that are related to the language domain allow your application to process natural language and learn how to recognize what users want. You can add textual and linguistic analysis to your application, as well as natural language understanding.

The following five APIs can be found in the language domain.

Bing Spell Check

The **Bing Spell Check** API allows you to add advanced spell checking to your application.

This API will be covered in *Chapter 6, Understanding Text*.

Language Understanding Intelligent Service (LUIS)

LUIS is an API that can help your application understand commands from your users. Using this API, you can create language models that understand intents. By using models from Bing and Cortana, you can make these models recognize common requests and entities (such as places, times, and numbers). You can add conversational intelligence to your applications.

LUIS will be covered in *Chapter 4, Let Applications Understand Commands*.

Text analytics

The **text analytics** API will help you in extracting information from text. You can use it to find the sentiment of a text (whether the text is positive or negative), and will also be able to detect the language, topic, key phrases, and entities that are used throughout the text.

We will also cover the text analysis API in *Chapter 6, Understanding Text*.

Translator Text API

By adding the **translator text** API, you can get textual translations for over 60 languages. It can detect languages automatically, and you can customize the API to your needs. In addition, you can improve translations by creating user groups, utilizing the power of crowdsourcing.

The translator text API will not be covered in this book.

Knowledge

When we talk about **knowledge** APIs, we are talking about APIs that allow you to tap into rich knowledge. This may be knowledge from the web or from academia, or it may be your own data. Using these APIs, you will be able to explore the different nuances of knowledge.

The following four APIs are contained in the knowledge API domain.

Project Academic Knowledge

Using the **Project Academic Knowledge** API, you can explore relationships among academic papers, journals, and authors. This API allows you to interpret natural language user query strings, which allows your application to anticipate what the user is typing. It will evaluate what is being typed and return academic knowledge entities.

This API will be covered in more detail in *Chapter 8, Query Structured Data in a Natural Way*.

Knowledge exploration

The **knowledge exploration** API will let you add the possibility of using interactive searches for structured data in your projects. It interprets natural language queries and offers autocompletions to minimize user effort. Based on the query expression received, it will retrieve detailed information about matching objects.

Details on this API will be covered in *Chapter 8, Query Structured Data in a Natural Way.*

Recommendations solution

The **recommendations solution** API allows you to provide personalized product recommendations for your customers. You can use this API to add a frequently-bought-together functionality to your application. Another feature that you can add is item-to-item recommendations, which allows customers to see what other customers like. This API will also allow you to add recommendations based on the prior activity of the customer.

We will go through this API in *Chapter 7, Building Recommendation Systems for Businesses.*

QnA Maker

The **QnA Maker** is a service to distill information for frequently asked questions (FAQ). Using existing FAQs, either online or in a document, you can create question and answer pairs. Pairs can be edited, removed, and modified, and you can add several similar questions to match a given pair.

We will cover QnA Maker in *Chapter 8, Query Structured Data in a Natural Way.*

Project Custom Decision Service

Project Custom Decision Service is a service designed to use reinforced learning to personalize content. The service understands any context and can provide context-based content.

This book does not cover Project Custom Decision Service.

Search

Search APIs give you the ability to make your applications more intelligent with the power of Bing. Using these APIs, you can use a single call to access data from billions of web pages, images, videos, and news articles.

The search domain contains the following APIs.

Bing Web Search

With **Bing Web Search**, you can search for details in billions of web documents that are indexed by Bing. All the results can be arranged and ordered according to a layout that you specify, and the results are customized to the location of the end user.

Bing Web Search will be covered in *Chapter 9, Adding Specialized Search*.

Bing Image Search

Using the **Bing Image Search** API, you can add an advanced image and metadata search to your application. Results include URLs to images, thumbnails, and metadata. You will also be able to get machine-generated captions, similar images, and more. This API allows you to filter the results based on image type, layout, freshness (how new the image is), and license. Bing Image Search will be covered in *Chapter 9, Adding Specialized Search*.

Bing Video Search

Bing Video Search will allow you to search for videos and return rich results. The results could contain metadata from the videos, static or motion-based thumbnails, and the video itself. You can add filters to the results based on freshness, video length, resolution, and price.

Bing Video Search will be covered in *Chapter 9, Adding Specialized Search*.

Bing News Search

If you add **Bing News Search** to your application, you can search for news articles. Results can include authoritative images, related news and categories, information on the provider, URLs, and more. To be more specific, you can filter news based on topics.

Bing News Search will be covered in *Chapter 9, Adding Specialized Search*.

Bing Autosuggest

The **Bing Autosuggest** API is a small but powerful one. It will allow your users to search faster using their search suggestions, allowing you to connect a powerful search functionality to your apps.

Bing Autosuggest will be covered in *Chapter 9, Adding Specialized Search*.

Bing Visual Search

Using the **Bing Visual Search** API, you can identify and classify images. You can also acquire knowledge about images.

Bing Visual Search will be covered in *Chapter 9*, *Adding Specialized Search*.

Bing Custom Search

By utilizing the **Bing Custom Search** API, you can create a powerful, customized search that fits your needs. This tool is an ad-free commercial tool that allows you to deliver the search results you want.

Bing Custom Search will be covered in *Chapter 9*, *Adding Specialized Search*.

Bing Entity Search

Using the **Bing Entity Search** API, you can enhance your searches. The API will find the most relevant entity based on your search terms. It will find entities such as famous people, places, movies, and more.

We will not cover Bing Entity Search in this book.

Getting feedback on detected faces

Now that we have seen what else Microsoft Cognitive Services can offer, we are going to add an API to our face detection application. In this section, we will add the Bing Speech API to make the application say the number of faces out loud.

This feature of the API is not provided in the NuGet package, and as such, we are going to use the REST API.

To reach our end goal, we are going to add two new classes, `TextToSpeak` and `Authentication`. The first class will be in charge of generating the correct headers and making the calls to our service endpoint. The latter class will be in charge of generating an authentication token. This will be tied together in our `ViewModel`, where we will make the application speak back to us.

We need to get our hands on an API key first. Head over to the Microsoft Azure Portal. Create a new service for Bing Speech.

To be able to call the Bing Speech API, we need to have an authorization token. Go back to Visual Studio and create a new file called `Authentication.cs`. Place this in the `Model` folder.

We need to add two new references to the project. Find the `System.Runtime.Serialization` and `System.Web` packages in the **Assembly** tab in the **Add References** window and add them.

In our `Authentication` class, define four `private` variables and one `public` property, as follows:

```
private string _requestDetails;
private string _token;
private Timer _tokenRenewer;

private const int TokenRefreshInterval = 9;

public string Token { get { return _token; } }
```

The constructor should accept one string parameter, `clientSecret`. The `clientSecret` parameter is the API key you signed up for.

In the constructor, assign the `_clientSecret` variable, as follows:

```
_clientSecret = clientSecret;
```

Create a new function called `Initialize`, as follows:

```
public async Task Initialize()
{
    _token = GetToken();

    _tokenRenewer = new Timer(new TimerCallback(OnTokenExpiredCal
lback), this,
    TimeSpan.FromMinutes(TokenRefreshInterval),
    TimeSpan.FromMilliseconds(-1));

}
```

We then fetch the access token in a method that we will create shortly.

Finally, we create our `timer` class, which will call the `callback` function in nine minutes. The `callback` function will need to fetch the access token again and assign it to the `_token` variable. It also needs to ensure that we run the timer again in nine minutes.

Next, we need to create the `GetToken` method. This method should return a `Task<string>`object, and it should be declared as `private` and marked as `async`.

In the method, we start by creating an `HttpClient` object, pointing to an endpoint that will generate our token. We specify the root endpoint and add the token issue path, as follows:

```
using(var client = new HttpClient())

{

    client.DefaultRequestHeaders.Add ("Opc-Apim-Subscription-Key",
_clientSecret);

    UriBuilder uriBuilder = new UriBuilder (https://api.cognitive.
microsoft.com/sts/v1.0");

    uriBuilder.Path = "/issueToken";
```

We then go on to make a POST call to generate a token, as follows:

```
var result = await client.PostAsync(uriBuilder.Uri.AbsoluteUri, null);
```

When the request has been sent, we expect there to be a response. We want to read this response and return the response string:

```
return await result.Content.ReadAsStringAsync();
```

Add a new file called `TextToSpeak.cs`, if you have not already done so. Put this file in the `Model` folder.

Beneath the newly created class (but inside the namespace), we want to add two event argument classes. These will be used to handle audio events, which we will see later.

The `AudioEventArgs` class simply takes a generic `stream`, as shown in the following code. You can imagine it being used to send the audio stream to our application:

```
public class AudioEventArgs : EventArgs
{
    public AudioEventArgs(Stream eventData)
    {
        EventData = eventData;
    }

    public StreamEventData { get; private set; }
}
```

The next class allows us to send an event with a specific error message:

```
public class AudioErrorEventArgs : EventArgs
{
    public AudioErrorEventArgs(string message)
    {
        ErrorMessage = message;
    }

    public string ErrorMessage { get; private set; }
}
```

We move on to start on the TextToSpeak class, where we start off by declaring some events and class members, as follows:

```
public class TextToSpeak
{
    public event EventHandler<AudioEventArgs>OnAudioAvailable;
    public event EventHandler<AudioErrorEventArgs>OnError;

    private string _gender;
    private string _voiceName;
    private string _outputFormat;
    private string _authorizationToken;
    private AccessTokenInfo _token;

    private List<KeyValuePair<string, string>> _headers = new
List<KeyValuePair<string, string>>();
```

The first two lines in the class are events that use the event argument classes that we created earlier. These events will be triggered if a call to the API finishes (returning some audio), or if anything fails. The next few lines are string variables, which we will use as input parameters. We have one line to contain our access token information. The last line creates a new list, which we will use to hold our request headers.

We add two constant strings to our class, as follows:

```
private const string RequestUri =  "https://speech.platform.bing.com/
synthesize";

private const string SsmlTemplate =
    "<speak version='1.0'xml:lang='en-US'>
        <voice xml:lang='en-US'xml:gender='{0}'
        name='{1}'>{2}
        </voice>
    </speak>";
```

The first string contains the request URI. That is the REST API endpoint that we need to call to execute our request. Next, we have a string defining our **Speech Synthesis Markup Language (SSML)** template. This is where we will specify what the speech service should say, and how it should say it.

Next, we create our constructor, as follows:

```
public TextToSpeak()
{
    _gender = "Female";
    _outputFormat = "riff-16khz-16bit-mono-pcm";
    _voiceName = "Microsoft Server Speech Text to Speech Voice
(en-US, ZiraRUS)";
}
```

Here, we are just initializing some of the variables that we declared earlier. As you may see, we are defining the voice as female and we define it so that it uses a specific voice. In terms of gender, it can be either female or male. The voice name can be one of a long list of options. We will look more into the details of that list when we go through this API in a later chapter.

The last line specifies the output format of the audio. This will define the format and codec in use by the resultant audio stream. Again, this can be a number of varieties, which we will look into in a later chapter.

Following the constructor, there are three public methods that we will create. These will generate an authentication token and some HTTP headers, and finally execute our call to the API. Before we create these, you should add two helper methods to be able to raise our events. Call them the `RaiseOnAudioAvailable` and `RaiseOnError` methods. They should accept `AudioEventArgs` and `AudioErrorEventArgs` as parameters.

Next, add a new method called the `GenerateHeaders` method, as follows:

```
public void GenerateHeaders()
{
    _headers.Add(new KeyValuePair<string, string>("Content-
Type", "application/ssml+xml"));
    _headers.Add(new KeyValuePair<string, string>("X-
Microsoft-OutputFormat", _outputFormat));
    _headers.Add(new KeyValuePair<string,
string>("Authorization", _authorizationToken));
    _headers.Add(new KeyValuePair<string, string>("X-Search-
AppId", Guid.NewGuid().ToString("N")));
```

```
        _headers.Add(new KeyValuePair<string, string>("X-Search-
    ClientID", Guid.NewGuid().ToString("N")));
        _headers.Add(new KeyValuePair<string, string>("User-
    Agent", "Chapter1"));
    }
```

Here, we add the HTTP headers to our previously created list. These headers are required for the service to respond, and if any are missing, it will yield an HTTP/400 response. We will cover what we are using as headers in more detail later. For now, just make sure that they are present.

Following this, we want to add a new method called GenerateAuthenticationToken, as follows:

```
    public bool GenerateAuthenticationToken(string clientSecret)
    {
        Authentication auth = new Authentication(clientSecret);
```

This method accepts one string parameter, the client secret (your API key). First, we create a new object of the Authentication class, which we looked at earlier, as follows:

```
    try
    {
        _token = auth.Token;

        if (_token != null)
        {
            _authorizationToken = $"Bearer {_token}";

            return true;
        }
        else
        {
            RaiseOnError(new AudioErrorEventArgs("Failed to
    generate authentication token."));
            return false;
        }
    }
```

We use the authentication object to retrieve an access token. This token is used in our authorization token string, which, as we saw earlier, is being passed on in our headers. If the application for some reason fails to generate the access token, we trigger an error event.

Finish this method by adding the associated catch clause. If any exceptions occur, we want to raise a new error event.

The last method that we need to create in this class is going to be called the SpeakAsync method, as shown in the following screenshot. This method will actually perform the request to the Speech API:

```
public Task SpeakAsync(string textToSpeak,
CancellationTokencancellationToken)
    {
        varcookieContainer = new CookieContainer();
        var handler = new HttpClientHandler() {
            CookieContainer = cookieContainer
        };
        var client = new HttpClient(handler);
```

The method takes two parameters. One is the string, which will be the text that we want to be spoken. The next is cancellationToken; this can be used to propagate the command that the given operation should be cancelled.

When entering the method, we create three objects that we will use to execute the request. These are classes from the .NET library. We will not be going through them in any more detail.

We generated some headers earlier, and we need to add these to our HTTP client. We do this by adding the headers in the preceding foreach loop, basically looping through the entire list, as shown in the following code:

```
foreach(var header in _headers)
{
    client.DefaultRequestHeaders.TryAddWithoutValidation
(header.Key, header.Value);
}
```

Next, we create an HTTP Request Message, specifying the request URI and the fact that we will send data through the POST method. We also specify the content using the SSML template that we created earlier, adding the correct parameters (gender, voice name, and the text we want to be spoken), as shown in the following code:

```
var request = new HttpRequestMessage(HttpMethod.Post,
RequestUri)
    {
        Content = new StringContent(string.
Format(SsmlTemplate, _gender, _voiceName, textToSpeak))
    };
```

We use the HTTP client to send the HTTP request asynchronously, as follows:

```
var httpTask = client.SendAsync(request,
HttpCompletionOption.ResponseHeadersRead, cancellationToken);
```

The following code is a continuation of the asynchronous send call that we made previously. This will run asynchronously as well, and check the status of the response. If the response is successful, it will read the response message as a stream and trigger the audio event. If everything succeeds, then that stream should contain our text in spoken words:

```
var saveTask = httpTask.ContinueWith(async (responseMessage,
token) =>
    {
        try
        {
            if (responseMessage.IsCompleted &&
                responseMessage.Result != null &&
                responseMessage.Result.IsSuccessStatusCode) {
                var httpStream = await responseMessage. Result.
Content.ReadAsStreamAsync().ConfigureAwait(false);
                RaiseOnAudioAvailable(new AudioEventArgs
(httpStream));
            } else {
                RaiseOnError(new AudioErrorEventArgs($"Service
returned {responseMessage.Result.StatusCode}"));
            }
        }
        catch(Exception e)
        {
            RaiseOnError(new AudioErrorEventArgs
(e.GetBaseException().Message));
        }
    }
```

If the response indicates anything other than success, we will raise the error event.

We also want to add a catch clause and a `finally` clause to this. Raise an error if an exception is caught and dispose of all objects used in the `finally` clause.

The final code we need specifies that the continuation task is attached to the parent task. We also need to add `cancellationToken` to this task. Add the following code to finish off the method:

```
    }, TaskContinuationOptions.AttachedToParent, cancellationToken);
    return saveTask;
}
```

With this in place, we are now able to utilize this class in our application. Open the `MainViewModel.cs` file and declare a new class variable, as follows:

```
private TextToSpeak _textToSpeak;
```

Add the following code in the constructor to initialize the newly added object. We also need to call a function to generate the authentication token, as follows:

```
_textToSpeak = new TextToSpeak();
_textToSpeak.OnAudioAvailable += _textToSpeak_
OnAudioAvailable;
_textToSpeak.OnError += _textToSpeak_OnError;

GenerateToken();
```

After we have created the object, we hook up the two events to event handlers. Then we generate an authentication token by creating a `GenerateToken` function with the following content:

```
public async void GenerateToken()

{

    if (await _textToSpeak.GenerateAuthenticationToken("BING_SPEECH_
API_KEY_HERE"))

        _textToSpeak.GenerateHeaders();

}
```

Then we generate an authentication token, specifying the API key for the Bing Speech API. If that call succeeds, we generate the HTTP headers required.

We need to add the event handlers, so create the `_textToSpeak_OnError` method first, as follows:

```
private void _textToSpeak_OnError(object sender,
AudioErrorEventArgs e)
    {
        StatusText = $"Status: Audio service failed -
{e.ErrorMessage}";
    }
```

It should be a rather simple method, just outputting the error message to the user in the status text field.

Next, we need to create a `_textToSpeak_OnAudioAvailable` method, as follows:

```
        private void _textToSpeak_OnAudioAvailable(object sender,
    AudioEventArgs e)
        {
            SoundPlayer player = new SoundPlayer(e.EventData);
            player.Play();
            e.EventData.Dispose();
        }
```

Here, we utilize the `SoundPlayer` class from the .NET framework. This allows us to add the stream data directly and simply play the message.

The last part that we need for everything to work is to make the call to the `SpeakAsync` method. We can make this by adding the following at the end of our `DetectFace` method:

```
    await _textToSpeak.SpeakAsync(textToSpeak, CancellationToken.
    None);
```

With that in place, you should now be able to compile and run the application. By loading a photo and clicking on **Detect face**, you should be able to get the number of faces in the image spoken back to you. Just remember to have your audio turned on!

Summary

This chapter was a brief introduction to Microsoft Cognitive Services. We started off by creating a template project to easily create new projects for the coming chapters. We tried this template by creating an example project for this chapter. Then you learned how to detect faces in images by utilizing the Face API. From there, we took a quick tour of what Cognitive Services has to offer. We finished off by adding text-to-speech capabilities to our application by using the Bing Speech API.

The next chapter will go into more detail of the vision part of the APIs. There, you will learn how to analyze images using the computer vision API. You will go into more detail about the Face API and will learn how to detect emotions in faces by using the emotion API. We will use some of this to start building our smart-house application.

2
Analyzing Images to Recognize a Face

"We can use the Computer Vision API to prove to our clients the reliability of the data, so they can be confident making important business decisions based on that information."

- Leendert de Voogd, CEO of Vigiglobe

In the previous chapter, you were briefly introduced to Microsoft Cognitive Services. Throughout this chapter, we will dive into image-based APIs from the vision API. We will learn how to perform image analysis. Moving on, we will dive deeper into the Face API, which we briefly looked at in the previous chapter, and we will learn how you can identify people. Next, we will learn how to use the Face API to recognize emotions in faces. Finally, we will learn about the different ways to moderate content.

In this chapter, we will cover the following topics:

- Analyzing images to identify content, metadata, and adult ratings.
- Recognizing celebrities in images and reading text in images.
- Diving into the Face API:
  - Learning to find the likelihood of two faces belonging to the same person
  - Grouping faces based on visual similarities and searching similar faces
  - Identifying a person from a face
  - Recognizing emotions
- Content moderation.

Analyze an image using the Computer Vision API

The Computer Vision API allows us to process an image and retrieve information about it. It relies on advanced algorithms to analyze the content of the image in different ways, based on our needs.

Throughout this section, we will learn how to take advantage of this API. We will look at the different ways to analyze an image through standalone examples. Some of the features we will cover will also be incorporated into our end-to-end application in a later chapter.

Calling any of the APIs will return one of the following response codes:

Code	Description
200	Information of the extracted features in JSON format.
400	Typically, this means bad request. It may be an invalid image URL, an image that is too small or too large, an invalid image format, or any other errors to do with the request body.
415	Unsupported media type.
500	Possible errors may include a failure to process the image, image processing timing out, or an internal server error.

Setting up a chapter example project

Before we go into the specifics of the API, we need to create an example project for this chapter. This project will contain all of the examples, which will not be put into the end-to-end application at this stage:

 If you have not already done so, sign up for an API key for Computer Vision by visiting `https://portal.azure.com`.

1. Create a new project in Visual Studio using the template we created in *Chapter 1, Getting Started with Microsoft Cognitive Services*.

2. Right-click on the project and choose **Manage NuGet Packages**. Search for the `Microsoft.ProjectOxford.Vision` package and install it into the project, as shown in the following screenshot:

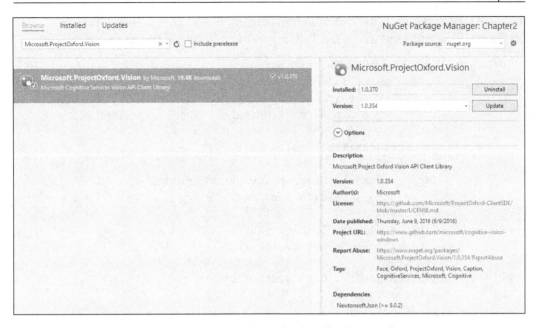

3. Create the following `UserControls` files and add them into the `ViewModel` folder:

   ° `CelebrityView.xaml`

   ° `DescriptionView.xaml`

   ° `ImageAnalysisView.xaml`

   ° `OcrView.xaml`

   ° `ThumbnailView.xaml`

4. Also, add the corresponding `ViewModel` instances from the following list into the `ViewModel` folder:

   ° `CelebrityViewModel.cs`

   ° `DescriptionViewModel.cs`

   ° `ImageAnalysisViewModel.cs`

   ° `OcrViewModel.cs`

   ° `ThumbnailViewModel.cs`

Go through the newly created `ViewModel` instances and make sure that all classes are public.

We will switch between the different views using a `TabControl` tag. Open the `MainView.xaml` file and add the following in the precreated `Grid` tag:

```
<TabControl x: Name = "tabControl"
               HorizontalAlignment = "Left"
               VerticalAlignment = "Top"
               Width = "810" Height = "520">
    <TabItem Header="Analysis" Width="100">
        <controls:ImageAnalysisView />
    </TabItem>
    <TabItem Header="Description" Width="100">
        <controls:DescriptionView />
    </TabItem>
    <TabItem Header="Celebs" Width="100">
        <controls:CelebrityView />
    </TabItem>
    <TabItem Header="OCR" Width="100">
        <controls:OcrView />
    </TabItem>
    <TabItem Header="Thumbnail" Width="100">
        <controls:ThumbnailView />
    </TabItem>
</TabControl>
```

This will add a tab bar at the top of the application that will allow you to navigate between the different views.

Next, we will add the properties and members required in our `MainViewModel.cs` file.

The following is the variable used to access the Computer Vision API:

```
private IVisionServiceClient _visionClient;
```

The following code declares a private variable holding the `CelebrityViewModel` object. It also declares the `public` property that we use to access the `ViewModel` in our `View`:

```
private CelebrityViewModel _celebrityVm;
public CelebrityViewModel CelebrityVm
{
```

```
        get { return _celebrityVm; }
        set
        {
            _celebrityVm = value;
            RaisePropertyChangedEvent("CelebrityVm");
        }
    }
}
```

Following the same pattern, add properties for the rest of the created `ViewModel` instances.

With all the properties in place, create the `ViewModel` instances in our constructor using the following code:

```
    public MainViewModel()
    {
        _visionClient = new VisionServiceClient("VISION_API_KEY_HERE",
"ROOT_URI");

        CelebrityVm = new CelebrityViewModel(_visionClient);
        DescriptionVm = new DescriptionViewModel(_visionClient);
        ImageAnalysisVm= new ImageAnalysisViewModel(_visionClient);
        OcrVm = new OcrViewModel(_visionClient);
        ThumbnailVm = new ThumbnailViewModel(_visionClient);
    }
```

Note how we first create the `VisionServiceClient` object with the API key that we signed up for earlier and the root URI, as described in *Chapter 1, Getting Started with Microsoft Cognitive Services*. This is then injected into all the `ViewModel` instances to be used there.

This should now compile and present you with the application shown in the following screenshot:

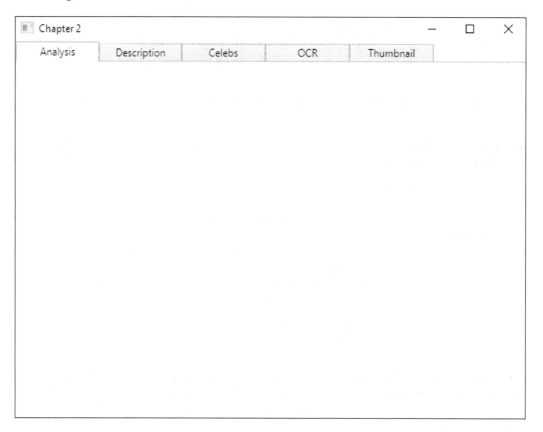

Generic image analysis

We start enabling generic image analysis by adding a UI to the `ImageAnalysis.xaml` file. All the Computer Vision example UIs will be built in the same manner.

The UI should have two columns, as shown in the following code:

```
<Grid.ColumnDefinitions>
    <ColumnDefinition Width="*" />
    <ColumnDefinition Width="*" />
</Grid.ColumnDefinitions>
```

The first one will contain the image selection, while the second one will display our results.

In the left-hand column, we create a vertically oriented `StackPanel` label. To this, we add a label and a `ListBox` label. The list box will display a list of visual features that we can add to our analysis query. Note how we have a `SelectionChanged` event hooked up in the `ListBox` label in the following code. This will be added behind the code, and will be covered shortly:

```
<StackPanel Orientation="Vertical"Grid.Column="0">

<TextBlock Text="Visual Features:"
           FontWeight="Bold"
           FontSize="15"
           Margin="5, 5" Height="20" />

<ListBox: Name = "VisualFeatures"
      ItemsSource = "{Binding ImageAnalysisVm.Features}"
      SelectionMode = "Multiple" Height="150" Margin="5, 0, 5, 0"
      SelectionChanged = "VisualFeatures_SelectionChanged" />
```

The list box will be able to select multiple items, and the items will be gathered in the `ViewModel`.

In the same stack panel, we also add a button element and an image element. These will allow us to browse for an image, show it, and analyze it. Both the `Button` command and the image source are bound to the corresponding properties in the `ViewModel`, as shown in the following code:

```
<Button Content = "Browse and analyze"
        Command = "{Binding ImageAnalysisVm.
BrowseAndAnalyzeImageCommand}"
        Margin="5, 10, 5, 10" Height="20" Width="120"
        HorizontalAlignment="Right" />

<Image Stretch = "Uniform"
       Source="{Binding ImageAnalysisVm.ImageSource}"
       Height="280" Width="395" />
</StackPanel>
```

We also add another vertically oriented stack panel. This will be placed in the right-hand column. It contains a title label, as well as a textbox, bound to the analysis result in our `ViewModel`, as shown in the following code:

```
<StackPanel Orientation= "Vertical"Grid.Column="1">
    <TextBlock Text="Analysis Results:"
               FontWeight = "Bold"
```

```
                FontSize="15" Margin="5, 5" Height="20" />
        <TextBox Text = "{Binding ImageAnalysisVm.AnalysisResult}"
                Margin="5, 0, 5, 5" Height="485" />
    </StackPanel>
```

Next, we want to add our `SelectionChanged` event handler to our code-behind. Open the `ImageAnalysisView.xaml.cs` file and add the following:

```
    private void VisualFeatures_SelectionChanged(object sender,
SelectionChangedEventArgs e) {
        var vm = (MainViewModel) DataContext;
        vm.ImageAnalysisVm.SelectedFeatures.Clear();
```

The first line of the function will give us the current `DataContext`, which is the `MainViewModel` class. We access the `ImageAnalysisVm` property, which is our `ViewModel`, and clear the selected visual features list.

From there, we loop through the selected items from our list box. All items will be added to the `SelectedFeatures` list in our `ViewModel`:

```
        foreach(VisualFeature feature in VisualFeatures.SelectedItems)
        {
            vm.ImageAnalysisVm.SelectedFeatures.Add(feature);
        }
    }
```

Open the `ImageAnalysisViewModel.cs` file. Make sure that the class inherits the `ObservableObject` class.

Declare a `private` variable, as follows:

```
    private IVisionServiceClient _visionClient;
```

This will be used to access the Computer Vision API, and it is initialized through the constructor.

Next, we declare a private variable and the corresponding property for our list of visual features, as follows:

```
    private List<VisualFeature> _features=new List<VisualFeature>();
    public List<VisualFeature> Features {
        get { return _features; }
        set {
            _features = value;
            RaisePropertyChangedEvent("Features");
        }
    }
```

In a similar manner, create a `BitmapImage` variable and property called `ImageSource`. Create a list of `VisualFeature` types called `SelectedFeatures` and a string called `AnalysisResult`.

We also need to declare the property for our button, as follows:

```
public ICommandBrowseAndAnalyzeImageCommand {get; private set;}
```

With that in place, we create our constructor, as follows:

```
public ImageAnalysisViewModel(IVisionServiceClientvisionClient) {
    _visionClient = visionClient;
    Initialize();
}
```

The constructor takes one parameter, the `IVisionServiceClient` object, which we have created in our `MainViewModel` file. It assigns that parameter to the variable that we created earlier. Then we call an `Initialize` function, as follows:

```
private void Initialize() {
    Features = Enum.GetValues(typeof(VisualFeature))
                .Cast<VisualFeature>().ToList();

    BrowseAndAnalyzeImageCommand = new DelegateCommand(BrowseAndA
nalyze);
}
```

In the `Initialize` function, we fetch all the values from the `VisualFeature` variable of the `enum` type. These values are added to the features list, which is displayed in the UI. We also created our button, and now that we have done so, we need to create the corresponding action, as follows:

```
private async void BrowseAndAnalyze(object obj)
{
    var openDialog = new Microsoft.Win32.OpenFileDialog();

    openDialog.Filter = "JPEG Image(*.jpg)|*.jpg";
    bool? result = openDialog.ShowDialog();

    if (!(bool)result) return;

    string filePath = openDialog.FileName;

    Uri fileUri = new Uri(filePath);
    BitmapImage image = new BitmapImage(fileUri);
```

```
        image.CacheOption = BitmapCacheOption.None;
        image.UriSource = fileUri;

        ImageSource = image;
```

The first lines of the preceding code are similar to what we did in *Chapter 1, Getting Started with Microsoft Cognitive Services*. We open a file browser and get the selected image.

With an image selected, we run an analyze on it, as follows:

```
    try {
        using (StreamfileStream = File.OpenRead(filePath)) {
            AnalysisResult analysisResult = await  _visionClient.
AnalyzeImageAsync(fileStream, SelectedFeatures);
```

We call the `AnalyzeImageAsync` function of our `_visionClient`. This function has four overloads, all of which are quite similar. In our case, we pass on the image as a `Stream` type and the `SelectedFeatures` list, containing the `VisualFeatures` variable to analyze.

The request parameters are as follows:

Parameter	Description
Image (required)	<ul><li>Can be uploaded in the form of a raw image binary or URL.</li><li>Can be JPEG, PNG, GIF, or BMP.</li><li>File size must be less than 4 MB.</li><li>Image dimensions must be at least 50 x 50 pixels.</li></ul>
Visual features (optional)	A list indicating the visual feature types to return. It can include categories, tags, descriptions, faces, image types, color, and whether or not it is adult content.
Details (optional)	A list indicating what domain-specific details to return.

The response to this request is the `AnalysisResult` string.

We then check to see if the result is `null`. If it is not, we call a function to parse it and assign the result to our `AnalysisResult` string, as follows:

```
if (analysisResult != null)
    AnalysisResult = PrintAnalysisResult(analysisResult);
```

Remember to close the `try` clause and finish the method with the corresponding `catch` clause.

The `AnalysisResult` string contains data according to the visual features requested in the API call.

Data in the `AnalysisResult` variable is described in the following table:

Visual feature	Description
Categories	Images are categorized according to a defined taxonomy. This includes everything from animals, buildings, and outdoors, to people.
Tags	Images are tagged with a list of words related to the content.
Description	This contains a full sentence describing the image.
Faces	This detects faces in images and contains face coordinates, gender, and age.
ImageType	This detects whether an image is clipart or a line drawing.
Color	This contains information about dominant colors, accent colors, and whether or not the image is in black and white.
Adult	This detects whether an image is pornographic in nature and whether or not it is racy.

To retrieve data, for example for categories, you can use the following:

```
if (analysisResult.Description != null) {
    result.AppendFormat("Description: {0}\n", analysisResult.
Description.Captions[0].Text);
    result.AppendFormat("Probability: {0}\n\n", analysisResult.
Description.Captions[0].Confidence);

}
```

A successful call would present us with the following result:

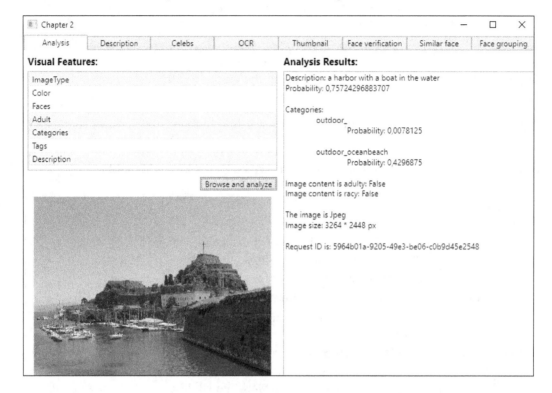

Sometimes, you may only be interested in the image description. In such cases, it is wasteful to ask for the kind of full analysis that we have just done. By calling the following function, you will get an array of descriptions:

```
AnalysisResultdescriptionResult = await _visionClient.
DescribeAsync(ImageUrl, NumberOfDescriptions);
```

In this call, we have specified a URL for the image and the number of descriptions to return. The first parameter must always be included, but it may be an image upload instead of a URL. The second parameter is optional, and in cases where it is not provided, it defaults to one.

A successful query will result in an `AnalysisResult` object, which is the same as the one that was described in the preceding code. In this case, it will only contain the request ID, image metadata, and an array of captions. Each caption contains an image description and the confidence of that description being correct.

We will add this form of image analysis to our smart-house application in a later chapter.

Recognizing celebrities using domain models

One of the features of the Computer Vision API is the ability to recognize domain-specific content. At the time of writing, the API only supports celebrity recognition, where it is able to recognize around 200,000 celebrities.

For this example, we choose to use an image from the internet. The UI will then need a textbox to input the URL. It will need a button to load the image and perform the domain analysis. There should be an image element to see the image and a textbox to output the result.

The corresponding `ViewModel` should have two `string` properties for the URL and the analysis result. It should have a `BitmapImage` property for the image and an `ICommand` property for our button.

Add a `private` variable for the `IVisionServiceClient` type at the start of the `ViewModel`, as follows:

```
private IVisionServiceClient _visionClient;
```

This should be assigned in the constructor, which will take a parameter of the `IVisionServiceClient` type.

As we need a URL to fetch an image from the internet, we need to initialize the `Icommand` property with both an action and a predicate. The latter checks whether the URL property is set or not, as shown in the following code:

```
public CelebrityViewModel(IVisionServiceClient visionClient) {
    _visionClient = visionClient;
    LoadAndFindCelebrityCommand = new DelegateCommand(LoadAndFindC
elebrity, CanFindCelebrity);
}
```

The `LoadAndFindCelebrity` load creates a `Uri` with the given URL. Using this, it creates a `BitmapImage` and assigns this to `ImageSource`, the `BitmapImage` property, as shown in the following code. The image should be visible in the UI:

```
private async void LoadAndFindCelebrity(object obj) {
    UrifileUri = new Uri(ImageUrl);
    BitmapImage image = new BitmapImage(fileUri);

    image.CacheOption = BitmapCacheOption.None;
    image.UriSource = fileUri;

    ImageSource = image;
```

We call the `AnalyzeImageInDomainAsync` type with the given URL, as shown in the following code. The first parameter we pass in is the image URL. Alternatively, this could have been an image that was opened as a `Stream` type:

```
try {
    AnalysisInDomainResultcelebrityResult = await _visionClient.An
alyzeImageInDomainAsync(ImageUrl, "celebrities");

    if (celebrityResult != null)
        Celebrity = celebrityResult.Result.ToString();
}
```

The second parameter is the domain model name, which is in a `string` format. As an alternative, we could have used a specific `Model` object, which can be retrieved by calling the following:

```
VisionClient.ListModelsAsync();
```

This would return an array of `Models`, which we can display and select from. As there is only one available at this time, there is no point in doing so.

The result from `AnalyzeImageInDomainAsync` is an object of the `AnalysisInDomainResult` type. This object will contain the request ID, metadata of the image, and the result, containing an array of celebrities. In our case, we simply output the entire result array. Each item in this array will contain the name of the celebrity, the confidence of a match, and the face rectangle in the image. Do try it in the example code provided.

Utilizing optical character recognition

For some tasks, **optical character recognition (OCR)** can be very useful. Say that you took a photo of a receipt. Using OCR, you can read the amount from the photo itself and have it automatically added to accounting.

OCR will detect text in images and extract machine-readable characters. It will automatically detect language. Optionally, the API will detect image orientation and correct it before reading the text.

To specify a language, you need to use the **BCP-47** language code. At the time of writing, the following languages are supported: simplified Chinese, traditional Chinese, Czech, Danish, Dutch, English, Finnish, French, German, Greek, Hungarian, Italian, Japanese, Korean, Norwegian, Polish, Portuguese, Russian, Spanish, Swedish, Turkish, Arabic, Romanian, Cyrillic Serbian, Latin Serbian, and Slovak.

In the code example, the UI will have an image element. It will also have a button to load the image and detect text. The result will be printed to a textbox element.

The `ViewModel` will need a `string` property for the result, a `BitmapImage` property for the image, and an `ICommand` property for the button.

Add a `private` variable to the `ViewModel` for the Computer Vision API, as follows:

```
private IVisionServiceClient _visionClient;
```

The constructor should have one parameter of the `IVisionServiceClient` type, which should be assigned to the preceding variable.

Create a function as a command for our button. Call it `BrowseAndAnalyze` and have it accept `object` as the parameter. Then, open a file browser and find an image to analyze. With the image selected, we run the OCR analysis, as follows:

```
using (StreamfileStream = File.OpenRead(filePath)) {
    OcrResultsanalysisResult = await _visionClient.
RecognizeTextAsync (fileStream);

    if(analysisResult != null)
        OcrResult = PrintOcrResult(analysisResult);
}
```

With the image opened as a `Stream` type, we call the `RecognizeTextAsync` method. In this case, we pass on the image as a `Stream` type, but we could just as easily have passed on a URL to an image.

Two more parameters may be specified in this call. First, you can specify the language of the text. The default is unknown, which means that the API will try to detect the language automatically. Second, you can specify whether or not the API should detect the orientation of the image. The default is set to `false`.

If the call succeeds, it will return data in the form of an `OcrResults` object. We send this result to a function, the `PrintOcrResult` function, where we will parse it and print the text, as follows:

```
private string PrintOcrResult(OcrResultsocrResult)
{
    StringBuilder result = new StringBuilder();

    result.AppendFormat("Language is {0}\n", ocrResult.Language);
    result.Append("The words are:\n\n");
```

First, we create a `StringBuilder` object, which will hold all the text. The first content we add to it is the language of the text in the image, as follows:

```
foreach(var region in ocrResult.Regions) {
    foreach(var line in region.Lines) {
        foreach(var text in line.Words) {
            result.AppendFormat("{0} ", text.Text);
        }
        result.Append("\n");
    }
    result.Append("\n\n");
}
```

The result has an array, which contains the `Regions` property. Each item represents recognized text, and each region contains multiple lines. The `line` variables are arrays, where each item represents recognized text. Each line contains an array of the `Words` property. Each item in this array represents a recognized word.

With all the words appended to the `StringBuilder` function, we return it as a string. This will then be printed in the UI, as shown in the following screenshot:

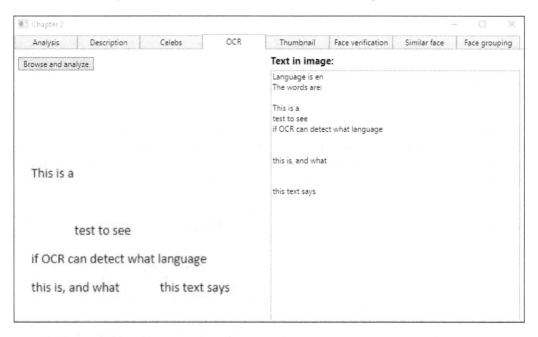

The result also contains the orientation and angle of the text. Combining this with the bounding box, also included, you can mark each word in the original image.

Generating image thumbnails

In today's world, we, as developers, have to consider different screen sizes when displaying images. The Computer Vision API offers some help with this by providing the ability to generate thumbnails.

Thumbnail generation, in itself, is not that big a deal. What makes the API clever is that it analyzes the image and determines the region of interest.

It will also generate smart cropping coordinates. This means that if the specified aspect ratio differs from the original, it will crop the image, with a focus on the interesting regions.

In the example code, the UI consists of two image elements and one button. The first image is the image in its original size. The second is for the generated thumbnail, which we specify to be 250 x 250 pixels in size.

The `View` model will need the corresponding properties, two `BitmapImages` methods to act as image sources, and one `ICommand` property for our button command.

Define a private variable in the `ViewModel`, as follows:

```
private IVisionServiceClient _visionClient;
```

This will be our API access point. The constructor should accept an `IVisionServiceClient` object, which should be assigned to the preceding variable.

For the `ICommand` property, we create a function, `BrowseAndAnalyze`, accepting an `object` parameter. We do not need to check whether we can execute the command. We will browse for an image each time.

In the `BrowseAndAnalyze` function, we open a file dialog and select an image. When we have the image file path, we can generate our thumbnail, as follows:

```
using (StreamfileStream = File.OpenRead(filePath))
{
    byte[] thumbnailResult = await _visionClient.
GetThumbnailAsync(fileStream, 250, 250);

    if(thumbnailResult != null &&thumbnailResult.Length != 0)
        CreateThumbnail(thumbnailResult);
}
```

We open the image file so that we have a `Stream` type. This stream is the first parameter in our call to the `GetThumbnailAsync` method. The next two parameters indicate the width and height that we want for our thumbnail.

By default, the API call will use smart cropping, so we do not have to specify it. If we have a case where we do not want smart cropping, we could add a `bool` variable as the fourth parameter.

If the call succeeds, we get a `byte` array back. This is the image data. If it contains data, we pass it on to a new function, `CreateThumbnail`, to create a `BitmapImage` object from it, as follows:

```
private void CreateThumbnail(byte[] thumbnailResult)
{
    try {
        MemoryStreamms = new MemoryStream(thumbnailResult);
        ms.Seek(0, SeekOrigin.Begin);
```

To create an image from a `byte` array, we create a `MemoryStream` object from it. We make sure that we start at the beginning of the array.

Next, we create a `BitmapImage` object and begin to initialize it. We specify the `CacheOption` and set the `StreamSource` to the `MemoryStream` variables we created earlier. Finally, we stop the `BitmapImage` initialization and assign the image to our `Thumbnail` property, as shown in the following code:

```
BitmapImage image = new BitmapImage();
image.BeginInit();
image.CacheOption = BitmapCacheOption.None;
image.StreamSource = ms;
image.EndInit();

Thumbnail = image;
```

Close up the `try` clause and add the corresponding `catch` clause. You should now be able to generate thumbnails.

Diving deep into the Face API

The Face API has two main features. The first one is face detection and the other is face recognition.

Face detection allows us to detect up to 64 faces in one image. We have already seen the basic usage. The features of face recognition are implied in its name: using it, we can detect whether two faces belong to the same person. We can find similar faces, or one in particular, and we can group similar faces. We will learn how to do all of this in the following sections.

When calling any of the APIs, it will respond with one of the following responses:

Code	Description
200	Successful call. It returns an array containing data related to the API call.
400	Request body is invalid. This can be a number of errors, depending on the API call. Typically, the request code is invalid.
401	Access denied because of an invalid subscription key. The key may be wrong or the account/subscription plan may be blocked.
403	Out of call volume data. You have made all the available calls to the API for this month.
415	Invalid media type.
429	Rate limit is exceeded. You will need to wait a period of time (less than one minute in the free preview) before you try again.

Retrieving more information from the detected faces

In *Chapter 1*, *Getting Started with Microsoft Cognitive Services*, we learned the very basic form of face detection. In the example, we retrieved a `Face` array. This contained information on all faces that were found in an image. In that specific example, we obtained information about the face rectangle, face ID, face landmarks, and age.

When calling the API, there are four request parameters, as shown in the following table:

Parameter	Description
image	<ul><li>The image in which to search for faces. It will either be in the form of a URL or binary data.</li><li>Supported formats are JPEG, PNG, GIF, and BMP.</li><li>The maximum file size is 4 MB.</li><li>The size of detectable faces is between 36 x 36 pixels and 4096 x 4096 pixels.</li></ul>
return FaceId (optional)	Boolean value. This specifies whether the response should include the face ID or not.
return FaceLandmarks (optional)	Boolean value. This specifies whether the response should include `FaceLandmarks` in detected faces.

Parameter	Description
`return FaceAttributes` (optional)	• String value. This is a comma-separated string containing all face attributes that are to be analyzed. • Supported attributes are age, gender, head pose, smile, facial hair, emotion, and glasses. • These attributes are still experimental, and should be treated as such.

If a face is successfully discovered, it will expire in 24 hours. When calling other parts of the Face API, you are often required to have a face ID as an input. In those cases, we need to detect a face first, followed by the call to the API we wish to use, using the detected face as a parameter.

Using this knowledge, I challenge you to play around with the example in *Chapter 1, Getting Started with Microsoft Cognitive Services*. Draw a rectangle around the face. Mark the eyes in the image.

Deciding whether two faces belong to the same person

To decide whether two faces belong to the same person, we are going to call the `Verify` function of the API. The API allows us to detect when two faces are of the same person, which is called **face-to-face verification**. Detecting whether a face belongs to a specific person is called **face-to-person verification**.

The UI will consist of three button elements, two image elements, and one text block element. Two of the buttons will be used to browse for images, which are then shown in each image element. The last button will run the verification. The text block will output the result.

Lay out the UI how you want and bind the different elements to properties in the `ViewModel`, as we have done previously. In the `ViewModel`, there should be two `BitmapImage` properties for the image elements. There should be one `string` property, containing the verification result. Finally, there should be three `ICommand` properties, one for each of our buttons.

Remember to add the UI to the `MainView.xaml` file as a new `TabItem`. In addition, add the `ViewModel` to the `MainViewModel.cs` file, where you will also need to add a new variable for the `FaceServiceClient` variable. This should be created with the Face API key, which we signed up for in *Chapter 1, Getting Started with Microsoft Cognitive Services*.

In the `ViewModel`, we need to declare the following three `private` variables:

```
private FaceServiceClient _faceServiceClient;
private Guid _faceId1 = Guid.Empty;
private Guid _faceId2 = Guid.Empty;
```

We have seen the first one before; it will access the Face API. The two `Guid` variables will be assigned when we have run the face detection.

The constructor accepts one parameter, which is our `FaceServiceClient` object. This is assigned to the previously created variable, as shown in the following code:

```
public FaceVerificationViewModel
(FaceServiceClientfaceServiceClient)
    {
        _faceServiceClient = faceServiceClient;
        Initialize();
    }
```

From the constructor, we call the `Initialize` function to create the `DelegateCommand` properties, as follows:

```
private void Initialize()
    {
        BrowseImage1Command = new DelegateCommand(BrowseImage1);
        BrowseImage2Command = new DelegateCommand(BrowseImage2);
        VerifyImageCommand = new DelegateCommand(VerifyFace,
CanVerifyFace);
    }
```

The browse commands do not need to be disabled at any point, so we just pass on the command function, as follows:

```
private async void BrowseImage1(object obj) {
        Image1Source = await BrowseImageAsync(1);
    }
```

Both functions will look similar. We call another function to browse for an image and detect a face. To separate each image, we pass on the image number.

The `BrowseImageAsync` function will accept an `int` type as a parameter. It returns a `BitmapImage` object, which we assign to the `BitmapImage` property bound to our UI. The first part opens a browse dialog and returns the selected image. We will jump in when we have the image and the path to that image.

We open the image as a `Stream` object. The `Stream` object is used in the API call to detect faces. When we call the API, we can use the default call, as it will return the value we are interested in, as shown in the following code:

```
try {
    using (Stream fileStream = File.OpenRead(filePath)) {
        Face[] detectedFaces = await  _faceServiceClient.
DetectAsync(fileStream);
```

When the detection process has completed, we check to see which image this is and assign the `FaceId` parameter to the correct `Guid` variable using the following code. For this example, we are assuming that there will be only one face per image:

```
        if (imagenumber == 1)
            _faceId1 = detectedFaces[0].FaceId;
        else
            _faceId2 = detectedFaces[0].FaceId;
    }
}
```

Finish off the function by adding catch clauses as you see fit. You also need to create and return a `BitmapImage` parameter from the selected image.

Before the button for the face verification is enabled, we perform a check to see if both face IDs have been set using the following code:

```
private bool CanVerifyFace(object obj)
{
    return !_faceId1.Equals(Guid.Empty) &&! _faceId2.Equals(Guid.
Empty);
}
```

The `VerifyFace` function is not a complex one, as you can see in the following code:

```
private async void VerifyFace(object obj) {
    try {
        VerifyResultverificationResult = await  _
faceServiceClient.VerifyAsync(_faceId1, _faceId2);
```

With the face IDs set, we can make a call to the `VerifyAsync` function of the API. We pass on the face IDs as parameters and get a `VerifyResult` object in return. We use this object to provide the output, as follows:

```
        FaceVerificationResult = $"The two provided faces is
identical: {verificationResult.IsIdentical}, with confidence:
{verificationResult.Confidence}";
    }
```

A successful call will return a code `200` response. The response data is a `bool` type variable, `isIdentical`, and a number, `confidence`:

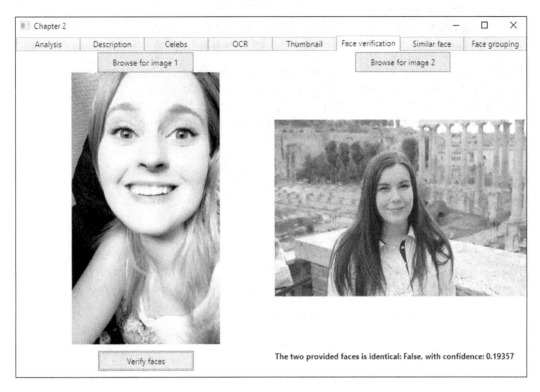

At the time of writing, the `NuGet` package for the Face API only allows for face-to-face verification. If we were calling directly to the REST API, we could have utilized face-to-person verification as well.

To use face-to-person verification, only one image is required. You will need to pass on the face ID for that image. You will also need to pass on a person group ID, and a person ID. These are to specify a specific person group to search in and a certain person within that group. We will cover person groups and persons later in this chapter.

Finding similar faces

Using the Face API, you can find faces similar to a provided face. The API allows for two search modes. Match person mode is the default mode. This will match faces to the same person, according to an internal same-person threshold. The other is match face mode, which will ignore the same-person threshold. This returns matches that are similar, but the similarity may be low.

In the example code provided, we have three buttons in our UI: one for generating a face list, another for adding faces to the list, and, finally, one to find similar faces. We need a textbox to specify a name for the face list. For convenience, we add a list box, outputting the persisted face IDs from the face list. We also add an image element to show the image we are checking, and a textbox outputting the result.

In the corresponding `ViewModel`, we need to add a `BitmapImage` property for the image element. We need two `string` properties: one for our face-list name and one for the API call result. To get data to our list box, we need an `ObservableCollection` property containing `Guids`. The buttons need to be hooked up to individual `ICommand` properties.

We declare two `private` variables at the start of the `ViewModel`, as shown in the following code. The first one is a `bool` variable to indicate whether or not the face list already exists. The other is used to access the Face API:

```
private bool _faceListExists = false;
private FaceServiceClient _faceServiceClient;
```

The constructor should accept the `FaceServiceClient` parameter, which it assigns to the preceding variable. It will then call an `Initialize` function, as follows:

```
private async void Initialize()
{
    FaceListName = "Chapter2";

    CreateFaceListCommand = new DelegateCommand(CreateFaceListAsy
nc, CanCreateFaceList);
    FindSimilarFaceCommand = new DelegateCommand(FindSimilarFace);
    AddExampleFacesToListCommand = new DelegateCommand(AddExampleF
acesToList, CanAddExampleFaces);
```

First, we initialize the `FaceListName` property to `Chapter2`. Next, we create the command objects, specifying actions and predicates.

We finish the `Initialize` function by calling two functions, as shown in the following code. One checks whether the face list exists, while the second updates the list of face IDs:

```
    await DoesFaceListExistAsync();
    UpdateFaceGuidsAsync();
}
```

To check whether a given face list exists, we first need to get a list of all face lists. We do this by calling the `ListFaceListsAsync` method, which will return a `FaceListMetadata` array. We make sure that the result has data before we loop through the array, as shown in the following code:

```
private async Task DoesFaceListExistAsync()
{
    FaceListMetadata[] faceLists = await _faceServiceClient.
ListFaceListsAsync();
```

Each `FaceListMetadata` array, from the resultant array, contains a face-list ID, a name of the face list, and user-provided data. For this example, we are just interested in the name. If the face-list name that we have specified is the name of any face list returned, we set the `_faceListExists` parameter to `true`, as shown in the following code:

```
foreach (FaceListMetadatafaceList in faceLists) {
    if (faceList.Name.Equals(FaceListName)) {
        _faceListExists = true;
        break;
    }
}
```

If the face list exists, we can update the list of face IDs.

To get the faces in a face list, we need to get the face list first. This is done with a call to the Face API's function, the `GetFaceListAsync` method. This requires the face-list ID to be passed as a parameter. The face-list ID needs to be in lowercase or digits, and can contain a maximum of 64 characters. For the sake of simplicity, we use the face-list name as the face ID, as follows:

```
private async void UpdateFaceGuidsAsync() {
    if (!_faceListExists) return;

    try {
        FaceListfaceList = await _faceServiceClient.
GetFaceListAsync(FaceListName.ToLower());
```

The result of this API call is a `FaceList` object, containing the face-list ID and face-list name. It also contains user-provided data and an array of persisted faces.

We check whether we have any data and then get the array of persisted faces. Looping through this array, we are able to get the `PersistedFaceId` parameter (as a `guid` variable) and user-provided data of each item. The persisted face ID is added to the `FaceIds ObservableCollection`, as shown in the following code:

```
if (faceList == null) return;

PersonFace[] faces = faceList.PersistedFaces;

foreach (PersonFace face in faces) {
    FaceIds.Add(face.PersistedFaceId);
}
```

Finish the function by adding the corresponding `catch` clause.

If the face list does not exist and we have specified a face-list name, then we can create a new face list, as follows:

```
private async void CreateFaceListAsync(object obj) {
    try {
        if (!_faceListExists) {
            await _faceServiceClient.CreateFaceListAsync (
FaceListName.ToLower(), FaceListName, string.Empty);
            await DoesFaceListExistAsync();
        }
    }
}
```

First, we check to see that the face list does not exist. Using the `_faceServiceClient` parameter, you are required to pass on a face-list ID, a face-list name, and user data. As seen previously, the face-list ID needs to be lowercase characters or digits.

Using the REST API, the user parameter is optional, and as such, you would not have to provide it.

After we have created a face list, we want to ensure that it exists. We do this by a call to the previously created `DoesFaceListExistAsync` function. Add the `catch` clause to finish the function.

If the named face list exists, we can add faces to this list. Add the `AddExampleFacesToList` function. It should accept `object` as a parameter. I will leave the details of adding the images up to you. In the provided example, we get a list of images from a given directory and loop through it.

With the file path of a given image, we open the image as a `Stream`. To optimize it for our similarity operation, we find the `FaceRectangle` parameter in an image. As there should be only one face per image in the face list, we select the first element in the `Face` array, as follows:

```
    using (StreamfileStream = File.OpenRead(image))
    {
        Face[] faces = await _faceServiceClient.
DetectAsync(fileStream);
        FaceRectanglefaceRectangle = faces[0].FaceRectangle;
```

Adding the face to the face list is as simple as calling the `AddFaceToFaceListAsync` function. We need to specify the face-list ID and the image. The image may come from a `Stream` (as in our case) or a URL. Optionally, we can add user data and the face rectangle of the image, as follows:

```
AddPersistedFaceResult addFacesResult = await _faceServiceClient.
AddFaceToFaceListAsync(FaceListName.ToLower(), fileStream, null,
faceRectangle);
UpdateFaceGuidsAsync();
```

The result of the API call is an `AddPersistedFaceResult` variable. This contains the persisted face ID, which is different from a face ID in the `DetectAsync` call. A face added to a face list will not expire until it is deleted.

We finish the function by calling the `UpdateFaceGuidsAsync` method.

Finally, we create our `FindSimilarFace` function, also accepting `object` as a parameter. To be able to search for similar faces, we need a face ID (the `Guid` variable) from the `DetectAsync` method. This can be called with a local image or from a URL. The example code opens a file browser and allows the user to browse for an image.

With the face ID, we can search for similar faces, as shown in the following code:

```
    try {
        SimilarPersistedFace[] similarFaces = await _
faceServiceClient.FindSimilarAsync (findFaceGuid, FaceListName.
ToLower(), 3);
```

We call the `FindSimilarAsync` function. The first parameter is the face ID of the face we specified. The next parameter is the face-list ID, and the final parameter is the number of candidate faces returned. The default for this is 20, so it is often best to specify a number.

Instead of using a face list to find similar faces, you can use an array of the Guid variable. That array should contain face IDs retrieved from the DetectAsync method.

At the time of writing, the NuGet API package only supports match person mode. If you are using the REST API directly, you can specify the mode as a parameter.

Depending on the mode selected, the result will contain either the face ID or the persisted face ID of similar faces. It will also contain the confidence of the similarity of the given face.

To delete a face from the face list, call the following function in the Face API:

```
DeleteFaceFromFaceListAsync(FACELISTID, PERSISTEDFACEID)
```

To delete a face list, call the following function in the Face API:

```
DeleteFaceListAsync(FACELISTID)
```

To update a face list, call the following function in the Face API:

```
UpdateFaceListAsync(FACELISTID, FACELISTNAME, USERDATA)
```

Grouping similar faces

If you have several images of faces, one thing you may want to do is group the faces. Typically, you will want to group faces based on similarity, which is a feature the Face API provides.

By providing the API with a list of face IDs, it will respond with one or more groups. One group consists of faces that are similar looking. Usually, this means that the faces belong to the same person. Faces that cannot find any similar counterparts are placed in a group we'll call MessyGroup.

Create a new View called FaceGroupingView.xaml. The View should have six image elements, with corresponding titles and textboxes for face IDs. It should also have a button for our group command and a textbox to output the grouping result.

In the corresponding FaceGroupingViewModel.xaml View model, you should add the BitmapImage properties for all images. You should also add the string properties for the face IDs and one for the result. There is also a need for an ICommand property.

At the start of the `ViewModel`, we declare some `private` variables, as follows:

```
private FaceServiceClient _faceServiceClient;
private List<string> _imageFiles = new List<string>();
private List<Guid> _faceIds = new List<Guid>();
```

The first one is used to access the Face API. The second one contains a list of strings that in turn contain the location of our images. The last list contains the detected face IDs.

The constructor accepts a parameter of the `FaceServiceClient` type. It assigns it to the corresponding variable and calls the `Initialize` function. This creates our `ICommand` object and calls a function to add our images to the application.

In the function that adds images, we add hardcoded image paths to our _
`imageFiles` list. For this example, we add six. Using a `for` loop, we generate each `BitmapImage` property. When we have an image, we want to detect faces in it:

```
try {
    using (Stream fileStream = File.OpenRead(_imageFiles[i])) {
        Face[] faces = await
        _faceServiceClient.DetectAsync(fileStream);
```

We do not need any more data than the generated face ID, which we know is stored for 24 hours after detection:

```
        _faceIds.Add(faces[0].FaceId);
        CreateImageSources(image, i, faces[0].FaceId);
    }
}
```

Assuming that there is only one face per image, we add that face ID to our _faceIds list. The image, face ID, and current iteration number in the loop are passed on to a new function, `CreateImageSources`. This function contains a `switch` case based on the iteration number. Based on the number, we assign the image and face ID to the corresponding image and image ID property. This is then shown in the UI.

We have a button to group the images. To group the images, we call the Face API's `GroupAsync` method, passing on an array of face IDs, as shown in the following code. The array of face IDs must contain at least two elements, and it cannot contain more than 1,000 elements:

```
private async void GroupFaces(object obj) {
    try {
        GroupResultfaceGroups = await _faceServiceClient.
GroupAsync(_faceIds.ToArray());
```

The response is a `GroupResult` type, which may contain one or more groups, as well as the messy group. We check to see whether there is a response and then we parse it, as shown in the following code:

```
if (faceGroups != null)
    FaceGroupingResult = ParseGroupResult(faceGroups);
}
```

Before looking at the `ParseGroupResult` method, add the corresponding `catch` clause and close-up `GroupFaces` function.

When parsing the results, we first create a `StringBuilder` class to hold our text. Then we get the `groups` from the result. A group is an array of face IDs of the images in that group. All groups are stored in a list, and we append the number of groups to the `StringBuilder` class, as shown in the following code:

```
private string ParseGroupResult(GroupResultfaceGroups) {
    StringBuilder result = new StringBuilder();
    List<Guid[]>groups = faceGroups.Groups;
    result.AppendFormat("There are {0} group(s)\n", groups.Count);
```

We loop through the list of groups. Inside this loop, we loop through each item in the group. For the sake of readability, we have a helper function to find the image name from the ID. It finds the index in our `_faceIds` list. This is then used in the image name, so if the index is 2, the image name would be `Image 3`. For this to give the intended effect, you must have placed the images in a logical order, as follows:

```
result.Append("Groups:\t");

foreach(Guid[] guid in groups)
{
    foreach(Guid id in guid)
    {
        result.AppendFormat("{0} - ", GetImageName(id));
    }
    result.Append("\n");
}
```

The `GroupResult` method may also contain a `MessyGroup` array. This is an array of `Guid` variables containing the face IDs in that group. We loop through this array and append the image name, the same way we did with the regular groups, as shown in the following code:

```
result.Append("Messy group:\t");

Guid[] messyGroup = faceGroups.MessyGroup;
```

```
foreach(Guidguid in messyGroup)
{
    result.AppendFormat("{0} - ", GetImageName(guid));
}
```

We end the function by returning the `StringBuilder` function's text, which will output it to the screen, as follows:

```
        return result.ToString();
    }
```

Make sure that the `ViewModel` instances have been created in the `MainViewModel.cs` file. Also, make sure that the `View` has been added as a `TabItem` property in the `MainView.xaml` file. Compile and test the application.

If you are using the sample images provided, you may end up with something like the following:

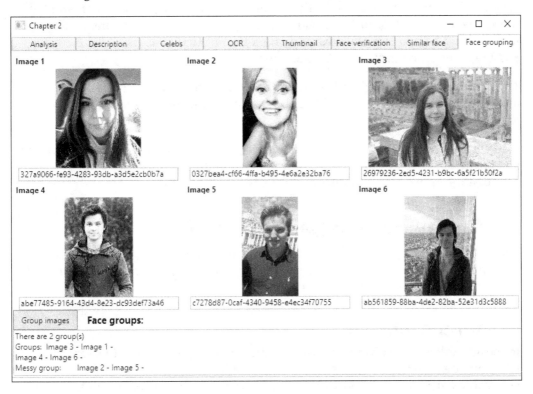

Adding identification to our smart-house application

As a part of our smart-house application, we want the application to recognize who we are. Doing so opens up the opportunity to get responses and actions from the application, tailored to you.

Creating our smart-house application

Create a new project for the smart-house application, based on the MVVM template we created earlier.

With the new project created, add the `Microsoft.ProjectOxford.Face` NuGet package.

As we will be building this application throughout this book, we will start small. In the `MainView.xaml` file, add a `TabControl` property containing two items. The two items should be two user controls, one called the `AdministrationView.xaml` file and the other called the `HomeView.xaml` file.

The administration control will be where we administer different parts of the application. The home control will be the starting point and the main control to use.

Add corresponding `ViewModel` instances to the `Views`. Make sure they are declared and created in `MainViewModel.cs`, as we have seen throughout this chapter. Make sure that the application compiles and runs before moving on.

Adding people to be identified

Before we can go on to identify a person, we need to have something to identify them from. To identify a person, we need a `PersonGroup` property. This is a group that contains several `Persons` properties.

Creating a view

In the administration control, we will execute several operations in this regard. The UI should contain two textbox elements, two list box elements, and six buttons. The two textbox elements will allow us to input a name for the person group and a name for the person. One list box will list all person groups that we have available. The other will list all the persons in any given group.

We have buttons for each of the operations that we want to execute, which are as follows:

- Add person group
- Delete person group
- Train person group
- Add person
- Delete person
- Add person face

The View model should have two ObservableCollection properties: one of a PersonGroup type and the other of a Person type. We should also add three string properties. One will be for our person group name, the other for our person name. The last will hold some status text. We also want a PersonGroup property for the selected person group. Finally, we want a Person property holding the selected person.

In our View model, we want to add a private variable for the FaceServiceClient method, as shown in the following code:

```
private FaceServiceClient _faceServiceClient;
```

This should be assigned in the constructor, which should accept a parameter of a FaceServiceClient type. It should also call an initialization function, which will initialize six ICommand properties. These maps to the buttons, created earlier. The initialization function should call the GetPersonGroups function to list all person groups available, as shown in the following code:

```
private async void GetPersonGroups() {
    try {
        PersonGroup[] personGroups = await
        _faceServiceClient.ListPersonGroupsAsync();
```

The ListPersonGroupsAsync function does not take any parameters, and returns a PersonGroup array if successfully executed, as shown in the following code:

```
        if(personGroups == null || personGroups.Length == 0)
        {
            StatusText = "No person groups found.";
            return;
        }

        PersonGroups.Clear();
```

```
        foreach (PersonGrouppersonGroup in personGroups)
        {
            PersonGroups.Add(personGroup);
        }
    }
```

We then check to see whether the array contains any elements. If it does, we clear out the existing `PersonGroups` list. Then we loop through each item of the `PersonGroup` array and add them to the `PersonGroups` list.

If no person groups exist, we can add a new one by filling in a name. The name you fill in here will also be used as a person group ID. This means that it can include numbers and English lowercase letters, the "-" character (hyphen), and the "_" character (underscore). The maximum length is 64 characters. When it is filled in, we can add a person group.

Adding person groups

First, we call the `DoesPersonGroupExistAsync` function, specifying `PersonGroupName` as a parameter, as shown in the following code. If this is `true`, then the name we have given already exists, and as such, we are not allowed to add it. Note how we call the `ToLower` function on the name. This is so we are sure that the ID is in lowercase:

```
    private async void AddPersonGroup(object obj) {
        try {
            if(await DoesPersonGroupExistAsync(PersonGroupName.
ToLower())) {
                StatusText = $"Person group {PersonGroupName} already
exist";

                return;
            }
```

If the person group does not exist, we call the `CreatePersonGroupAsync` function, as shown in the following code. Again, we specify the `PersonGroupName` as lowercase in the first parameter. This represents the ID of the group. The second parameter indicates the name we want. We end the function by calling the `GetPersonGroups` function again, so we get the newly added group in our list:

```
            await _faceServiceClient.CreatePersonGroupAsync
(PersonGroupName.ToLower(), PersonGroupName);
            StatusText = $"Person group {PersonGroupName} added";
            GetPersonGroups();
        }
```

The DoesPersonGroupExistAsync function makes one API call. It tries to call the
GetPersonGroupAsync function, with the person group ID specified as a parameter.
If the resultant PersonGroup list is anything but null, we return true.

To delete a person group, a group must be selected as follows:

```
private async void DeletePersonGroup(object obj)
{
    try
    {
        await _faceServiceClient.DeletePersonGroupAsync
(SelectedPersonGroup.PersonGroupId);
        StatusText = $"Deleted person group {SelectedPersonGroup.
Name}";

        GetPersonGroups();
    }
```

The API call to the DeletePersonGroupAsync function requires a person group ID
as a parameter. We get this from the selected person group. If no exception is caught,
then the call has completed successfully, and we call the GetPersonGroups function
to update our list.

When a person group is selected from the list, we make sure that we call the
GetPersons function. This will update the list of persons, as follows:

```
private async void GetPersons()
{
    if (SelectedPersonGroup == null)
        return;

    Persons.Clear();

    try
    {
        Person[] persons = await _faceServiceClient.GetPersonsAsyn
c(SelectedPersonGroup.PersonGroupId);
```

We make sure the selected person group is not null. If it is not, we clear our
persons list. The API call to the GetPersonsAsync function requires a person
group ID as a parameter. A successful call will result in a Person array.

If the resultant array contains any elements, we loop through it. Each `Person` object is added to our `persons` list, as shown in the following code:

```
if (persons == null || persons.Length == 0)
{
    StatusText = $"No persons found in
{SelectedPersonGroup.Name}.";
    return;
}

foreach (Person person in persons)
{
    Persons.Add(person);
}
}
```

Adding new persons

If no persons exist, we can add new ones. To add a new one, a person group must be selected, and a name of the person must be filled in. With this in place, we can click on the **Add** button:

```
private async void AddPerson(object obj)
{
    try
    {
        CreatePersonResultpersonId = await _faceServiceClient.Crea
tePersonAsync(SelectedPersonGroup.PersonGroupId, PersonName);
        StatusText = $"Added person {PersonName} got ID:
{personId.PersonId.ToString()}";

        GetPersons();
    }
```

The API call to the `CreatePersonAsync` function requires a person group ID as the first parameter. The next parameter is the name of the person. Optionally, we can add user data as a third parameter. In this case, it should be a string. When a new person has been created, we update the `persons` list by calling the `GetPersons` function again.

If we have selected a person group and a person, then we will be able to delete that person, as shown in the following code:

```
private async void DeletePerson(object obj)
{
    try
    {
        await _faceServiceClient.DeletePersonAsync
(SelectedPersonGroup.PersonGroupId, SelectedPerson.PersonId);

        StatusText = $"Deleted {SelectedPerson.Name} from
{SelectedPersonGroup.Name}";

        GetPersons();
    }
```

To delete a person, we make a call to the `DeletePersonAsync` function. This requires the person group ID of the person group the person lives in. It also requires the ID of the person we want to delete. If no exceptions are caught, then the call succeeded, and we call the `GetPersons` function to update our person list.

Our administration control now looks similar to the following screenshot:

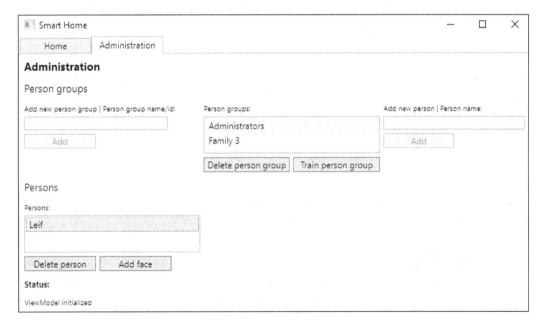

Associating faces with a person

Before we can identify a person, we need to associate faces with that person. With a given person group and person selected, we can add faces. To do so, we open a file dialog. When we have an image file, we can add the face to the person, as follows:

```
using (StreamimageFile = File.OpenRead(filePath))
{
    AddPersistedFaceResultaddFaceResult = await _
faceServiceClient.AddPersonFaceAsync(
    SelectedPersonGroup.PersonGroupId,
    SelectedPerson.PersonId, imageFile);

    if (addFaceResult != null)
    {
        StatusText = $"Face added for {SelectedPerson.Name}.
Remember to train the person group!";
    }
}
```

We open the image file as a `Stream`. This file is passed on as the third parameter in our call to the `AddPersonFaceAsync` function. Instead of a stream, we could have passed a URL to an image.

The first parameter in the call is the person group ID of the group in which the person lives. The next parameter is the person ID.

Some optional parameters to include are user data in the form of a string and a `FaceRectangle` parameter for the image. The `FaceRectangle` parameter is required if there is more than one face in the image.

A successful call will result in an `AddPersistedFaceResult` object. This contains the persisted face ID for the person.

Each person can have a maximum of 248 faces associated with it. The more faces you can add, the more likely it is that you will receive a solid identification later. The faces that you add should from slightly different angles.

Training the model

With enough faces associated with the persons, we need to train the person group. This is a task that is required after any change to a person or person group.

We can train a person group when one has been selected, as shown in the following code:

```
private async void TrainPersonGroup(object obj)
{
    try
    {
        await _faceServiceClient.TrainPersonGroupAsync(
SelectedPersonGroup.PersonGroupId);
```

The call to the `TrainPersonGroupAsync` function takes a person group ID as a parameter, as shown in the following code. It does not return anything, and it may take a while to execute:

```
while(true)
{
    TrainingStatustrainingStatus = await _
faceServiceClient.GetPersonGroupTrainingStatusAsync
(SelectedPersonGroup.PersonGroupId);
```

We want to ensure that the training completed successfully. To do so, we call the `GetPersonGroupTrainingStatusAsync` function inside a `while` loop. This call requires a person group ID, and a successful call results in a `TrainingStatus` object, as shown in the following code:

```
if(trainingStatus.Status != Status.Running)
{
    StatusText = $"Person group finished with status:
{trainingStatus.Status}";
    break;
}

StatusText = "Training person group...";
await Task.Delay(1000);
    }
}
```

We check the status and we show the result if it is not running. If the training is still running, we wait for one second and run the check again.

When the training has succeeded, we are ready to identify people.

Additional functionality

There are a few API calls that we have not looked at, which will be mentioned briefly in the following bullet list:

- To update a person group, call the following; this function does not return anything:

  ```
  UpdatePersonGroupAsync(PERSONGROUPID, NEWNAME, USERDATA)
  ```

- To get a person's face, call the following:

  ```
  GetPersonFaceAsync(PERSONGROUPID, PERSONID,
  PERSISTEDFACEID)
  ```

  A successful call returns the persisted face ID and user-provided data.

- To delete a person's face, call the following; this call does not return anything:

  ```
  DeletePersonFaceAsync(PERSONGROUPID, PERSONID,
  PERSISTEDFACeID)
  ```

- To update a person, call the following; this call does not return anything:

  ```
  UpdatePersonAsync(PERSONGROUPID, PERSONID, NEWNAME,
  USERDATA)
  ```

- To update a person's face, call the following; this call does not return anything:

  ```
  UpdatePersonFaceAsync(PERSONGROUID, PERSONID,
  PERSISTEDFACEID, USERDATA)
  ```

Identifying a person

To identify a person, we are first going to upload an image. Open the `HomeView.xaml` file and add a `ListBox` element to the UI. This will contain the person groups to choose from when identifying a person. We will need to add a button element to find an image, upload it, and identify the person. A `TextBox` element is added to show the working response. For our own convenience, we also add an image element to show the image we are using.

In the `View` model, add an `ObservableCollection` property of a `PersonGroup` type. We need to add a property for the selected `PersonGroup` type. Also, add a `BitmapImage` property for our image, and a string property for the response. We will also need an `ICommand` property for our button.

Add a `private` variable for the `FaceServiceClient` type, as follows:

```
private FaceServiceClient _faceServiceClient;
```

This will be assigned in our constructor, which should accept a parameter of a `FaceServiceClient` type. From the constructor, call on the `Initialize` function to initialize everything, as shown in the following code:

```
private void Initialize()
{
    GetPersonGroups();
    UploadOwnerImageCommand = new DelegateCommand(UploadOwnerImage
,CanUploadOwnerImage);
}
```

First, we call the `GetPersonGroups` function to retrieve all the person groups. This function makes a call to the `ListPersonGroupsAsync` API, which we saw earlier. The result is added to our `PersonGroup` list's `ObservableCollection` parameter.

Next, we create our `ICommand` object. The `CanUploadOwnerImage` function will return `true` if we have selected an item from the `PersonGroup` list. If we have not, it will return `false`, and we will not be able to identify anyone.

In the `UploadOwnerImage` function, we first browse to an image and then load it. With an image loaded and a file path available, we can start to identify the person in the image, as shown in the following code:

```
using (StreamimageFile = File.OpenRead(filePath))
{
    Face[] faces = await _faceServiceClient.
DetectAsync(imageFile);
    Guid[] faceIds = faces.Select(face =>face.FaceId).ToArray();
```

We open the image as a `Stream` type, as shown in the following code. Using this, we detect faces in the image. From the detected faces, we get all the face IDs in an array:

```
IdentifyResult[] personsIdentified = await _faceServiceClient.
IdentifyAsync (SelectedPersonGroup.PersonGroupId,
faceIds, 1);
```

The array of face IDs will be sent as the second parameter to the `IdentifyAsync` API call. Remember that when we detect a face, it is stored for 24 hours. Proceeding to use the corresponding face ID will make sure that the service knows which face to use for identification.

The first parameter used is the ID of the person group we have selected. The last parameter in the call is the number of candidates returned. As we do not want to identify more than one person at a time, we specify one. Because of this, we should ensure that there is only one face in the image we upload.

A successful API call will result in an array of the `IdentifyResult` parameter, as shown in the following code. Each item in this array will contain candidates:

```
foreach(IdentifyResultpersonIdentified in personsIdentified) {
    if(personIdentified.Candidates.Length == 0) {
        SystemResponse = "Failed to identify you.";
        break;
    }
    GuidpersonId = personIdentified.Candidates[0].PersonId;
```

We loop through the array of results, as shown in the following code. If we do not have any candidates, we just break out of the loop. If, however, we do have candidates, we get the `PersonId` parameter of the first candidate (we asked for only one candidate earlier, so this is okay):

```
    Person person = await faceServiceClient.GetPersonAsync(
SelectedPersonGroup.PersonGroupId, personId);

    if(person != null) {
        SystemResponse = $"Welcome home, {person.Name}";
        break;
    }
  }
}
```

With the `personId` parameter, we get a single `Person` object, using the API to call the `GetPersonAsync` function. If the call is successful, we print a welcome message to the correct person (as shown in the following screenshot) and break out of the loop:

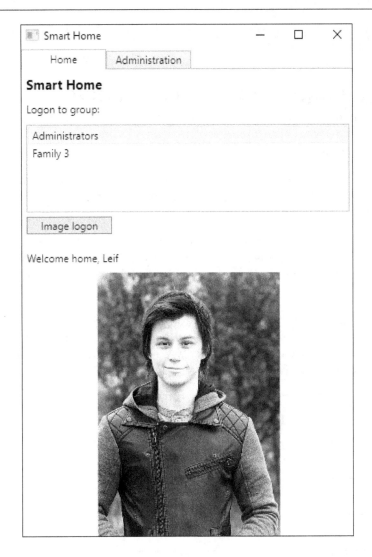

Knowing your mood using the Face API

The Face API allows you to recognize emotions from faces.

Research has shown that there are some key emotions that can be classified as cross-cultural. These are happiness, sadness, surprise, anger, fear, contempt, disgust, and neutral. All of these are detected by the API, which allows your applications to respond in a more personalized way by knowing the user's mood.

We will learn how to recognize emotions from images so that our smart-house application can know our mood.

Getting images from a web camera

Imagine that there are several cameras around your house. The smart-house application can see what your mood is at any time. By knowing this, it can utilize the mood to better predict your needs.

We are going to add web-camera capabilities to our application. If you do not have a web camera, you can follow along, but load images using the techniques we have already seen.

First we need to add a NuGet package to our smart-house application. Search for `OpenCvSharp3-AnyCPU` and install the package by **shimat**. This is a package that allows for the processing of images, and is utilized by the next dependency we are going to add.

In the example code provided, there is a project called `VideoFrameAnalyzer`. This is a project written by Microsoft that allows us to grab frame-by-frame images from a web camera. Using this, we are able to analyze emotions in our application. The use case we will execute is as follows:

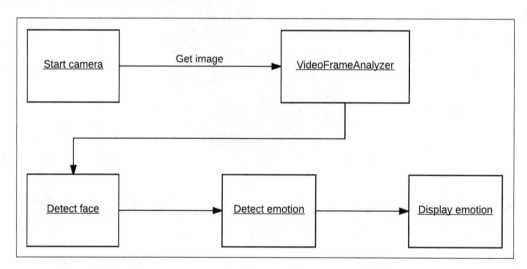

In our `HomeView.xaml` file, add two new buttons. One will be to start the web camera while the other will be to stop it.

In the corresponding `View` model, add two `ICommand` properties for each of the buttons. Also add the following `private` members:

```
private FrameGrabber<CameraResult> _frameGrabber;
private static readonly ImageEncodingParam[] s_jpegParams = {
    new ImageEncodingParam(ImwriteFlags.JpegQuality, 60)
};
```

The first one is a `FrameGrabber` object, which is from the `VideoFrameAnalyzer` project. The `static` member is an array of parameters for images, and is used when fetching web camera images. Additionally, we need to add a `CameraResult` class, which should be within the `ViewModel` file.

We initialize the `EmotionScores` to `null`, as shown in the following code. This is done so that new emotion scores always will be assigned from the most resent analysis result:

```
internal class CameraResult {
    public EmotionScores EmotionScores { get; set; } = null;
}
```

Add an initialization of the `_frameGrabber` member in the constructor and add the following in the `Initialization` function:

```
_frameGrabber.NewFrameProvided += OnNewFrameProvided;
```

Each time a new frame is provided from the camera, an event is raised.

When we receive new frames, we want to create a `BitmapImage` from it to show it in the UI. To do so requires us to invoke the action from the current dispatcher, as the event is triggered from a background thread, as shown in the following code:

```
private void OnNewFrameProvided(object sender,
FrameGrabber<CameraResult>.NewFrameEventArgs e) {
    Application.Current.Dispatcher.Invoke(() => {
        BitmapSource bitmapSource = e.Frame.Image.ToBitmapSource();

        JpegBitmapEncoder encoder = new JpegBitmapEncoder();
        MemoryStream memoryStream = new MemoryStream();
        BitmapImage image = new BitmapImage();
```

We get the `BitmapSource` of the `Frame` and create some required variables.

Using the encoder we created, we add the bitmapSource and save it to the memoryStream, as follows:

```
encoder.Frames.Add(BitmapFrame.Create(bitmapSource));
encoder.Save(memoryStream);
```

This memoryStream is then assigned to the BitmapImage we created, as shown in the following code. This is in turn assigned to the ImageSource, which will show the frame in the UI:

```
memoryStream.Position = 0;
image.BeginInit();
image.CacheOption = BitmapCacheOption.OnLoad;
image.StreamSource = memoryStream;
image.EndInit();

memoryStream.Close();
ImageSource = image;
```

As this event will be triggered a lot, we will get a fluent stream in the UI, and it will seem like it is a direct video feed.

In our Initialization function, we will also need to create our ICommand for the buttons, as follows:

```
StopCameraCommand = new DelegateCommand(StopCamera);
StartCameraCommand = new DelegateCommand(StartCamera,
CanStartCamera);
```

To be able to start the camera, we need to have selected a person group, and we need to have at least one camera available:

```
private bool CanStartCamera(object obj) {
    return _frameGrabber.GetNumCameras() > 0 &&
SelectedPersonGroup != null;
}
```

To start a camera, we need to specify which camera to use and how often we want to trigger an analysis using the following code:

```
private async void StartCamera(object obj) {
    _frameGrabber.TriggerAnalysisOnInterval(TimeSpan.
FromSeconds(5));
    await _frameGrabber.StartProcessingCameraAsync();
}
```

If no camera is specified in `StartProcessingCameraAsync`, the first one available is chosen by default.

We will get back to the analysis part of this process soon.

To stop the camera, we run the following command:

```
private async void StopCamera(object obj) {
    await _frameGrabber.StopProcessingAsync();
}
```

Letting the smart house know your mood

We now have a video from the web camera available for our use.

In the `FrameGrabber` class, there is a `Func`, which will be used for analysis functions. We need to create the function that will be passed on this that will enable emotions to be recognized.

Create a new function, `EmotionAnalysisAsync`, that accepts a `VideoFrame` as a parameter. The return type should be `Task<CameraResult>` and the function should be marked as `async`.

The `frame` we get as a parameter is used to create a `MemoryStream` containing the current frame. This will be in the JPG file format. We will find a face in this image, and we want to ensure that we specify that we want emotion attributes using the following code:

```
private async Task<CameraResult> EmotionAnalysisAsync (VideoFrame
frame) {
    MemoryStream jpg = frame.Image.ToMemoryStream(".jpg", s_
jpegParams);
    try {
        Face[] face = await _faceServiceClient.DetectAsync(jpg, true,
false, new List<FaceAttributeType>
            { FaceAttributeType.Emotion });
        EmotionScores emotions = face.First()?.FaceAttributes?.Emotion;
```

A successful call will result in an object containing all the emotion scores, as shown in the following code. The scores are what we want to return:

```
return new CameraResult {
    EmotionScores = emotions
};
```

Catch any exceptions that may be thrown, returning `null` when they are.

We need to assign the `Initialize` function to the `Func`. We also need to add an event handler each time we have a new result.

When a new result is obtained, we grab the `EmotionScore` that is received, as shown in the following code. If it is `null` or does not contain any elements, then we do not want to do anything else:

```
_frameGrabber.NewResultAvailable += OnResultAvailable;
_frameGrabber.AnalysisFunction = EmotionAnalysisAsync;
private void OnResultAvailable(object sender,
FrameGrabber<CameraResult>.NewResultEventArgs e)
{
    var analysisResult = e.Analysis.EmotionScores;
    if (analysisResult == null)
        return;
```

In the following code, we parse the emotion scores in `AnalyseEmotions`, which we will look at in a bit:

```
string emotion = AnalyseEmotions(analysisResult);

Application.Current.Dispatcher.Invoke(() => {
    SystemResponse = $"You seem to be {emotion} today.";
});
}
```

Using the result from `AnalyseEmotions`, we print a string to the result to indicate the current mood. This will need to be invoked from the current dispatcher, as the event has been triggered in another thread.

To get the current mood in a readable format, we parse the emotion scores in `AnalyseEmotions` as follows:

```
private string AnalyseEmotions(Scores analysisResult) {
    string emotion = string.Empty;
    var sortedEmotions = analysisResult.ToRankedList();
    string currentEmotion = sortedEmotions.First().Key;
```

With the `Scores` we get, we call a `ToRankedList` function. This will return a list of `KeyValuePair`, containing each emotion, along with the corresponding confidence. The first one will be the most likely, the second will be the second most likely, and so on. We only care about the most likely one, so we select it.

With the top emotion score selected, we use a `switch` statement to find the correct emotion. This is returned and printed to the result, as follows:

```
switch(currentEmotion)
{
    case "Anger":
        emotion = "angry";
        break;
    case "Contempt":
        emotion = "contempt";
        break;
    case "Disgust":
        emotion = "disgusted";
        break;
    case "Fear":
        emotion = "scared";
        break;
    case "Happiness":
        emotion = "happy";
        break;
    case "Neutral":
        default:
        emotion = "neutral";
        break;
    case "Sadness":
        emotion = "sad";
        break;
    case "Suprise":
        emotion = "suprised";
        break;
}
return emotion;
}
```

The last piece of the puzzle is to make sure that the analysis is being executed at a specified interval. In the `StartCamera` function, add the following line, just before calling `StartProcessingCamera`:

```
_frameGrabber.TriggerAnalysisOnInterval(TimeSpan.FromSeconds(5));
```

This will trigger an emotion analysis to be called every fifth second.

When I have a smile on my face, the application now knows that I am happy and can provide further interaction accordingly. If we compile and run the example, we should get results like those shown in the following screenshots:

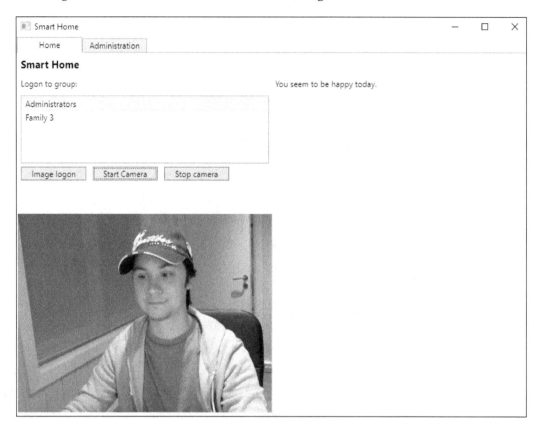

As my mood changes to neutral, the application detects this as well:

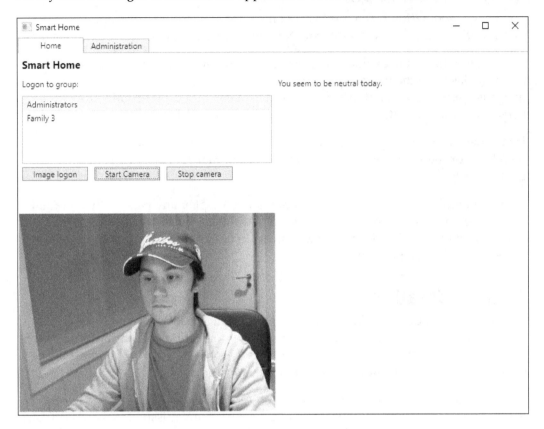

Automatically moderating user content

Using the content moderator API, we can add monitoring to user-generated content. The API is created to assist with flags and to assess and filter offensive and unwanted content.

Types of content moderation APIs

We will quickly go through the key features of the moderation APIs in this section.

> A reference to the documentation for all APIs can be found at `https://docs.microsoft.com/nb-no/azure/cognitive-services/content-moderator/api-reference`.

Image moderation

The image moderation API allows you to moderate images for adult and inappropriate content. It can also extract textual content and detect faces in images.

When using the API to evaluate inappropriate content, the API will take an image as input. Based on the image, it will return a Boolean value, indicating whether the image is appropriate or not. It will also contain a corresponding confidence score between 0 and 1. The Boolean value is set based on a set of default thresholds.

If the image contains any text, the API will use OCR to extract the text. It will then look for the same adult or racy content as text moderation, which we will get to shortly.

Some content-based applications may not want to display any personally identifiable information, in which case it can be wise to detect faces in images. Based on the information retrieved in the face-detection evaluation, you can ensure that no user content contains images of people.

Text moderation

Using the text moderation API, you can screen text against custom and shared lists of text. It is able to detect personally identifiable information and profanity in text. In this case, personally identifiable information is the presence of information such as email addresses, phone numbers, and mailing addresses.

When you submit a text to be moderated, the API can detect the language used, if it is not stated. Screening text will automatically correct any misspelled words (to catch deliberately misspelled words). The results will contain the location of profanities and personal identifiable information in the text, as well as the original text, autocorrected text, and the language. Using these results, you can moderate content appropriately.

Moderation tools

There are three ways to moderate content, enabled by the content moderator:

- **Human moderation**: Using teams and community to manually moderate all content
- **Automated moderation**: Utilizing machine learning and AI to moderate at scale with no human interaction
- **Hybrid moderation**: A combination of the preceding two, where people typically occasionally do reviews

The common scenario used is the last one. This is where machine learning is used to automate the moderation process and teams of people can review the moderation. Microsoft have created a review tool to ease this process. This allows you to see through all the items for review in a web browser while using the APIs in your application. We will look into this tool in the following section.

Using the review tool

To get started with the review tool, head over to `https://contentmoderator.cognitive.microsoft.com/`. From here, you can sign in using your Microsoft account. On your first sign-in, you will need to register by adding your name to the account. You will then go on to create a *review team*, as shown in the following screenshot:

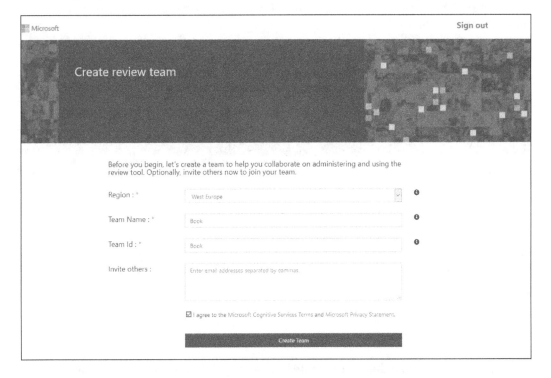

You can do this by selecting the region and entering a team name. You can optionally enter the email addresses of other people who should be part of the team. Click on **Create Team**.

Once in, you will be presented with the following dashboard:

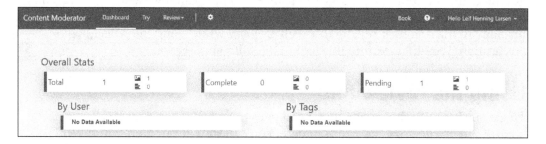

You will be presented with the total number of images and textual content that are for review. You will also be presented with the total number of completed and pending reviews. The dashboard also lists the users that have completed reviews, as well as any tags used for content.

By selecting the **Try** option in the menu, you have the option to upload images or text to execute moderation online. Do this by either uploading an image or entering sample text in the textbox. Once done, you can select the **Review** option, where you will be presented with the following screen:

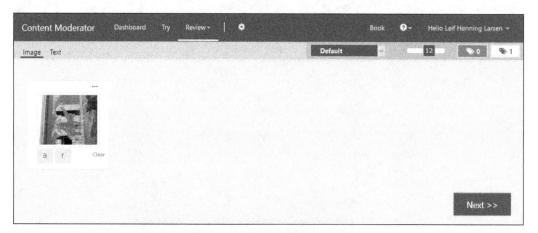

If the given content is either adult content or racist, you can click on the **a** or **r** buttons, respectively. For text, any profanities will be displayed. Once you are done marking reviews, click on **Next**. This will go through a process of moderating the given content.

Other tools

Apart from the APIs and the review tool, there are two other tools you can use, as follows:

- **List manager API**: Using custom lists of images and text to moderate pre-identified content that you don't wish to scan for repeatedly
- **Workflow API**: Using this API, you can define conditional logic and actions to specify the policies used by your specific content

To use any of these APIs, or to use the moderator APIs, you can make calls to specific REST APIs. To do so, you will need to use an API key and a base URL. These settings can be found under **Settings | Credentials** on the review tool website, as shown in the following screenshot:

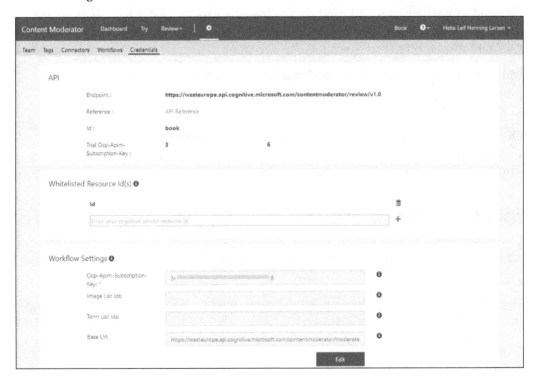

Building your own image classifiers

The **Custom Vision** service allows you to build your own image classifiers. There might be cases where you require special images to use the image APIs. Such cases may be from a factory, where the equipment you need to recognize is not very available. You can start to build a prototype, using as little as 50 images.

 To get started with the Custom Vision service, head over to `https://customvision.ai/` and log on using your Microsoft account.

Building a classifier

To build a classifier, you will need to create a new project. Doing so will allow you to specify what category the images will be in. You will also select the classification type and project type.

Moving on, you will need to upload images. This can be done through the web page or through a REST API. All images must be tagged so that the classifier will recognize similar images later.

Once all images (at least 50) are uploaded, you must train your model. Once the training is complete, you will be presented with a precision percentage per tag. This is a measurement of the accuracy of the model.

Improving the model

On the website, you can test your models. Doing so will allow you to upload images, which will be classified by the model. If it turns out that the model performs poorly, you can improve the model.

Improving the model involves uploading more images. Some general guidelines to improve the model are as follows:

- Have enough images
- Make sure that the balance between tags is good (so that there is an equal number of images per tag)
- Use a diverse set of images for training
- Use images that have been used for prediction
- Inspect the predictions

Using the trained model

Once you are happy with the model, you can use it for predictions. The model can be used in one of the two following ways:

- With a REST API
- Export it to a model file

The first choice involves uploading an image. Calling the generated endpoint for your model, along with the image data, will result in a prediction. The result will contain the predicted tags, ordered by their probability.

The second choice allows you to run the prediction offline. This means that you can utilize different frameworks, such as TensorFlow, CoreML, and ONNX, for different platforms. How to use the model with these frameworks is beyond the scope of this book. The downside of using an offline model is that the accuracy may suffer a bit compared to the online version.

Summary

In this chapter, we took a deep dive into a big part of the vision APIs. You first learned how to get good descriptions of images. Next, you learned how to recognize celebrities and text in images, and you learned how to generate thumbnails. Following this, we moved on to the Face API, where we got more information about detected faces. We found out how to verify whether two faces were the same. After this, you learned how to find similar faces and group similar faces. Then we added identification to our smart-house application, allowing it to know who we are. We also added the ability to recognize emotions in faces. We took a quick look into the content moderator to see how you can add automatic moderation to user-generated content. Finally, we briefly looked at the Custom Vision service, and how you can use it to generate specific prediction models.

The next chapter will continue with the final vision API. We will focus on videos, learning what the video indexer API has to offer.

3
Analyzing Videos

In the previous chapter, we looked at different APIs for processing images. We are going to cover one new API: the Video Indexer API.

In this chapter, we will cover the following topics:

- General overview of Video Indexer
- Guide to Video Indexer using the prebuilt UI

Diving into Video Indexer

Video Indexer is a service that allows you to upload videos and gain insights from the videos that you upload. These insights can be used to make videos (and by extension your content) more discoverable. They can also be used to improve user engagement.

General overview

Using artificial intelligence technologies, Video Indexer enables you to extract a great deal of information. It can gain insights from the following list of features:

- Audio transcript, with language detection
- Creation of closed captions
- Noise reduction
- Face tracking and identification
- Speaker indexing
- Visual-text recognition
- Voice-activity detection
- Scene detection

- Keyframe extraction
- Sentiment analysis
- Translation
- Visual-content moderation
- Keyword extraction
- Annotations
- Detection of brands
- Object and action labeling
- Textual-content moderation
- Emotion detection

Typical scenarios

The following list shows a few typical scenarios where one might want to use Video Indexer:

- **Search**: If you have a library of videos, you can use the insights gained from Video Indexer to index each video. Indexing by (for example) spoken word or where two specific people are seen together can provide a much better search experience for users.

- **Monetization**: The value of each video can be improved by using the insights gained from Video Indexer. For example, you can deliver more relevant ads by using the video insights to present ads that are contextually correct. For instance, by using the insights, you can display ads for sports shoes in the middle of a football match instead of a swimming competition.

- **User engagement**: By using the insights gained from Video Indexer, you can improve user engagement by displaying relevant elements of the video. If you have a video covering different material for 60 minutes, placing video moments over that time allows the user to jump straight to the relevant section.

Key concepts

The following sections describe the key concepts that are important to understand when discussing Video Indexer.

Breakdowns

A breakdown is a complete list containing all details of all the insights. This is where a full video transcript comes from; however, breakdowns are mostly too detailed for users. Instead, you typically want to use summarized insights to obtain only the most relevant knowledge. If more detailed insights is required, you would go from the summarized insights to the full breakdowns.

Summarized insights

Instead of going through several thousand time ranges and checking for given data, one can use summarized insights. This will provide you with an aggregated view of the data, such as faces, keywords, and sentiments, and the time ranges they appear in.

Keywords

From any transcribed audio in the video, Video Indexer will extract a list of keywords and topics that may be relevant to the video.

Sentiments

When a video is transcribed, it is also analyzed for sentiment. This means that you can gauge whether or not the video is more positive or negative.

Blocks

Blocks are used to move through the data in an easy way. If there are changes to speakers or long pauses between audio, these might be indexed as separate blocks.

Unlocking video insights using Video Indexer

In this section, we will look at how to use Video Indexer.

How to use Video Indexer

We are going to take a quick look at how you can utilize Video Indexer.

Through a web portal

To use the prebuilt Video Indexer tool from Microsoft, head over to
`https://vi.microsoft.com/`. Sign up or log in with your Microsoft account.
When you have signed in, you will be asked to register the account by filling out
some information, as shown in the following screenshot:

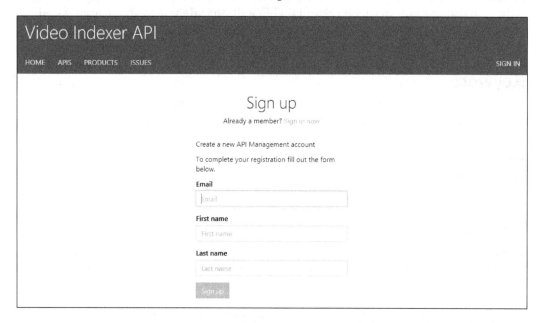

Once you have logged in, you will find yourself at a dashboard, as shown in the
following screenshot:

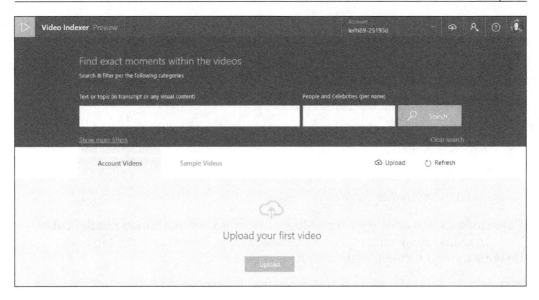

To get started, you can upload your videos by clicking on **Upload**. This will open a popup that you can use to either upload a video or enter a URL to a video. Alternatively, you can get started quickly by selecting a sample video by clicking on **Sample Videos** in the menu.

When you have chosen a video, or when the video you have uploaded has completed its indexing, you will be taken to a page to see the insights. This page will show you the video in full, along with any insights that are found, as shown in the following screenshot:

In addition to the keywords and people that were discovered in the video, you will get a list of annotations and sentiments of the speech throughout the video. These insights will give the following list of information (if such information is detected):

- People appearing in the video
- Keywords about the video content
- Labels related to the video
- Brands detected
- Emotions
- List of keyframes

Video Indexer will also create a timeline of every key event throughout the video. You can follow along with this timeline by selecting **Timeline** at the top of the **Insights** frame, as shown in the following screenshot:

This timeline will automatically move forward as the video moves forward.

The timeline will display the transcript of any audio in the video. In addition, it will show any objects that were detected and any people recognized.

Video Indexer API

Apart from the premade Video Indexer site, there is also a Video Indexer API present. This allows you to gain the exact same insights as the web tool from your own application.

To get started with the API, head over to `https://api-portal.videoindexer.ai/`. Once here, log in with your Microsoft account. The first step is to subscribe to the API product. You can do this by clicking on the **Products** tab. This will present you with the following:

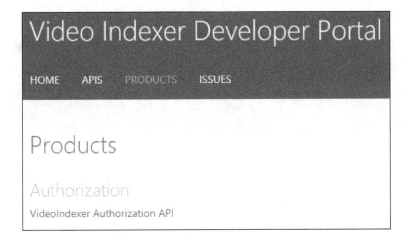

By clicking on **Authorization**, you will be taken to another page, as shown in the following screenshot:

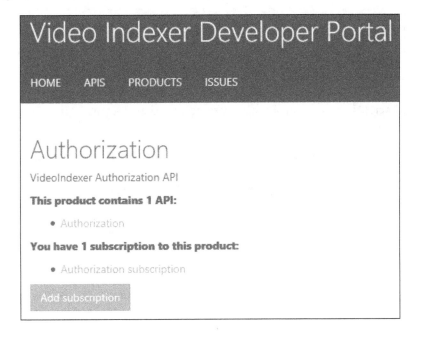

Click on **Add subscription**. This will display the following:

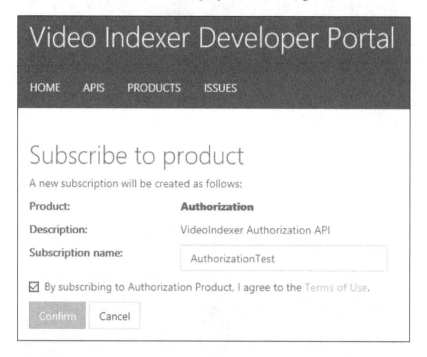

Fill in a **Subscription name** and make sure you read and agree to the terms of use. Click **Confirm**.

Once you have subscribed to the product, you will be taken to a page to see the API keys, as shown in the following screenshot. This can always be reached by going to the **Products** tab and selecting the product you have subscribed to:

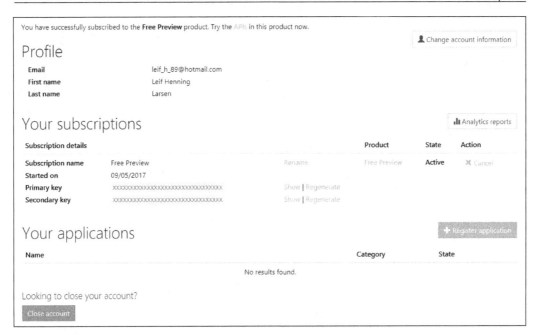

Once you have the key, select the **APIs** tab and select your subscribed product. This will present all the API calls that are available for you to use. The entire API is REST-based and, as such, you are able to use it from any application as long as you provide the correct request parameters and API keys.

Summary

In this chapter, we covered Video Indexer. We started with a general overview, learning what Video Indexer is. We then learned how to analyze videos in the Video Indexer web application. We ended the chapter by looking at how to sign up for the REST API, allowing us to utilize the power of Video Indexer in our own applications.

In the next chapter, we will move away from the vision APIs and into the first language API. You will learn how to configure the API to understand intent in sentences, using the power of LUIS.

4
Letting Applications Understand Commands

"LUIS saved us tremendous time while going from a prototype to production."

- Eyal Yavor, Cofounder and CTO of Meekan

Throughout the previous chapters, we have focused on vision APIs. Starting with this chapter, we will move on to language APIs, where we will start with the **Language Understanding Intelligent Service** (**LUIS**). Throughout this chapter, you will learn how to create and maintain language-understanding models.

By the end of this chapter, we will have covered the following topics:

- Creating language-understanding models
- Handling common requests using prebuilt models from Bing and Cortana

Creating language-understanding models

Sometimes, we might wish that our computer could understand what we want. As we go on with our day-to-day business, we want to be able to talk to our computer, or mobile phone, using regular sentences. This is hard to do without any extra help.

Utilizing the power of LUIS, we can now solve this problem. By creating language-understanding models, we can allow applications to understand what users want. We can also recognize key data, which is, typically, data that you want to be part of a query or command. If you are asking for the latest news on a certain issue, then the key data would be the topic of the news that you are asking for.

Creating an application

To get started with LUIS, you should head over to `https://www.luis.ai`. This is where we will set up our application. Click on the **Sign in or create an account** button to get started.

Let's create our first application. Click on **My Apps** from the top menu. This should take you back to the application list, which should be empty. Click on **New App**.

In the form that is shown, we fill in the given information about our application. We are required to give the application a name. We also need to indicate an atypical usage scenario, which will be set by default to **Other (please specify)**. Instead, set this to **SmartHouseApplication**. This application falls under the **Tools** domain. We will choose an English **Application Culture**.

The other languages that are available are Brazilian, Portuguese, Chinese, French, German, Italian, Japanese, and Spanish.

The following screenshot shows how we can define the application:

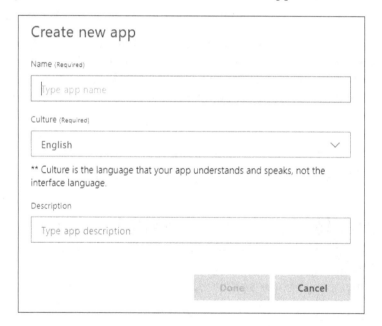

When you click on the **Create** button, the application will be created. This process will take about a minute or so to complete, so just be patient.

When the application has been created, you will be taken to the application's home base, as shown in the following screenshot:

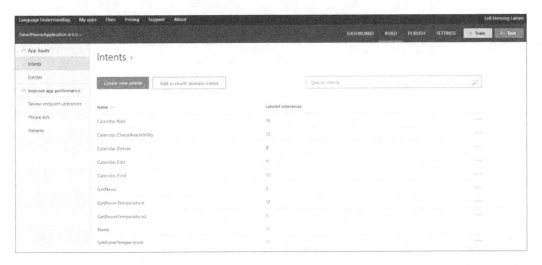

As you can see, we have a variety of features to use, and we will cover the important ones here.

The application we will build will be aimed at our smart house application. We will configure the application to recognize commands to set the temperature in different rooms. In addition, we would like it to tell us what the temperatures in the different rooms are.

Recognizing key data using entities

One of the key features of LUIS is the ability to recognize key data in sentences. The instances of this key data are known as entities. In a news application, an example of an entity would be the topic. If we ask to get the latest news, we could specify a topic for the service to recognize.

For our application, we want to add an entity for our rooms. We do this by selecting **Entities** in the left-hand pane. Then we click on **Add custom entity**.

We will be presented with the following screen:

Enter the name of the entity and click on the **Save** button. That's it—you have now created the first entity. We will see how to use this in a bit.

As you may have noticed, there is a drop-down list called **Entity type** in the entity creation form. Entity types are a way to create hierarchical entities, which is basically about defining relationships between entities.

As an example, you can imagine searching for news inside a given time frame. The generic top-level entity is Date. Going from there, you can define two children, StartDate and EndDate. These will be recognized by the service, where models will be built for the entity and its children.

To add a hierarchical child entity, check the checkbox and select **Hierarchical** from the selection. Click on the + button next to **Entity Children** for each child you want to add, as shown in the following screenshot. Enter the name of the child:

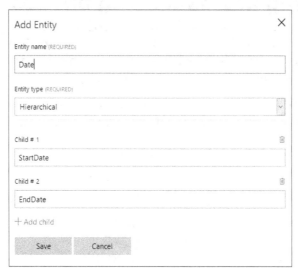

The other types of entities you can add are called **composite entities**. This is a type of entity that is formed by a set of existing entities. This is what we would call a *has-a* relationship, so the components are children, but not in a parent-child relationship.

Composite entities do not share common traits as hierarchical entities do. When deleting the top-level entity, you do not delete components. Using composite entities, LUIS can identify groups of entities, which are then treated as a single entity.

Using composite entities is like ordering a pizza. You can order a pizza by stating *I want a large pizza with mushrooms and pepperoni*. In this example, we can see the size as an entity, and we can also see the two toppings as entities. Combining these could make a composite entity, which is called an order.

The last type of entity you can add is called a **list entity**. This is a customized list of entity values to be used as keywords or identifiers within utterances.

When using entities, there may be times where an entity consists of several words. In our case, with the Rooms entity, we may ask for the living room. To be able to identify such phrasings, we can define a feature list. This is a comma-separated list that can contain some or all of the expected phrases.

Let's add one for our application. On the left-hand side, at the bottom of the pane, you will see **Features**. Select this and click on **Add phrase list** to create a new list. Call it Rooms and add the different rooms that you would expect to find in a house, as shown in the following screenshot:

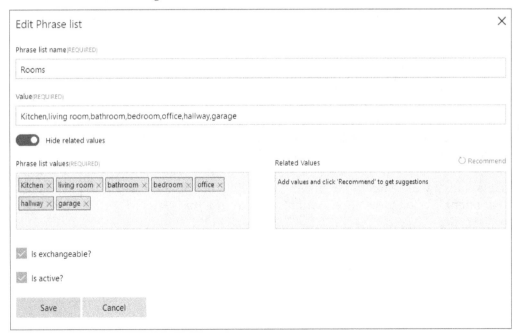

By clicking on **Recommend** on the right-hand side, LUIS will recommend more values related to the ones you have already entered.

We will see how this is utilized later.

In addition to creating phrase lists, we can create **pattern features**. The typical use case of using pattern features is when you have data that matches patterns but it is not feasible to enter them as a phrase list. Pattern features are typically used with product numbers.

Understanding what the user wants using intents

Now that we have defined an entity, it is time to see how it fits in with intents. An **intent** is basically the purpose of a sentence.

We can add intents to our application by selecting the **Intents** option in the left-hand pane. Click on **Add intent**. When we add an intent, we give it a name. The name should be descriptive of what the intent is. We want to add an intent named `GetRoomTemperature`, where the goal is to get the temperature of a given room, as shown in the following screenshot:

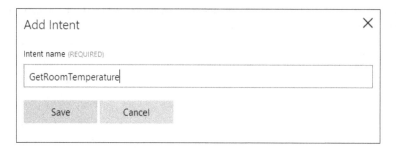

When you click on the **Save** button, you will be taken to the utterance page. Here, we can add sentences that we can use for the intent, so let's add one. Enter `what is the temperature in the kitchen?` and press *Enter*. The sentence (or utterance, as it is called) will be ready for labeling. Labeling an utterance means that we define what intent it belongs to. We should also make sure that we mark entities with the correct type.

The following screenshot shows the labeling process for our first utterance:

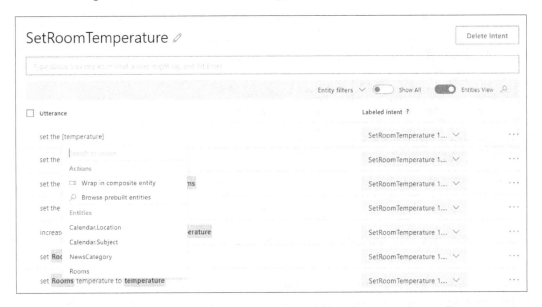

As you can see, the entity is marked. You can tell LUIS that a word is a given entity by clicking on the word. This will pop up a menu containing all the available entities, and you can then select the correct one. Also, note how the **GetRoomTemperature** intent is selected in the drop-down list. Click **Train** once you are done labeling your utterances.

All applications are created with a default intent called **None**. This intent will encompass sentences that do not belong to our application at all. If we were to say *Order a large pizza with mushrooms and pepperoni*, this would end up with **None** as the intent.

When you are creating intents, you should define at least three to five utterances. This will give LUIS something to work with, and, as such, it can create better models. We will see how we can improve performance later in this chapter.

Simplifying development using prebuilt models

Building entities and intents can be easy or it can be intricate. Fortunately, LUIS provides a set of prebuilt entities that stem from Bing. These entities will be included in the applications, as well as on the web, while going through the labeling process.

The following table describes all the available prebuilt entities:

Entity	Example
builtin.number	Five, 23.21
builtin.ordinal	Second, 3rd
builtin.temperature	2 degrees Celsius, 104 F
builtin.dimension	231 square kilometers
builtin.age	27 years old
builtin.geography	City, country, point of interest
builtin.encyclopedia	Person, organization, event, TV episode, product, film, and so on
builtin.datetime	Date, time, duration, set

The last three have several subentities, as described in the **Example** column of the table.

We are going to add one of these prebuilt entities, so select **Entities** in the menu. Click on **Add prebuilt entity**, select **temperature** from the list, and click on **Save**.

With the newly created entity, we want to add a new intent called **SetTemperature**. If the example utterance is *Set the temperature in the kitchen to 22 degrees Celsius*, we can label the utterance as shown in the following screenshot:

As you can see, we have a room entity. We also have the prebuilt temperature entity clearly labeled. As the correct intent should be selected in the drop-down menu, we can click on the **Train** button to save the utterance.

Prebuilt domains

In addition to using prebuilt entities, we can use prebuilt domains. These are entities and intents that already exist, leveraging commonly used intents and entities from different domains. By using these intents and entities, you can use models that you would typically use in Windows. A very basic example is setting up appointments in the calendar.

To use Cortana's prebuilt domain, you can select **Prebuilt domains** from the left-hand menu. This will open a list of available domains. By clicking **Add domain**, you can add the selected domain, as shown in the following screenshot:

This will add the intents and entities for that specific domain to the list of intents and entities that is already defined, as shown in the following screenshot:

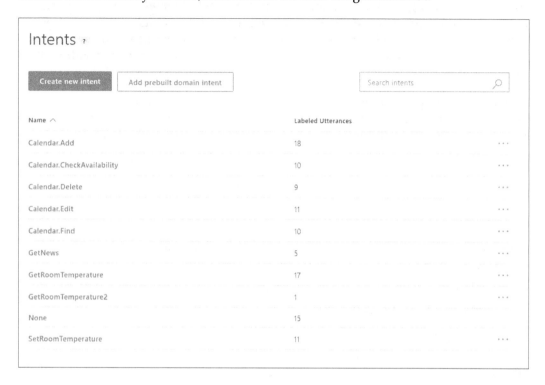

The following list shows the top-level domains that are available with Cortana's prebuilt domains. For a complete list of the available prebuilt domains, please refer to *Appendix A, LUIS Entities*:

- Calendar
- Camera
- Communication
- Entertainment
- Events
- Fitness
- Gaming
- HomeAutomation

- MovieTickets
- Music
- Note
- OnDevice
- Places
- Reminder
- RestaurantReservation
- Taxi
- Translate
- Utilities
- Weather
- Web

Training a model

Now that we have a working model, it is time to put it into action.

Training and publishing the model

The first step to using the model is to make sure that the model has some utterances to work with. Until now, we have added one utterance per intent. Before we deploy the application, we need more.

Think of three to four different ways to set or get the room temperature and add them, specifying the entities and intents. Also, add a couple of utterances that fall into the None intent, just for reference.

When we have added some new utterances, we need to train the model. Doing so will make LUIS develop code to recognize the relevant entities and intents in the future. This process is done periodically; however, it is wise to do it whenever you have made changes, before publication. This can be done by clicking **Train** in the top menu.

To test the application, you can simply enter test sentences in the **Interactive Testing** tab. This will show you how any given sentence is labeled, and what intents the service has discovered, as shown in the following screenshot:

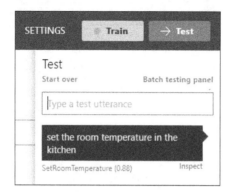

With the training completed, we can publish the application. This will deploy the models to an HTTP endpoint, which will interpret the sentences that we send to it.

Select **Publish** from the left-hand menu. This will present you with the following screen:

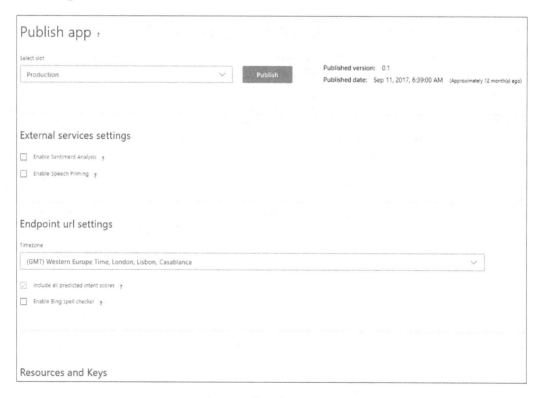

Click on the **Publish** button to deploy the application. The URL beneath the **Endpoint url settings** field is the endpoint where the model is deployed. As you can see, it specifies the application ID, as well as the subscription key.

Before we go any further, we can verify that the endpoint actually works. You can do this by entering a query into the text field (for instance, `get the bedroom temperature`) and clicking on the link. This should present you with something similar to the following screenshot:

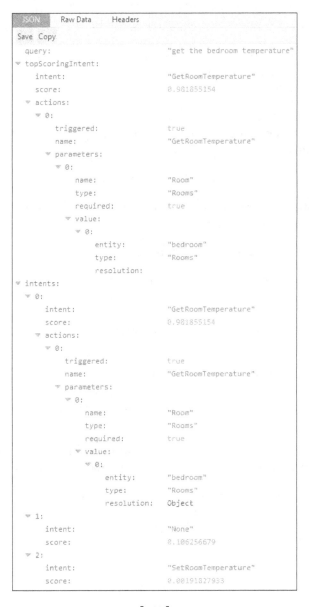

When the model has been published, we can move on to access it through the code.

Connecting to the smart house application

To be able to easily work with LUIS, we will want to add the NuGet client package. In the smart house application, go to the NuGet package manager and find the `Microsoft.Cognitive.LUIS` package. Install this into the project.

We will need to add a new class called `Luis`. Place the file under the `Model` folder. This class will be in charge of calling the endpoint and processing the result.

As we will need to test this class, we will need to add a `View` and a `ViewModel`. Add the file `LuisView.xaml` to the `View` folder, and add `LuisViewModel.cs` to the `ViewModel` folder.

The `View` should be rather simple. It should contain two `TextBox` elements, one for inputting requests and the other for displaying results. We also need a button to execute commands.

Add the `View` as a `TabItem` in the `MainView.xaml` file.

The `ViewModel` should have two `string` properties, one for each of the `TextBox` elements. It will also need an `ICommand` property for the `button` command.

We will create the `Luis` class first, so open the `Luis.cs` file. Make the class `public`.

When we have made requests and received the corresponding result, we want to trigger an event to notify the UI. We want some additional arguments with this event, so, below the `Luis` class, create a `LuisUtteranceResultEventArgs` class that inherits from the `EventArgs` class, as follows:

```
public class LuisUtteranceResultEventArgs : EventArgs {
    public string Status { get; set; }
    public string Message { get; set; }
    public bool RequiresReply { get; set; }
}
```

This will contain a `Status` string, a `Message` status, and the `Result` itself. Go back to the `Luis` class and add an event and a private member, as follows:

```
public event EventHandler<LuisUtteranceResultEventArgs>
OnLuisUtteranceResultUpdated;

private LuisClient _luisClient;
```

We have already discussed the event. The private member is the API access object, which we installed from NuGet:

```
public Luis(LuisClientluisClient) {
    _luisClient = luisClient;
}
```

The constructor should accept the `LuisClient` object as a parameter and assign it to the member we previously created.

Let's create a helper method to raise the `OnLuisUtteranceResultUpdated` event, as follows:

```
private void RaiseOnLuisUtteranceResultUpdated(
LuisUtteranceResultEventArgsargs)
{
    OnLuisUtteranceResultUpdated?.Invoke(this, args);
}
```

This is purely for our own convenience.

To be able to make requests, we will create a function called `RequestAsync`. This will accept a `string` as a parameter and have `Task` as the return type. The function should be marked as `async`, as follows:

```
public async Task RequestAsync(string input) {
    try {
        LuisResult result = await _luisClient.Predict(input);
```

Inside the function, we make a call to the `Predict` function of `_luisClient`. This will send a query to the endpoint we published earlier. A successful request will result in a `LuisResult` object that contains some data, which we will explore shortly.

We use the result in a new function, where we process it. We make sure that we catch any exceptions and notify any listeners about it using the following code:

```
        ProcessResult(result);
    }
    catch(Exception ex) {
        RaiseOnLuisUtteranceResultUpdated(new
LuisUtteranceResultEventArgs
        {
            Status = "Failed",
            Message = ex.Message
        });
    }
}
```

In the `ProcessResult` function, we create a new object of the `LuisUtteranceResultEventArgs` type. This will be used when notifying listeners of any results. In this argument object, we add the `Succeeded` status and the `result` object. We also write out a message, stating the top identified intent. We also add the likelihood of this intent being the top one out of all the intents we have. Finally, we also add the number of intents identified:

```
private void ProcessResult(LuisResult result) {
    LuisUtteranceResultEventArgsargs = new
LuisUtteranceResultEventArgs();

    args.Result = result;
    args.Status = "Succeeded";
    args.Message = $"Top intent is {result.TopScoringIntent.Name}
with score {result.TopScoringIntent.Score}. Found {result.Entities.
Count} entities.";

    RaiseOnLuisUtteranceResultUpdated(args);
}
```

With that in place, we head to our view model. Open the `LuisViewModel.cs` file. Make sure that the class is `public` and that it inherits from the `ObservableObject` class.

Declare a private member, as follows:

```
private Luis _luis;
```

This will hold the `Luis` object we created earlier:

```
public LuisViewModel() {
    _luis = new Luis(new LuisClient("APP_ID_HERE", "API_KEY_
HERE"));
```

Our constructor creates the `Luis` object, making sure it is initialized with a new `LuisClient`. As you may have noticed, this requires two parameters, the application ID and the subscription ID. There is also a third parameter, `preview`, but we will not need to set it at this time.

The application ID can be found either by looking at the URL in the publishing step or by going to **Settings** on the application's site at `https://www.luis.ai`. There, you will find the **Application ID**, as shown in the following screenshot:

App Settings

Application ID: 6877e272-a517-4574-a0af-06f730bbc4b3

With the `Luis` object created, we complete the constructor as follows:

```
    _luis.OnLuisUtteranceResultUpdated +=
OnLuisUtteranceResultUpdated;
    ExecuteUtteranceCommand = new DelegateCommand(ExecuteUtterance,
CanExecuteUtterance);
    }
```

This will hook up the `OnLuisUtteranceResultUpdated` event and create a new
`DelegateCommand` event for our button. For our command to be able to run,
we need to check that we have written some text in the input field. This is done
using `CanExecuteUtterance`.

The `ExecuteUtterance` command is itself rather simple, as shown in the
following code:

```
    private async void ExecuteUtterance(object obj) {
        await _luis.RequestAsync(InputText);
    }
```

All we do is make a call to the `RequestAsync` function in the `_luis` object. We do not
need to wait for any results, as these will be coming from the event.

The event handler, `OnLuisUtteranceResultUpdated`, will format the results and
print them to the screen.

First, we make sure that we invoke the methods in the current dispatcher thread.
This is done as the event is triggered in another thread. We create a `StringBuilder`,
which will be used to concatenate all the results, as shown in the following code:

```
    private void OnLuisUtteranceResultUpdated(object sender,
LuisUtteranceResultEventArgs e) {
        Application.Current.Dispatcher.Invoke(() => {
            StringBuilder sb = new StringBuilder();
```

First, we append the `Status` and the `Message` status. We then check to see if we have
any entities that were detected and append the number of entities, as follows:

```
        sb.AppendFormat("Status: {0}\n", e.Status);
        sb.AppendFormat("Summary: {0}\n\n", e.Message);

        if(e.Result.Entities != null&&e.Result.Entities.Count != 0) {
            sb.AppendFormat("Entities found: {0}\n", e.Result.Entities.
Count);
            sb.Append("Entities:\n");
```

If we do have any entities, we loop through each of them, printing out the entity name and the value:

```
foreach(var entities in e.Result.Entities) {
    foreach(var entity in entities.Value) {
        sb.AppendFormat("Name: {0}\tValue: {1}\n",
                        entity.Name, entity.Value);
    }
}
sb.Append("\n");
}
```

Finally, we add `StringBuilder` to our `ResultText` string, which should display it on screen, as follows:

```
ResultText = sb.ToString();
    });
}
```

With everything having compiled, the result should look something like the following screenshot:

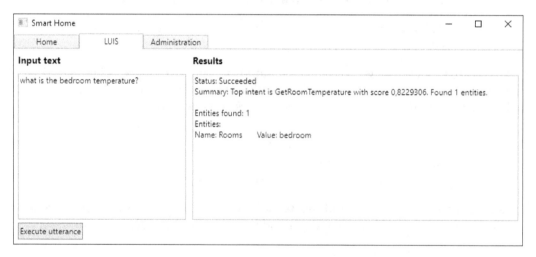

Model improvement through active usage

LUIS is a machine learning service. The applications we create, and the models that are generated, can therefore improve based on use. Throughout the development, it is a good idea to keep an eye on the performance. You may notice some intents that are often mislabeled, or entities that are hard to recognize.

Visualizing performance

On the LUIS website, the dashboard displays information about intent and entity breakdowns. This is basically information on how the intents and entities are distributed across the utterances that have been used.

The following diagram shows what the intent breakdown display looks like:

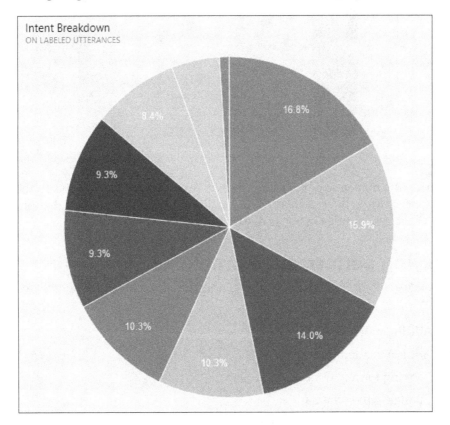

The following diagram shows what the entity breakdown looks like:

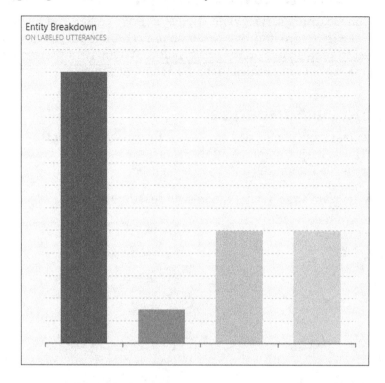

By hovering the mouse over the different bars (or sectors of the pie chart), the name of the intent/entity will be displayed. In addition, the percentage number of the total number of intents/entities in use is displayed.

Resolving performance problems

If you notice an error in your applications, there are typically four options to resolve it:

- Adding model features
- Adding labeled utterances
- Looking for incorrect utterance labels
- Changing the schema

We will now look briefly at each of these.

Adding model features

Adding model features is typically something we can do if we have phrases that should be detected as entities, but are not. We have already seen an example of this with the room entity, where one room could be the living room.

The solution is, of course, to add phrase lists or regex features. There are three scenarios where this will likely help:

- When LUIS fails to see words or phrases that are similar.
- When LUIS has trouble identifying entities. Adding all possible entity values in a phrase list should help.
- When rare or proprietary words are used.

Adding labeled utterances

Adding and labeling more utterances will always improve performance. This will most likely help in the following scenarios:

- When LUIS fails to differentiate between two intents
- When LUIS fails to detect entities between surrounding words
- If LUIS systematically assigns low scores to an intent

Looking for incorrect utterance labels

A common mistake is mislabeling an utterance or entity. In such cases, you will need to find the incorrect utterance and correct it. This will likely resolve problems in the following scenarios:

- If LUIS fails to differentiate between two intents, even when similar utterances have been labeled
- If LUIS consistently misses an entity

Changing the schema

If all the preceding solutions fail and you still have problems with the model, you may consider changing the schema, meaning combining, regrouping, and/or dropping intents and entities.

Keep in mind that if it is hard for humans to label an utterance, it is even harder for a machine.

Active learning

A very nice feature of LUIS is the power of active learning. When we are using the service actively, it will log all queries, and, as such, we will then be able to analyze usage. Doing so allows us to quickly correct errors and label utterances we have not seen before.

Using the application we have built—the smart house application—if we run a query with the utterance `can you tell me the bedroom temperature?`, the model will likely not recognize this. If we debug the process, stepping through the `ProcessResult` function, we will see the following values returned:

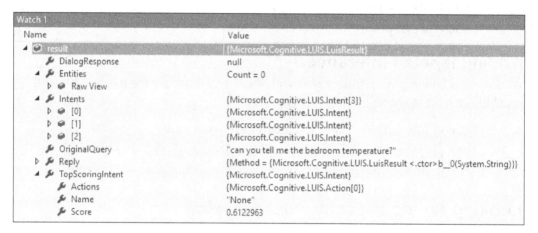

As you can see from the preceding screenshot, the top-scoring intent is `None`, with a score of `0.61`. In addition, no entities have been recognized, so this is not good.

Head back to the LUIS website. Move to the **Review endpoint utterances** page, which can be found in the left-hand menu. Here, we can see that the utterance we just tried has been added. We can now label the intent and entity correctly, as shown in the following screenshot:

By labeling the utterance with the correct intent and entity, we will get a correct result the next time we query in this way, as you can see in the following screenshot:

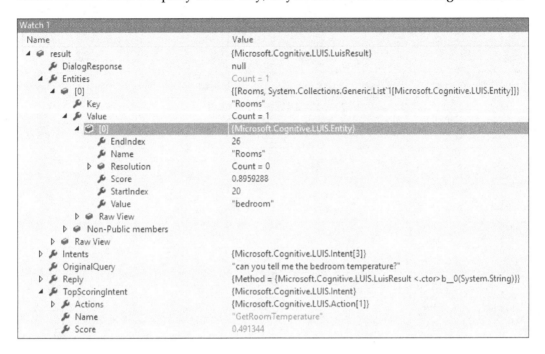

Summary

In this chapter, we created a LUIS application. You learned how to create language-understanding models, which can recognize entities in sentences. You learned how to understand the user's intent and how we can trigger actions from this. An important step was to see how to improve the model in various ways.

In the next chapter, we will utilize what you have learned here, using LUIS with speech APIs, giving us the ability to speak to our application.

5
Speaking with Your Application

In the previous chapter, we learned how to discover and understand the intent of a user, based on utterances. In this chapter, we will learn how to add audio capabilities to our applications, convert text to speech and speech to text, and learn how to identify the person speaking. Throughout this chapter, we will learn how you can utilize spoken audio to verify a person. Finally, we will briefly touch on how to customize speech recognition to make it unique for your application's usage.

By the end of this chapter, we will have covered the following topics:

- Converting spoken audio to text and text to spoken audio
- Recognizing intent from spoken audio by utilizing LUIS
- Verifying that the speaker is who they claim to be
- Identifying the speaker
- Tailoring the Speaker Recognition API to recognize custom speaking styles and environments

Converting text to audio and vice versa

In *Chapter 1, Getting Started with Microsoft Cognitive Services*, we utilized a part of the Bing Speech API. We gave the example application the ability to say sentences to us. We will use the code that we created in that example now, but we will dive a bit deeper into the details.

We will also go through the other feature of Bing Speech API, that is, converting spoken audio to text. The idea is that we can speak to the smart-house application, which will recognize what we are saying. Using the textual output, the application will use LUIS to gather the intent of our sentence. If LUIS needs more information, the application will politely ask us for more via audio.

To get started, we want to modify the build definition of the smart-house application. We need to specify whether we are running it on a 32-bit or 64-bit OS. To utilize speech-to-text conversion, we want to install the Bing Speech NuGet client package. Search for `Microsoft.ProjectOxford.SpeechRecognition` and install either the 32-bit version or the 64-bit version, depending on your system.

Further on, we need to add references to `System.Runtime.Serialization` and `System.Web`. These are needed so that we are able to make web requests and deserialize response data from the APIs.

Speaking to the application

Add a new file to the `Model` folder, called `SpeechToText.cs`. Beneath the automatically created `SpeechToText` class, we want to add an `enum` type variable called `SttStatus`. It should have two values, `Success` and `Error`.

In addition, we want to define an `EventArgs` class for events that we will raise during execution. Add the following class at the bottom of the file:

```
public class SpeechToTextEventArgs : EventArgs
{
    public SttStatus Status { get; private set; }
    public string Message { get; private set; }
    public List<string> Results { get; private set; }

    public SpeechToTextEventArgs(SttStatus status,
    string message, List<string> results = null)
    {
        Status = status;
        Message = message;
        Results = results;
    }
}
```

As you can see, the `event` argument will hold the operation status, a message of any kind, and a list of strings. This will be a list with potential speech-to-text conversions.

The `SpeechToText` class needs to implement `IDisposable`. This is done so that we can clean up the resources used for recording spoken audio and shut down the application properly. We will add the details presently, so for now, just make sure to add the `Dispose` function.

Now, we need to define a few private members in the class, as well as an event:

```
public event EventHandler<SpeechToTextEventArgs>
OnSttStatusUpdated;

    private DataRecognitionClient _dataRecClient;
    private MicrophoneRecognitionClient _micRecClient;
    private SpeechRecognitionMode _speechMode = SpeechRecognitionMode.
ShortPhrase;

    private string _language = "en-US";
    private bool _isMicRecording = false;
```

The `OnSttStatusUpdated` event will be triggered whenever we have a new operation status. `DataRecognitionClient` and `MicrophoneRecognitionClient` are the two objects that we can use to call the Bing Speech API. We will look at how they are created presently.

We define `SpeechRecognitionMode` as `ShortPhrase`. This means that we do not expect any spoken sentences longer than 15 seconds. The alternative is `LongDictation`, which means that we can convert spoken sentences to be up to 2 minutes long.

Finally, we specify the language to be English, and define a `bool` type variable, which indicates whether or not we are currently recording anything.

In our constructor, we accept the Bing Speech API key as a parameter. We will use this in the creation of our API clients:

```
public SpeechToText(string bingApiKey)
{
    _dataRecClient = SpeechRecognitionServiceFactory.
CreateDataClientWithIntentUsingEndpointUrl(_language, bingApiKey,
"LUIS_ROOT_URI");

    _micRecClient = SpeechRecognitionServiceFactory.
CreateMicrophoneClient(_speechMode, _language, bingApiKey);

    Initialize();
}
```

As you can see, we create both `_dataRecClient` and `_micRecClient` by calling `SpeechRecognitionServiceFactory`. For the first client, we state that we want to use intent recognition as well. The parameters required are the language, Bing API key, the LUIS app ID, and the LUIS API key. By using a `DataRecognitionClient` object, we can upload audio files with speech.

By using `MicrophoneRecognitionClient`, we can use a microphone for real-time conversion. For this, we do not want intent detection, so we call `CreateMicrophoneClient`. In this case, we only need to specify the speech mode, the language, and the Bing Speech API key.

Before leaving the constructor, we call the `Initialize` function. In this, we subscribe to certain events on each of the clients:

```
private void Initialize()
{
    _micRecClient.OnMicrophoneStatus += OnMicrophoneStatus;
    _micRecClient.OnPartialResponseReceived +=
OnPartialResponseReceived;
    _micRecClient.OnResponseReceived += OnResponseReceived;
    _micRecClient.OnConversationError +=
OnConversationErrorReceived;

    _dataRecClient.OnIntent += OnIntentReceived;
    _dataRecClient.OnPartialResponseReceived +=
    OnPartialResponseReceived;
    _dataRecClient.OnConversationError +=
OnConversationErrorReceived;
    _dataRecClient.OnResponseReceived += OnResponseReceived;
}
```

As you can see, there are quite a few similarities between the two clients. The two differences are that `_dataRecClient` will get intents through the `OnIntent` event, and `_micRecClient` will get the microphone status through the `OnMicrophoneStatus` event.

We do not really care about partial responses. However, they may be useful in some cases, as they will continuously give the currently completed conversion:

```
private void OnPartialResponseReceived(object sender,
PartialSpeechResponseEventArgs e)
{
    Debug.WriteLine($"Partial response received:{e.
PartialResult}");
}
```

For our application, we will choose to output it to the debug console window. In this case, `PartialResult` is a string with the partially converted text:

```
private void OnMicrophoneStatus(object sender, MicrophoneEventArgs e)
{
    Debug.WriteLine($"Microphone status changed to recording:
{e.Recording}");
}
```

We do not care about the current microphone status, either. Again, we output the status to the debug console window.

Before moving on, add a helper function, called `RaiseSttStatusUpdated`. This should raise `OnSttStatusUpdated` when called.

When we are calling `_dataRecClient`, we may recognize intents from LUIS. In these cases, we want to raise an event, where we output the recognized intent. This is done with the following code:

```
private void OnIntentReceived(object sender, SpeechIntentEventArgs e)
{
    SpeechToTextEventArgs args = new SpeechToTextEventArgs(SttStatus.
Success, $"Intent received: {e.Intent.ToString()}.\n Payload:
{e.Payload}");
    RaiseSttStatusUpdated(args);
}
```

We choose to print out intent information and the `Payload`. This is a string containing recognized entities, intents, and actions that are triggered from LUIS.

If any errors occur during the conversion, there are several things we will want to do. First and foremost, we want to stop any microphone recordings that may be running. There is really no point in trying to convert more in the current operation if it has failed:

```
    private void OnConversationErrorReceived(object sender,
SpeechErrorEventArgs e)
    {
        if (_isMicRecording) StopMicRecording();
```

We will create `StopMicRecording` presently.

In addition, we want to notify any subscribers that the conversion failed. In such cases, we want to give details about error codes and error messages:

```
        string message = $"Speech to text failed with status code:{e.
SpeechErrorCode.ToString()}, and error message: {e.SpeechErrorText}";
```

```
        SpeechToTextEventArgs args = new
    SpeechToTextEventArgs(SttStatus.Error, message);

        RaiseSttStatusUpdated(args);
    }
```

The `OnConversationError` event does, fortunately, provide us with detailed information about any errors.

Now, let's look at the `StopMicRecording` method:

```
    private void StopMicRecording()
    {
        _micRecClient.EndMicAndRecognition();
        _isMicRecording = false;
    }
```

This is a simple function that calls `EndMicAndRecognition` on the `_micRecClient` `MicrophoneRecognitionClient` object. When this is called, we stop the client from recording.

The final event handler that we need to create is the `OnResponseReceived` handler. This will be triggered whenever we receive a complete, converted response from the service.

Again, we want to make sure we do not record any more if we are currently recording:

```
    private void OnResponseReceived(object sender,
    SpeechResponseEventArgs e)
    {
        if (_isMicRecording) StopMicRecording();
```

The `SpeechResponseEventArgs` argument contains a `PhraseResponse` object. This contains an array of `RecognizedPhrase`, which we want to access. Each item in this array contains the confidence of correct conversion. It also contains the converted phrases as `DisplayText`. This uses inverse text normalization, proper capitalization, and punctuation, and it masks profanities with asterisks:

```
    RecognizedPhrase[] recognizedPhrases = e.PhraseResponse.Results;
    List<string> phrasesToDisplay = new List<string>();

    foreach(RecognizedPhrase phrase in recognizedPhrases)
    {
        phrasesToDisplay.Add(phrase.DisplayText);
    }
```

We may also get the converted phrases in other formats, as described in the following table:

Format	Description
LexicalForm	This is the raw, unprocessed recognition result.
InverseTextNormalizationResult	This displays phrases such as *one two three four* as *1234*, so it is ideal for usages such as *go to second street*.
MaskedInverseTextNormalizationResult	Inverse text normalization and the profanity mask. No capitalization or punctuation is applied.

For our use, we are just interested in the `DisplayText`. With a populated list of recognized phrases, we raise the status update event:

```
        SpeechToTextEventArgs args = new
    SpeechToTextEventArgs(SttStatus.Success, $"STT completed with status:
    {e.PhraseResponse.RecognitionStatus.ToString()}", phrasesToDisplay);


        RaiseSttStatusUpdated(args);
    }
```

To be able to use this class, we need a couple of public functions so that we can start speech recognition:

```
    public void StartMicToText()
    {
        _micRecClient.StartMicAndRecognition();
        _isMicRecording = true;
    }
```

The `StartMicToText` method will call the `StartMicAndRecognition` method on the `_micRecClient` object. This will allow us to use the microphone to convert spoken audio. This function will be our main way of accessing this API:

```
    public void StartAudioFileToText(string audioFileName) {
        using (FileStream fileStream = new FileStream(audioFileName,
    FileMode.Open, FileAccess.Read))
        {
            int bytesRead = 0;
            byte[] buffer = new byte[1024];
```

The second function will require a filename for the audio file, with the audio we want to convert. We open the file, with read access, and are ready to read it:

```
try {
    do {
        bytesRead = fileStream.Read(buffer, 0, buffer.Length);
        _dataRecClient.SendAudio(buffer, bytesRead);
    } while (bytesRead > 0);
}
```

As long as we have data available, we read from the file. We will fill up the `buffer`, and call the `SendAudio` method. This will then trigger a recognition operation in the service.

If any exceptions occur, we make sure to output the exception message to a debug window. Finally, we need to call the `EndAudio` method so that the service does not wait for any more data:

```
catch(Exception ex) {
    Debug.WriteLine($"Exception caught: {ex.Message}");
}
finally {
    _dataRecClient.EndAudio();
}
```

Before leaving this class, we need to dispose of our API clients. Add the following in the `Dispose` function:

```
if (_micRecClient != null) {
    _micRecClient.EndMicAndRecognition();
    _micRecClient.OnMicrophoneStatus -= OnMicrophoneStatus;
    _micRecClient.OnPartialResponseReceived -=
OnPartialResponseReceived;
    _micRecClient.OnResponseReceived -= OnResponseReceived;
    _micRecClient.OnConversationError -=
OnConversationErrorReceived;

    _micRecClient.Dispose();
    _micRecClient = null;
}

if(_dataRecClient != null) {
    _dataRecClient.OnIntent -= OnIntentReceived;
    _dataRecClient.OnPartialResponseReceived -=
OnPartialResponseReceived;
```

```
        _dataRecClient.OnConversationError -=
    OnConversationErrorReceived;
        _dataRecClient.OnResponseReceived -= OnResponseReceived;

        _dataRecClient.Dispose();
        _dataRecClient = null;
    }
```

We stop microphone recording, unsubscribe from all events, and dispose and clear the client objects.

Make sure that the application compiles before moving on. We will look at how to use this class presently.

Letting the application speak back

We have already seen how to make the application speak back to us. We are going to use the same classes we created in *Chapter 1, Getting Started with Microsoft Cognitive Services*. Copy Authentication.cs and TextToSpeech.cs from the example project from *Chapter 1, Getting Started with Microsoft Cognitive Services,* into the Model folder. Make sure that the namespaces are changed accordingly.

As we have been through the code already, we will not go through it again. We will instead look at some of the details left out in *Chapter 1, Getting Started with Microsoft Cognitive Services.*

Audio output format

The audio output format can be one of the following formats:

- raw-8khz-8bit-mono-mulaw
- raw-16khz-16bit-mono-pcm
- riff-8khz-8bit-mono-mulaw
- riff-16khz-16bit-mono-pcm

Error codes

There are four possible error codes that can occur in calls to the API. These are described in the following table:

Code	Description
400 / BadRequest	A required parameter is missing, empty, or null. Alternatively, a parameter is invalid. An example may be a string that's longer than the allowed length.
401 / Unauthorized	The request is not authorized.
413 / RequestEntityTooLarge	The SSML input is larger than what's supported.
502 / BadGateway	A network-related or server-related issue.

Supported languages

The following languages are supported:

English (Australia), English (United Kingdom), English (United States), English (Canada), English (India), Spanish, Mexican Spanish, German, Arabic (Egypt), French, Canadian French, Italian, Japanese, Portuguese, Russian, Chinese (S), Chinese (Hong Kong), and Chinese (T).

Utilizing LUIS based on spoken commands

To utilize the features that we have just added, we are going to modify `LuisView` and `LuisViewModel`. Add a new `Button` in the View, which will make sure that we record commands. Add a corresponding `ICommand` in the ViewModel.

We also need to add a few more members to the class:

```
private SpeechToText _sttClient;
private TextToSpeech _ttsClient;
private string _bingApiKey = "BING_SPEECH_API_KEY";
```

The first two will be used to convert between spoken audio and text. The third is the API key for the Bing Speech API.

Make the ViewModel implement `IDisposable`, and explicitly dispose the `SpeechToText` object.

Create the objects by adding the following in the constructor:

```
_sttClient = new SpeechToText(_bingApiKey);
_sttClient.OnSttStatusUpdated += OnSttStatusUpdated;

_ttsClient = new TextToSpeech();
_ttsClient.OnAudioAvailable += OnTtsAudioAvailable;
_ttsClient.OnError += OnTtsError;
GenerateHeaders();
```

This will create the client objects and subscribe to the required events. Finally, it will call a function to generate authentication tokens for the REST API calls. This function should look like this:

```
private async void GenerateHeaders()
{
    if (await _ttsClient.GenerateAuthenticationToken(_bingApiKey))
    _ttsClient.GenerateHeaders();
}
```

If we receive any errors from _ttsClient, we want to output it to the debug console:

```
private void OnTtsError(object sender, AudioErrorEventArgs e)
{
    Debug.WriteLine($"Status: Audio service failed -
{e.ErrorMessage}");
}
```

We do not need to output this to the UI, as this is a nice-to-have feature.

If we have audio available, we want to make sure that we play it. We do so by creating a SoundPlayer object:

```
private void OnTtsAudioAvailable(object sender, AudioEventArgs e)
{
    SoundPlayer player = new SoundPlayer(e.EventData);
    player.Play();
    e.EventData.Dispose();
}
```

Using the audio stream we got from the event arguments, we can play the audio to the user.

If we have a status update from _sttClient, we want to display this in the textbox.

If we have successfully recognized spoken audio, we want to show the `Message` string if it is available:

```
    private void OnSttStatusUpdated(object sender,
SpeechToTextEventArgs e) {
        Application.Current.Dispatcher.Invoke(() => {
            StringBuilder sb = new StringBuilder();

        if(e.Status == SttStatus.Success) {
            if(!string.IsNullOrEmpty(e.Message)) {
                sb.AppendFormat("Result message: {0}\n\n",
e.Message);
            }
```

We also want to show all recognized phrases. Using the first available phrase, we make a call to LUIS:

```
        if(e.Results != null && e.Results.Count != 0) {
            sb.Append("Retrieved the following results:\n");
                foreach(string sentence in e.Results) {
                    sb.AppendFormat("{0}\n\n", sentence);
                }
                sb.Append("Calling LUIS with the top result\n");
                CallLuis(e.Results.FirstOrDefault());
            }
        }
```

If the recognition failed, we print out any error messages that we may have. Finally, we make sure that the `ResultText` is updated with the new data:

```
        else {
                sb.AppendFormat("Could not convert speech to
    text:{0}\n", e.Message);
            }

            sb.Append("\n");
            ResultText = sb.ToString();
        });
    }
```

The newly created `ICommand` needs to have a function to start the recognition process:

```
    private void RecordUtterance(object obj) {
        _sttClient.StartMicToText();
    }
```

The function starts the microphone recording.

Finally, we need to make some modifications to `OnLuisUtteranceResultUpdated`. Make the following modifications, where we output any `DialogResponse`:

```
    if (e.RequiresReply && !string.IsNullOrEmpty(e.DialogResponse))
    {
        await _ttsClient.SpeakAsync(e.DialogResponse,
CancellationToken.None);
        sb.AppendFormat("Response: {0}\n", e.DialogResponse);
        sb.Append("Reply in the left textfield");

        RecordUtterance(sender);
    }
    else
    {
        await _ttsClient.SpeakAsync($"Summary: {e.Message}",
CancellationToken.None);
    }
```

This will play the `DialogResponse` if it exists. The application will ask you for more information if required. It will then start the recording, so we can answer without clicking any buttons.

If no `DialogResponse` exists, we simply make the application say the summary to us. This will contain data on intents, entities, and actions from LUIS.

Knowing who is speaking

Using the **Speaker Recognition** API, we can identify who is speaking. By defining one or more speaker profiles with corresponding samples, we can identify whether any of them are speaking at any time.

To be able to utilize this feature, we need to go through a few steps:

1. We need to add one or more speaker profiles to the service.
2. Each speaker profile enrolls several spoken samples.
3. We call the service to identify a speaker based on audio input.

If you have not already done so, sign up for an API key for the Speaker Recognition API at `https://portal.azure.com`.

Start by adding a new NuGet package to your smart-house application. Search for and add `Microsoft.ProjectOxford.SpeakerRecognition`.

Add a new class called `SpeakerIdentification` to the `Model` folder of your project. This class will hold all of the functionality related to speaker identification.

Beneath the class, we will add another class, containing `EventArgs` for status updates:

```
    public class SpeakerIdentificationStatusUpdateEventArgs :
EventArgs
    {
        public string Status { get; private set; }
        public string Message { get; private set; }
        public Identification IdentifiedProfile { get; set; }

        public SpeakerIdentificationStatusUpdateEventArgs (string
status, string message)
        {
            Status = status;
            Message = message;
        }
    }
```

The two first properties should be self-explanatory. The last one, `IdentificationProfile`, will hold the results of a successful identification process. We will look at what information this contains presently.

We also want to send events for errors, so let's add an `EventArgs` class for the required information:

```
    public class SpeakerIdentificationErrorEventArgs : EventArgs {
        public string ErrorMessage { get; private set; }

        public SpeakerIdentificationErrorEventArgs(string
errorMessage)
        {
            ErrorMessage = errorMessage;
        }
    }
```

Again, the property should be self-explanatory.

In the `SpeakerIdentification` class, add two events and one private member at the top of the class:

```
    public event EventHandler
  <SpeakerIdentificationStatusUpdateEventArgs>
        OnSpeakerIdentificationStatusUpdated;
    public event EventHandler <SpeakerIdentificationErrorEventArgs>
        OnSpeakerIdentificationError;


    private ISpeakerIdentificationServiceClient _
  speakerIdentificationClient;
```

The events will be triggered if we have any status updates, a successful identification, or errors. The `ISpeakerIdentificationServiceClient` object is the access point for the Speaker Recognition API. Inject this object through the constructor.

To make it easier to raise events, add two helper functions, one for each event. Call these `RaiseOnIdentificationStatusUpdated` and `RaiseOnIdentificationError`. They should accept the corresponding `EventArgs` object as a parameter and trigger the corresponding event.

Adding speaker profiles

To be able to identify speakers, we need to add profiles. Each profile can be seen as a unique person who we can identify later.

At the time of writing, each subscription allows for 1,000 speaker profiles to be created. This also includes profiles that are created for verification, which we will look at presently.

To facilitate creating profiles, we need to add some elements to our `AdministrationView` and `AdministrationViewModel` properties, so open these files.

In the View, add a new button for adding speaker profiles. Also, add a list box, which will show all of our profiles. How you lay out the UI is up to you.

The ViewModel will need a new `ICommand` property for the button. It will also need an `ObservableObject` property for our profile list; make sure it is of type `Guid`. We will also need to be able to select a profile, so add a `Guid` property for the selected profile.

Additionally, we need to add a new member to the ViewModel:

```
private SpeakerIdentification _speakerIdentification;
```

This is the reference to the class we created earlier. Create this object in the constructor, passing on an `ISpeakerIdentificationServiceClient` object, which you inject via the ViewModel's constructor. In the constructor, you should also subscribe to the events we created:

```
_speakerIdentification.OnSpeakerIdentificationError +=
OnSpeakerIdentificationError;
_speakerIdentification.OnSpeakerIdentificationStatusUpdated +=
OnSpeakerIdentificationStatusUpdated;
```

Basically, we want both event handles to update the status text with the message they carry:

```
Application.Current.Dispatcher.Invoke(() =>
{
    StatusText = e.Message;
});
```

The preceding code is for `OnSpeakerIdentificationStatusUpdated`. The same should be used for `OnSpeakerIdentificationError`, but set `StatusText` to be `e.ErrorMessage` instead.

In the function created for our `ICommand` property, we do the following to create a new profile:

```
private async void AddSpeaker(object obj)
{
    Guid speakerId = await _speakerIdentification.
CreateSpeakerProfile();
```

We make a call to our `_speakerIdentification` object's `CreateSpeakerProfile` function. This function will return a `Guid`, which is the unique ID of that speaker. In our example, we do not do anything further with this. In a real-life application, I would recommend mapping this ID to a name in some way. As you will see presently, identifying people through GUIDs is for machines, not people:

```
GetSpeakerProfiles();
}
```

We finish this function by calling a `GetSpeakerProfile` function, which we will create next. This will fetch a list of all the profiles we have created so that we can use these throught the further process:

```
private async void GetSpeakerProfiles()
{
    List<Guid> profiles = await _speakerIdentification.
ListSpeakerProfiles();

    if (profiles == null) return;
```

In our `GetSpeakerProfiles` function, we call `ListSpeakerProfiles` on our `_speakerIdentification` object. This will, as we will see presently, fetch a list of GUIDs, containing the profile IDs. If this list is null, there is no point in moving on:

```
foreach(Guid profile in profiles)
{
    SpeakerProfiles.Add(profile);
}
}
```

If the list does contain anything, we add these IDs to our `SpeakerProfiles`, which is the `ObservableCollection` property. This will show all of our profiles in the UI.

This function should also be called from the `Initialize` function, so we populate the list when we start the application.

Back in the `SpeakerIdentification` class, create a new function called `CreateSpeakerProfile`. This should have the return type `Task<Guid>` and be marked as `async`:

```
public async Task<Guid> CreateSpeakerProfile()
{
    try
    {
        CreateProfileResponse response = await _
speakerIdentificationClient.CreateProfileAsync("en-US");
```

We will then make a call to `CreateProfileAsync` on the API object. We need to specify the locale, which is used for the speaker profile. At the time of writing, `en-US` is the only valid option.

If the call is successful, we get a `CreateProfileResponse` object in response. This contains the ID of the newly created speaker profile:

```
    if (response == null)
    {
        RaiseOnIdentificationError(
            new SpeakerIdentificationErrorEventArgs
                ("Failed to create speaker profile."));
        return Guid.Empty;
    }


    return response.ProfileId;
}
```

If the `response` is null, we raise an error event. If it contains data, we return the `ProfileId` to the caller.

Add the corresponding `catch` clause to finish the function.

Create a new function called `ListSpeakerProfile`. This should return `Task<List<Guid>>` and be marked as `async`:

```
public async Task<List<Guid>> ListSpeakerProfiles()
{
    try
    {
        List<Guid> speakerProfiles = new List<Guid>();

        Profile[] profiles = await _speakerIdentificationClient.
GetProfilesAsync();
```

We will then create a list of type `Guid`, which is the list of speaker profiles we will return. Then, we call the `GetProfilesAsync` method on our `_speakerIdentificationClient` object. This will get us an array of type `Profile`, which contains information on each profile. This is information such as creation time, enrollment status, last modified, and so on. We are interested in the IDs of each profile:

```
        if (profiles == null || profiles.Length == 0)
        {
            RaiseOnIdentificationError(new SpeakerIdentificationEr
rorEventArgs("No profiles exist"));
            return null;
        }
```

```
        foreach (Profile profile in profiles)
        {
            speakerProfiles.Add(profile.ProfileId);
        }

        return speakerProfiles;
    }
```

If any profiles are returned, we loop through the array and add each `profileId` to the previously created list. This list is then returned to the caller, which in our case will be the ViewModel.

End the function with the corresponding `catch` clause. Make sure that the code compiles and executes as expected before continuing. This means that you should now be able to add speaker profiles to the service and get the created profiles displayed in the UI.

To delete a speaker profile, we will need to add a new function to `SpeakerIdentification`. Call this function `DeleteSpeakerProfile`, and let it accept a `Guid` as its parameter. This will be the ID of the given profile we want to delete. Mark the function as `async`. The function should look as follows:

```
public async void DeleteSpeakerProfile(Guid profileId)
{
    try
    {
        await _speakerIdentificationClient.
DeleteProfileAsync(profileId);
    }
    catch (IdentificationException ex)
    {
        RaiseOnIdentificationError(new SpeakerIdentificationErrorEventAr
gs($"Failed to
        delete speaker profile: {ex.Message}"));
    }
    catch (Exception ex)
    {
        RaiseOnIdentificationError(new SpeakerIdentificationErrorEventAr
gs($"Failed to
        delete speaker profile: {ex.Message}"));
    }
}
```

As you can see, the call to the `DeleteProfileAsync` method expects a `Guid` type, `profileId`. There is no return value and, as such, when we call this function, we need to call the `GetSpeakerProfile` method in our ViewModel.

To facilitate the deletion of speaker profiles, add a new button to the UI and a corresponding `ICommand` property in the ViewModel.

Enrolling a profile

With a speaker profile in place, we need to associate spoken audio with the profile. We do this through a process called **enrolling**. For speaker identification, enrolling is text-independent. This means that you can use whatever sentence you want for enrollment. Once the voice is recorded, a number of features will be extracted to form a unique voice-print.

When enrolling, the audio file you are using must be 5 seconds at least and 5 minutes at most. Best practice states that you should accumulate at least 30 seconds of speech. This is 30 seconds *after* silence has been removed, so several audio files may be required. This recommendation can be avoided by specifying an extra parameter, as we will see presently.

How you choose to upload the audio file is up to you. In the smart-house application, we will use a microphone to record live audio. To do so, we will need to add a new NuGet package called **NAudio**. This is an audio library for .NET, which simplifies audio work.

We will also need a class to deal with recording, which is out of the scope of this book. As such, I recommend you copy the `Recording.cs` file, which can be found in the sample project in the `Model` folder.

In the `AdministrationViewModel` ViewModel, add a private member for the newly copied class. Create the class and subscribe to the events defined in the `Initialize` function:

```
_recorder = new Recording();
_recorder.OnAudioStreamAvailable +=
OnRecordingAudioStreamAvailable;
_recorder.OnRecordingError += OnRecordingError;
```

We have an event for errors and one for available audio stream. Let `OnRecordingError` print the `ErrorMessage` to the status text field.

In `OnAudioStreamAvailable`, add the following:

```
Application.Current.Dispatcher.Invoke(() =>
{
    _speakerIdentification.CreateSpeakerEnrollment(e.AudioStream,
SelectedSpeakerProfile);
});
```

Here, we call `CreateSpeakerEnrollment` on the `_speakerIdentification` object. We will cover this function presently. The parameters we pass on are the `AudioStream`, from the recording, as well as the ID of the selected profile.

To be able to get audio files for enrollment, we need to start and stop the recording. This can be done by simply adding two new buttons, one for start and one for stop. They will then need to execute one of the following:

```
_recorder.StartRecording();
_recorder.StopRecording();
```

Back in the `SpeakerIdentification.cs` file, we need to create a new function, `CreateSpeakerEnrollment`. This should accept `Stream` and `Guid` as parameters, and be marked as `async`:

```
public async void CreateSpeakerEnrollment(Stream audioStream, Guid
profileId) {
    try {
        OperationLocation location = await _
speakerIdentificationClient.EnrollAsync(audioStream, profileId);
```

In this function, we call the `EnrollAsync` function on `_speakerIdentificationClient`. This function requires both the `audioStream` and `profileId` as parameters. An optional third parameter is a `bool` type variable, which lets you decide whether or not you would like to use the recommended speech length or not. The default is `false`, meaning that you use the recommended setting of at least 30 seconds of speech.

If the call is successful, we get an `OperationLocation` object back. This holds a URL that we can query for the enrollment status, which is precisely what we will do:

```
if (location == null) {
    RaiseOnIdentificationError(new SpeakerIdentificationErrorE
ventArgs("Failed to start enrollment process."));
    return;
}

GetEnrollmentOperationStatus(location);
}
```

First, we make sure that we have the `location` data. Without it, there is no point in moving on. If we do have the `location` data, we call a function, `GetEnrollmentOperationStatus`, specifying the `location` as the parameter.

Add the corresponding `catch` clause to finish the function.

The `GetEnrollmentOperationStatus` method accepts `OperationLocation` as a parameter. When we enter the function, we move into a `while` loop, which will run until the operation completes. We call `CheckEnrollmentStatusAsync`, specifying the `location` as the parameter. If this call is successful, it will return an `EnrollmentOperation` object, which contains data such as status, enrollment speech time, and an estimation of the time of enrollment left:

```
    private async void GetEnrollmentOperationStatus(OperationLocation
location) {
        try {
            while(true) {
                EnrollmentOperation result = await _
speakerIdentificationClient.CheckEnrollmentStatusAsync(location);
```

When we have retrieved the result, we check to see if the status is running or not. If it isn't, the operation has either failed, succeeded, or not started. In any case, we do not want to check any further, so we send an update with the status and break out of the loop:

```
                if(result.Status != Status.Running)
                {
                    RaiseOnIdentificationStatusUpdated(new SpeakerIden
tificationStatusUpdateEventArgs(result.Status.ToString(),
                        $"Enrollment finished. Enrollment status: {result.
ProcessingResult.EnrollmentStatus.ToString()}"));
                    break;
                }

                RaiseOnIdentificationStatusUpdated(new Speaker
IdentificationStatusUpdateEventArgs(result.Status.ToString(),
"Enrolling..."));
                await Task.Delay(1000);
            }
        }
```

If the status is still running, we update the status and wait for 1 second before trying again.

With enrollment completed, there may be times when we need to reset the enrollment for a given profile. We can do so by creating a new function in `SpeakerIdentification`. Name it `ResetEnrollments`, and let it accept a `Guid` as a parameter. This should be the profile ID of the speaker profile to reset. Execute the following inside a `try` clause:

```
await _speakerIdentificationClient .ResetEnrollmentsAsync(pro
fileId);
```

This will delete all audio files associated with the given profile and also reset the enrollment status. To call this function, add a new button to the UI and the corresponding `ICommand` property in the ViewModel.

If you compile and run the application, you may get a result similar to the following screenshot:

Identifying the speaker

The last step is to identify the speaker, which we will do in the `HomeView` and corresponding `HomeViewModel`. We do not need to modify the UI much, but we do need to add two buttons in order to start and stop the recording. Alternatively, if you are not using a microphone, you can get away with one button for browsing an audio file. Either way, add the corresponding `ICommand` properties in the ViewModel.

We also need to add private members for the `Recording` and `SpeakerIdentification` classes. Both should be created in the constructor, where we should inject `ISpeakerIdentificationServiceClient` as well.

In the `Initialize` function, subscribe to the required events:

```
    _speakerIdentification.OnSpeakerIdentificationError +=
OnSpeakerIdentificationError;
    _speakerIdentification.OnSpeakerIdentificationStatusUpdated +=
OnSpeakerIdentificationStatusReceived;

    _recording.OnAudioStreamAvailable += OnSpeakerRecordingAvailable;
    _recording.OnRecordingError += OnSpeakerRecordingError;
```

For both of the error event handlers, OnSpeakerRecordingError and OnSpeakerIdentificationError, we do not wish to print the error message here. For simplicity, we just output it to the debug console window.

The OnSpeakerRecordingAvailable event will be triggered when we have recorded some audio. This is the event handler that will trigger an attempt to identify the person speaking.

The first thing we need to do is get a list of speaker profile IDs. We do so by calling ListSpeakerProfiles, which we looked at earlier:

```csharp
    private async void OnSpeakerRecordingAvailable(object sender,
RecordingAudioAvailableEventArgs e)
    {
        try
        {
            List<Guid> profiles = await _speakerIdentification.
ListSpeakerProfiles();
```

With the list of speaker profiles, we call the IdentifySpeaker method on the _speakerIdentification object. We pass on the recorded audio stream and the profile list, as an array, as parameters to the function:

```csharp
            _speakerIdentification.IdentifySpeaker(e.AudioStream,
profiles.ToArray());
        }
```

Finish the event handler by adding the corresponding catch clause.

Back in the SpeakerIdentification.cs file, we add the new function, IdentifySpeaker:

```csharp
    public async void IdentifySpeaker(Stream audioStream, Guid[]
speakerIds)
    {
        try
        {
            OperationLocation location = await _
speakerIdentificationClient.IdentifyAsync(audioStream, speakerIds);
```

The function should be marked as async and accept a Stream and an array of Guid as parameters. To identify a speaker, we make a call to the IdentifyAsync function on the _speakerIdentificationClient object. This requires an audio file, in the form of a Stream, as well as an array of profile IDs. An optional third parameter is a bool, which you can use to indicate whether or not you want to deviate from the recommended speech length.

If the call succeeds, we get an `OperationLocation` object back. This contains a URL that we can use to retrieve the status of the current identification process:

```
if (location == null)
{
    RaiseOnIdentificationError(new
SpeakerIdentificationErrorEventArgs ("Failed to identify speaker."));
    return;
}
GetIdentificationOperationStatus(location);
}
```

If the resulting data contains nothing, we do not want to bother doing anything else. If it does contain data, we pass it on as a parameter to the `GetIdentificationOperationStatus` method:

```
private async void GetIdentificationOperationStatus
(OperationLocation location)
{
    try
    {
        while (true)
        {
            IdentificationOperation result = await _
speakerIdentificationClient.CheckIdentificationStatusAsync(location);
```

This function is quite similar to `GetEnrollmentOperationStatus`. We go into a `while` loop, which will run until the operation completes. We call `CheckIdentificationStatusAsync`, passing on the `location` as a parameter, getting `IdentificationOperation` as a result. This will contain data, such as a status, the identified profiles ID, and the confidence of a correct result.

If the operation is not running, we raise the event with the status message and the `ProcessingResult`. If the operation is still running, we update the status and wait for 1 second before trying again:

```
if (result.Status != Status.Running)
{
    RaiseOnIdentificationStatusUpdated(new SpeakerIdenti
ficationStatusUpdateEventArgs(result.Status.ToString(), $"Enrollment
finished with message:{result.Message}.") { IdentifiedProfile =
result.ProcessingResult });
    break;
}
```

```
            RaiseOnIdentificationStatusUpdated(new SpeakerIdentificati
    onStatusUpdateEventArgs(result.Status.ToString(), "Identifying..."));

            await Task.Delay(1000);
        }
    }
```

Add the corresponding `catch` clause before heading back to the `HomeViewModel`.

The last piece in the puzzle is to create `OnSpeakerIdentificationStatusReceived`. Add the following code inside HomeViewModel:

```
    Application.Current.Dispatcher.Invoke(() =>
    {
        if (e.IdentifiedProfile == null) return;

        SystemResponse = $"Hi there, {e.IdentifiedProfile.
    IdentifiedProfileId}";
    });
```

We need to check to see whether or not we have an identified profile. If we do not, we leave the function. If we have an identified profile, we give a response to the screen, stating who it is.

As with the administrative side of the application, this is a place where it would be convenient to have name-to-profile ID mapping. As you can see from the following resulting screenshot, recognizing one GUID among many is not that easy:

Verifying a person through speech

The process of verifying if a person is who they claim to be is quite similar to the identification process. To show how it is done, we will create a new example project, as we do not need this functionality in our smart-house application.

Add the `Microsoft.ProjectOxford.SpeakerRecognition` and `NAudio` NuGet packages to the project. We will need the `Recording` class that we used earlier, so copy this from the smart-house application's `Model` folder.

Open the `MainView.xaml` file. We need a few elements in the UI for the example to work. Add a `Button` element to add speaker profiles. Add two `Listbox` elements. One will hold available verification phrases while the other will list our speaker profiles.

Add `Button` elements for deleting a profile, starting and stopping enrollment recording, resetting enrollment, and starting/stopping verification recording.

In the ViewModel, you will need to add two `ObservableCollection` properties: one of type `string`, the other of type `Guid`. One will contain the available verification phrases, while the other will contain the list of speaker profiles. You will also need a property for the selected speaker profile, and we also want a string property to show the status.

The ViewModel will also need seven `ICommand` properties, one for each of our buttons.

Create a new class in the `Model` folder and call this `SpeakerVerification`. Add two new classes beneath this one, in the same file.

The first one is the event arguments that we will pass on when we raise a status update event. The `Verification` property will, if set, hold the verification result, which we will see presently:

```
public class SpeakerVerificationStatusUpdateEventArgs : EventArgs
{
    public string Status { get; private set; }
    public string Message { get; private set; }
    public Verification VerifiedProfile { get; set; }

    public SpeakerVerificationStatusUpdateEventArgs(string
status,string message)
    {
        Status = status;
        Message = message;
    }
}
```

The next class is a generic event argument, which is used when we raise an error event. In `SpeakerVerification` itself, add the following events:

```
public class SpeakerVerificationErrorEventArgs : EventArgs
{
    public string ErrorMessage { get; private set; }

    public SpeakerVerificationErrorEventArgs(string errorMessage)
    {
        ErrorMessage = errorMessage;
    }
}
```

For our convenience, add helper functions to raise these. Call them `RaiseOnVerificationStatusUpdated` and `RaiseOnVerificationError`. Raise the correct event in each of them:

```
public event EventHandler
<SpeakerVerificationStatusUpdateEventArgs>
OnSpeakerVerificationStatusUpdated;

public event EventHandler<SpeakerVerificationErrorEventArgs>
OnSpeakerVerificationError;
```

We also need to add a private member called `ISpeakerVerificationServiceClient`. This will be in charge of calling the API. We inject this through the constructor.

Add the following functions to the class:

- `CreateSpeakerProfile`: No parameters, the `async` function, and the return type `Task<Guid>`
- `ListSpeakerProfile`: No parameters, the `async` function, and the return type `Task<List<Guid>>`
- `DeleteSpeakerProfile`: `Guid` as the required parameter, the `async` function, no returned values
- `ResetEnrollments`: `Guid` as the required parameter, the `async` function, no returned values

The contents of these functions can be copied from the corresponding functions in the smart-house application, as they are exactly the same. The only difference is that you need to change the API call from `_speakerIdentificationClient` to `_speakerVerificationClient`. Also, raising the events will require the newly created event arguments.

Next, we need a function to list verification phrases. These are phrases that are supported for use with verification. When enrolling a profile, you are required to say one of the sentences in this list.

Create a function named `GetVerificationPhrase`. Have it return
`Task<List<string>>`, and mark it as `async`:

```
public async Task<List<string>> GetVerificationPhrase()
{
    try
    {
        List<string> phrases = new List<string>();

        VerificationPhrase[] results = await _
speakerVerificationClient.GetPhrasesAsync("en-US");
```

We will make a call to `GetPhrasesAsync`, specifying the language we want the
phrases to be in. At the time of writing, English is the only possible choice.

If this call is successful, we will get an array of `VerificationPhrases` in return.
Each element in this array contains a string with the following phrase:

```
foreach(VerificationPhrase phrase in results) {
    phrases.Add(phrase.Phrase);
}
return phrases;
}
```

We loop through the array and add the phrases to our list, which we will return
to the caller.

So, we have created a profile and we have the list of possible verification phrases.
Now, we need to do the enrollment. To enroll, the service requires at least three
enrollments from each speaker. This means that you choose a phrase and enroll
it at least three times.

When you do the enrollment, it is highly recommended to use the same recording
device that you will use for verification.

Create a new function called `CreateSpeakerEnrollment`. This should require a
`Stream` and a `Guid`. The first parameter is the audio to use for enrollment. The latter
is the ID of the profile we are enrolling. The function should be marked as `async`,
and have no return value:

```
public async void CreateSpeakerEnrollment(Stream audioStream, Guid
profileId) {
    try {
        Enrollment enrollmentStatus = await _
speakerVerificationClient.EnrollAsync(audioStream, profileId);
```

When we call `EnrollAsync`, we pass on the `audioStream` and `profileId` parameters. If the call is successful, we get an `Enrollment` object back. This contains the current status of enrollment and specifies the number of enrollments you need to add before completing the process.

If the `enrollmentStatus` is null, we exit the function and notify any subscribers. If we do have status data, we raise the event to notify it that there is a status update, specifying the current status:

```
if (enrollmentStatus == null) {
        RaiseOnVerificationError(new SpeakerVerificationErrorE
ventArgs("Failed to start enrollment process."));
        return;
}

        RaiseOnVerificationStatusUpdate(new SpeakerVerificationStat
usUpdateEventArgs("Succeeded", $"Enrollment status:{enrollmentStatus.
EnrollmentStatus}"));
    }
```

Add the corresponding `catch` clause to finish up the function.

The last function we need in this class is a function for verification. To verify a speaker, you need to send in an audio file. This file must be at least 1 second and at most 15 seconds long. You will need to record the same phrase that you used for enrollment.

Call the `VerifySpeaker` function and make it require a `Stream` and `Guid`. The stream is the audio file we will use for verification. The `Guid` is the ID of the profile we wish to verify. The function should be `async` and have no return type:

```
    public async void VerifySpeaker(Stream audioStream, Guid
speakerProfile) {
        try {
            Verification verification = await _
speakerVerificationClient.VerifyAsync(audioStream, speakerProfile);
```

We will make a call to `VerifyAsync` from `_speakerVerificationClient`. The required parameters are `audioStream` and `speakerProfile`.

A successful API call will result in a `Verification` object in response. This will contain the verification results, as well as the confidence of the results being correct:

```
if (verification == null) {
        RaiseOnVerificationError(new SpeakerVerificationErrorE
ventArgs("Failed to verify speaker."));
```

```
            return;
        }

        RaiseOnVerificationStatusUpdate(new SpeakerVerificationSta
    tusUpdateEventArgs("Verified", "Verified speaker") { VerifiedProfile =
    verification });
        }
```

If we do have a verification result, we raise the status update event. Add the corresponding `catch` clause to complete the function.

Back in the ViewModel, we need to wire up the commands and event handlers. This is done in a similar manner as for speaker identification, and as such we will not cover the code in detail.

With the code compiling and running, the result may look similar to the following screenshot:

Here, we can see that we have created a speaker profile. We have also completed the enrollment and are ready to verify the speaker.

Verifying the speaker profile may result in the following:

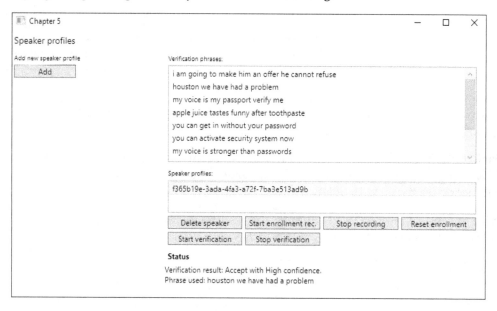

As you can see, the verification was accepted with high confidence.

If we try to verify this using a different phrase or let someone else try to verify as a particular speaker profile, we may end up with the following result:

Here, we can see that the verification has been rejected.

Customizing speech recognition

When we use speech recognition systems, there are several components that are working together. Two of the more important components are acoustic and language models. The first one labels short fragments of audio into sound units. The second helps the system decide the words, based on the likelihood of a given word appearing in certain sequences.

Although Microsoft has done a great job of creating comprehensive acoustic and language models, there may still be times when you need to customize these models.

Imagine that you have an application that is supposed to be used in a factory environment. Using speech recognition will require acoustic training of that environment so that the recognition can separate it from usual factory noises.

Another example is if your application is used by a specific group of people, say, an application for search, where programming is the main topic. You would typically use words such as *object-oriented*, *dot net*, or *debugging*. This can be recognized by customizing language models.

Creating a custom acoustic model

To create custom acoustic models, you will need audio files and transcripts. Each audio file must be stored as a WAV and be between 100 ms and 1 minute in length. It is recommended that there is at least 100 ms of silence at the start and end of the file. Typically, this will be between 500 ms and 1 second. With a lot of background noise, it is recommended to have silences in-between content.

Each file should contain one sentence or utterance. Files should be uniquely named, and an entire set of files can be up to 2 GB. This translates to about 17 to 34 hours of audio, depending on the sampling rate. All files in one set should be placed in a zipped folder, which then can be uploaded.

Accompanying the audio files is a single file with the transcript. This should name the file and have the sentence next to the name. The filename and sentence should be separated by a tab.

Uploading the audio files and transcript will make CRIS process it. When this process is done, you will get a report stating which sentences have failed or succeeded. If anything fails, you will get the reason for the failure.

When the dataset has been uploaded, you can create the acoustic model. This will be associated with the dataset you select. When the model has been created, you can start the process to train it. Once the training is completed, you can deploy the model.

Creating a custom language model

Creating custom language models will also require a dataset. This set is a single plain text file containing sentences or utterances unique to your model. Each new line marks a new utterance. The maximum file size is 2 GB.

Uploading the file will make CRIS process it. Once the processing is done, you will get a report, which will print any errors, with the reason of failure.

With the processing done, you can create a custom language model. Each model will be associated with a given dataset of your selection. Once created, you can train the model, and when the training complete, you can deploy it.

Deploying the application

To deploy and use the custom models, you will need to create a deployment. Here, you will name and describe the application. You can select acoustic models and language models. Be aware that you can only select one of each per deployed application.

Once created, the deployment will start. This process can take up to 30 minutes to complete, so be patient. When the deployment completes, you can get the required information by clicking on the application name. You will be given URLs you can use, as well as subscription keys to use.

To use the custom models with the Bing Speech API, you can overload `CreateDataClientWithIntent` and `CreateMicrophoneClient`. The overloads you will want to use specify both the primary and secondary API keys. You need to use the ones supplied by CRIS. Additionally, you need to specify the supplied URL as the last parameter.

Once this is done, you are able to use customized recognition models.

Translating speech on the fly

Using the **Translator Speech** API, you can add automatic end-to-end translation for speech. Utilizing this API, one can submit an audio stream of speech and retrieve a textual and audio version of translated text. It uses silent detection to detect when speech has ended. Results will be streamed back once the pause is detected.

For a comprehensive list of supported languages, please visit the following site: `https://www.microsoft.com/en-us/translator/business/languages/`.

The result recieved from the API, will contain a stream of audio- and text-based results. The results contain the source text in its original language and the translation in the target language.

For a thorough example on how to use the **Translator Speech** API, please visit the following sample at GitHub: `https://github.com/MicrosoftTranslator/SpeechTranslator`.

Summary

Throughout this chapter, we have focused on speech. We started by looking at how we can convert spoken audio to text and text to spoken audio. Using this, we modified our LUIS implementation so that we can say commands and have conversations with the smart-house application. From there, we moved on to see how we can identify a person speaking using the Speaker Recognition API. Using the same API, we also learned how to verify that a person is who they claim to be. We briefly looked at the core functionality of the Custom Speech Service. Finally, we briefly covered an introduction to the Translator Speech API.

In the following chapter, we will move back to textual APIs, where we will learn how to explore and analyze text in different ways.

6
Understanding Text

The previous chapter covered the speech APIs. Throughout this chapter, we will look closer at more language APIs. We will learn how to use spellcheck features. We will then discover how to detect languages, key phrases, and sentiment in text. Finally, we will look at the translator text API to see how we can detect languages and translate text.

By the end of this chapter, we will have covered the following topics:

- Checking spelling and recognizing slang and informal language, common names, homonyms, and brands
- Detecting language, key phrases, and sentiment in text
- Translating text on the fly

Setting up a common core

Before we get into the details, we want to set ourselves up for success. At the time of writing, none of the language APIs that we will be covering have NuGet client packages. As such, we will need to call directly to the REST endpoints. Because of this, we will do some work beforehand to make sure that we get away with writing less code.

New project

We will not be adding the APIs to our smart-house application. Using the following steps, create a new project using the MVVM template that we created in *Chapter 1, Getting Started with Microsoft Cognitive Services*:

1. Go into the NuGet package manager and install `Newtonsoft.Json`. This will help us deserialize API responses and serialize request bodies.

2. Right-click on **References**.

3. In the **Assemblies** tab, select **System.Web** and **System.Runtime. Serialization**.

4. Click **OK**.

5. In the `MainView.xaml` file, add a `TabControl` element. All our additional views will be added as `TabItems` in the `MainView`.

Web requests

All the APIs follow the same pattern. They call on their respective endpoints using either POST or GET requests. Further on, they pass on parameters as query strings, and some as request bodies. Since they have these similarities, we can create one class that will handle all API requests.

In the `Model` folder, add a new class and call it `WebRequest`.

We also need a few `private` variables, as follows:

```
private const string JsonContentTypeHeader = "application/json";

private static readonly JsonSerializerSettings _settings = new
JsonSerializerSettings
    {
        DateFormatHandling = DateFormatHandling.IsoDateFormat,
        NullValueHandling = NullValueHandling.Ignore,
        ContractResolver = new
CamelCasePropertyNamesContractResolver()
    };

private HttpClient _httpClient;
private string _endpoint;
```

The constant, `JsonContentTypeHeader`, defines the content type that we want to use for all API calls. The `_settings` phrase is a `JsonSerializerSettings` object, which specifies how we want JSON data to be (de)serialized.

The `_httpClient` is the object that will be used to make our API requests. The last member, `_endpoint`, will hold the API endpoint.

As shown in the following code, our constructor will accept two parameters: one string for the URI, and one string for the API key:

```
public WebRequest(string uri, string apiKey)
{
    _endpoint = uri;

    _httpClient = new HttpClient();
    _httpClient.DefaultRequestHeaders.Add("Ocp-Apim-Subscription-
Key", apiKey);
}
```

We assign the `uri` to the corresponding member. Next, we create a new object of a `HttpClient` type and add one request header. This is the header that contains the given `apiKey`.

The class will contain one function, `MakeRequest`. This should have the return type of `Task<TResponse>`, meaning a type that we specify when calling the function. As you can see in the following code, it should accept three parameters: a `HttpMethod`, a query `string`, and a `TRequest`, (which is a request body that we specify in the call). The function should be asynchronous:

```
public async Task <TResponse> MakeRequest <TRequest, TResponse>
(HttpMethod method, string queryString, TRequest requestBody =
default(TRequest))
```

The preceding lines show the complete function signature. Note how we do not need to specify a request body, as there are some cases where it may be empty. We will cover what `TRequest` and `TResponse` may be in a bit.

We enter a `try` clause, as shown in the following code:

```
try {
    string url = $"{_endpoint}{queryString}";
    var request = new HttpRequestMessage(method, url);

    if (requestBody != null)
        request.Content = new StringContent (JsonConvert.
SerializeObject(requestBody, _settings), Encoding.UTF8,
JsonContentTypeHeader);

    HttpResponseMessage response = await _httpClient.
SendAsync(request);
```

First, we create a url, consisting of our _endpoint and the queryString. Using this and the specified method, we create a HttpRequestMessage object.

If we have a requestBody, we add Content to the request object by serializing the requestBody.

With the request in order, we make an asynchronous call to SendAsync on the _httpClient object. This will call the API endpoint, returning a HttpResponseMessage containing the response.

If the response is successful, we want to get the Content as a string. This is done as follows:

1. Make an asynchronous call to ReadAsStringAsync. This will return a string.
2. Deserialize the string as a TResponse object.
3. Return the deserialized object to the caller.

In the case that there is no data in responseContent, we return a default TResponse. This will contain default values for all properties, as shown in the following code:

```
if (response.IsSuccessStatusCode)
{
    string responseContent = null;

    if (response.Content != null)
        responseContent = await response.Content.
ReadAsStringAsync();
        if (!string.IsNullOrWhiteSpace(responseContent))
            return JsonConvert.DeserializeObject<TResponse>(responseCo
ntent, _settings);

        return default(TResponse);
}
```

If the API response contains any error code, then we try to get the error message as a string (errorObjectString). In a typical application, you would want to deserialize this and propagate it to the user. However, as this is a simple example application, we will choose to output it to the Debug console window, as shown in the following code:

```
else
{
    if (response.Content != null && response.Content.Headers.
ContentType.MediaType.Contains (JsonContentTypeHeader))
        {
```

```
        var errorObjectString = await response.Content.
ReadAsStringAsync();
        Debug.WriteLine(errorObjectString);
    }
  }
```

Make sure you add the corresponding `catch` clause and output any exceptions to the `Debug` console window. Also, make sure that you return a default `TResponse` if any exceptions occur.

Data contracts

As we need to (de)serialize JSON data as a part of the requests and responses to the APIs, we need to create data contracts. These will act as the `TResponse` and `TRequest` objects, used in the `WebRequest` class.

Add a new folder called `Contracts` to the project. A typical data contract may look like the following:

```
[DataContract]
public class TextErrors {
    [DataMember]
    public string id { get; set; }

    [DataMember]
    public string message { get; set; }
}
```

This correlates to errors in the text analytics API. As you can see, it has two string properties for `id` and `message`. Both may appear in an API response.

When discussing each API, we will see all request and response parameters in either table form or JSON format. We will not look at how each of these translates into a data contract, but it will take a similar form to that previously shown. It is then up to you to create the contracts needed.

The most important thing to note is that the property names must be identical to the corresponding JSON property.

Make sure that the code compiles and that you can run the application before continuing.

Correcting spelling errors

The Bing Spell Check API leverages the power of machine learning and statistical machine translation to train and evolve a highly contextual algorithm for spellchecking. Doing so allows us to utilize this to perform spellchecking using context.

A typical spellchecker will follow dictionary-based rule sets. As you can imagine, this will need continuous updates and expansions.

Using the Bing Spell Check API, we can recognize and correct slang and informal language. It can recognize common naming errors and correct word-breaking issues. It can detect and correct words that sound the same, but differ in meaning and spelling (homophones). It can also detect and correct brands and popular expressions.

Create a new `View` in the `View` folder; call the file `SpellCheckView.xaml`. Add a `TextBox` element for the input query. We will also need two `TextBox` elements for the pre- and post-context. Add a `TextBox` element to show the result and a `Button` element to execute the spellcheck.

Add a new `ViewModel` in the folder named `ViewModel`; call the file `SpellCheckViewModel.cs`. Make the class `public`, and let it inherit from the `ObservableObject` class. Add the following `private` member:

```
private WebRequest _webRequest;
```

This is the `WebRequest` class that we created earlier.

We need properties corresponding to our `View`. This means that we need four `string` properties and one `ICommand` property.

If you have not already done so, register for a free API key at `https://portal.azure.com`.

The constructor should look like the following:

```
public SpellCheckViewModel()
{
    _webRequest = new WebRequest ("https://api.cognitive.
microsoft.com/bing/v7.0/spellcheck/?", "API_KEY_HERE");
    ExecuteOperationCommand = new DelegateCommand(
    ExecuteOperation, CanExecuteOperation);
}
```

We create a new object of a `WebRequest` type, specifying the Bing Spell Check API endpoint and the API key. We also create a new `DelegateCommand` for our `ExecuteOperationCommand`, `ICommand`, property.

The `CanExecuteOperation` property should return `true` if our input query is filled in and `false` otherwise.

To execute a call to the API, we do the following:

```
private async void ExecuteOperation(object obj)
{
    var queryString = HttpUtility.ParseQueryString(string.Empty);

    queryString["text"] = InputQuery;
    queryString["mkt"] = "en-us";
    //queryString["mode"] = "proof";

    if (!string.IsNullOrEmpty(PreContext))
queryString["preContextText"] = PreContext;

        if(!string.IsNullOrEmpty(PostContext))
    queryString["postContextText"] = PostContext;
```

First, we create a `queryString` using `HttpUtility`. This will format the string so that it can be used in a URI.

As we will be calling the API using a `GET` method, we need to specify all parameters in the string. The required parameters are `text` and `mkt`, which are the input query and language, respectively. If we have entered `PreContext` and/or `PostContext`, then we add these parameters as well. We will look at the different parameters in more detail in a bit.

To make the request, we need to make the following call:

```
        SpellCheckResponse response = await _webRequest.MakeRequest
    <object, SpellCheckResponse>(HttpMethod.Get, queryString.ToString());
        ParseResults(response);
    }
```

We call `MakeRequest` on the `_webRequest` object. As we are making a `GET` request, we do not need any request body, and we pass on `object` as `TRequest`. We expect a `SpellCheckResponse` contract in return. This will contain the resultant data, and we will look at the parameters in greater detail in a bit.

When we have a response, we pass that on to a function to parse it, as shown in the following code:

```
private void ParseResults(SpellCheckResponse response)
{
    if(response == null || response.flaggedTokens == null ||
response.flaggedTokens.Count == 0)
    {
        Result = "No suggestions found";
        return;
    }

    StringBuilder sb = new StringBuilder();
    sb.Append("Spell checking results:nn");
```

If we do not have any response, we exit the function. Otherwise, we create a `StringBuilder` to format the results, as shown in the following code:

```
foreach (FlaggedTokens tokens in response.flaggedTokens)
{
    if (!string.IsNullOrEmpty(tokens.token))
        sb.AppendFormat("Token is: {0}n", tokens.token);

    if(tokens.suggestions != null || tokens.suggestions.Count !=
0)
    {
        foreach (Suggestions suggestion in tokens.suggestions)
        {
            sb.AppendFormat("Suggestion: {0} - with score: {1}n",
suggestion.suggestion, suggestion.score);
        }
        sb.Append("n");
    }
}
Result = sb.ToString();
```

If we have any corrected spellings, we loop through them. We add all suggestions to the `StringBuilder`, making sure that we add the likelihood of the suggestion being correct. At the end, we make sure that we output the result to the UI.

The following table describes all the parameters we can add to the API call:

Parameter	Description
text	The text that we want to check for spelling and grammar errors.
mode	The current mode of the spellcheck. It can be either of the following: • **Proof**: Spelling corrections for long queries, as typically used in MS Word. • **Spell**: Used for search engine corrections. Can be used for queries up to nine words long (tokens).
preContextText	The string that gives context to the text. The petal parameter is valid, but if you specify bike in this parameter, it will be corrected to pedal.
postContextText	The string that gives context to the text. The read parameter is valid, but if you specify carpet in this parameter, it may be corrected to red.
mkt	For proof mode, the language must be specified. It can currently be en-us, es-es, or pt-br. For spell mode, all language codes are supported.

A successful response will be a JSON response, containing the following:

```
{
    "_type": "SpellCheck",
    "flaggedTokens": [
    {
        "offset": 5,
        "token": "Gatas",
        "type": "UnknownToken",
        "suggestions": [
        {
            "suggestion": "Gates",
            "score": 1
        }]
    }]
}
```

The offset is where the word appears in the text and token is the word that contains the error, while type describes the type of error. The suggestions phrase contains an array with the suggested correction and the probability of it being correct.

When the `View` and `ViewModel` have been correctly initialized, as seen in previous chapters, we should be able to compile and run the example.

An example output of running a spellcheck may give the following result:

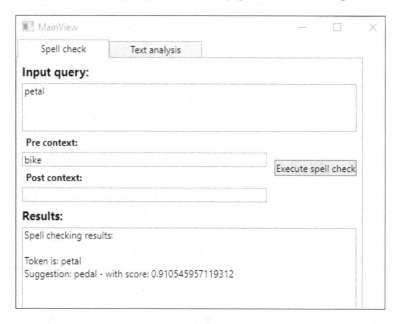

Extracting information through textual analysis

Using the **text analytics** API, we are able to analyze text. We will cover language detection, key-phrase analysis, and sentiment analysis. In addition, a new feature is the ability to detect topics. This does, however, require a lot of sample text, and as such, we will not go into detail on this last feature.

For all our text-analysis tasks, we will be using a new `View`. Add a new `View` into the `View` folder called `TextAnalysisView.xaml`. This should contain a `TextBox` element for the input query. It should also have a `TextBox` element for the result. We will need three `Button` elements, one for each detection analysis that we will perform.

We will also need a new `ViewModel`, so add `TextAnalysisViewModel.cs` to the `ViewModel` folder. In this, we need two `string` properties, one for each `TextBox`. Also add three `ICommand` properties, one for each of our buttons.

If you have not already done so, register for an API key at
`https://portal.azure.com`.

Add a `private` member called `_webRequest` of a `WebRequest` type. With that in
place, we can create our constructor, as shown in the following code:

```
public TextAnalysisViewModel()
{
    _webRequest = new WebRequest("ROOT_URI","API_KEY_HERE");
    DetectLanguageCommand = new DelegateCommand(DetectLanguage,
CanExecuteOperation);
    DetectKeyPhrasesCommand = new DelegateCommand(DetectKeyPhrases
, CanExecuteOperation);
    DetectSentimentCommand = new DelegateCommand(DetectSentiment,
CanExecuteOperation);
}
```

The constructor creates a new `WebRequest` object, specifying the API endpoint and
API key. We then go on to create the `DelegateCommand` objects for our `ICommand`
properties. The `CanExecuteOperation` function should return `true` if we have
entered the input query and `false` otherwise.

Detecting language

The API can detect which language is used in text from over 120 different languages.

This is a `POST` call, so we need to send in a request body. A request body should
consist of `documents`. This is basically an array containing a unique `id` for each
`text`. It also needs to contain the text itself, as shown in the following code:

```
private async void DetectLanguage(object obj)
{
    var queryString = HttpUtility.ParseQueryString("languages");
    TextRequests request = new TextRequests
    {
        documents = new List<TextDocumentRequest>
        {
            new TextDocumentRequest {id="FirstId", text=InputQue
ry}
        }
    };

    TextResponse response = await _webRequest.
MakeRequest<TextRequests, TextResponse>(HttpMethod.Post, queryString.
ToString(), request);
```

We create a `queryString` specifying the REST endpoint that we want to reach. Then we go on to create a `TextRequest` contract, which contains documents. As we only want to check one piece of text, we add one `TextDocumentRequest` contract, specifying an `id` and the `text`.

When the request is created, we call `MakeRequest`. We expect the response to be of a `TextResponse` type and the request body to be of a `TextRequests` type. We pass along `POST` as the call method, the `queryString`, and the `request` body.

If the response is successful, then we loop through the `detectedLanguages`. We add the languages to a `StringBuilder`, also outputting the probability of that language being correct. This is then displayed in the UI, as shown in the following code:

```
if(response.documents == null || response.documents.Count == 0)
{
    Result = "No languages was detected.";
    return;
}

StringBuilder sb = new StringBuilder();

foreach (TextLanguageDocuments document in response.documents)
{
    foreach (TextDetectedLanguages detectedLanguage in document.
detectedLanguages)
    {
        sb.AppendFormat("Detected language: {0} with score {1}n",
detectedLanguage.name, detectedLanguage.score);
    }
}

Result = sb.ToString();
```

A successful response will contain the following JSON:

```
{
    "documents": [
    {
        "id": "string",
        "detectedLanguages": [
        {
            "name": "string",
            "iso6391Name": "string",
            "score": 0.0
        }]
    }],
```

```
    "errors": [
    {
        "id": "string",
        "message": "string"
    }]
}
```

This contains an array of `documents` -, as many as were provided in the
request. Each document will be marked with a unique `id` and contain an array of
`detectedLanguage` instances. These languages will have the `name`, `iso6391Name`,
and the probability (`score`) of being correct.

If any errors occur for any document, we will get an array of `errors`. Each error will
contain the `id` of the document where the error occurred and the `message` as a string.

A successful call will create a result similar to the one shown in the
following screenshot:

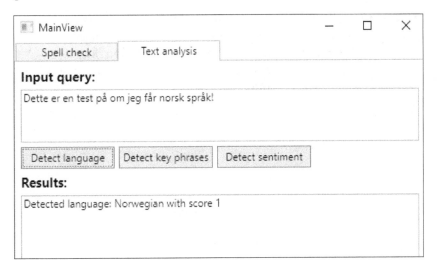

Extracting key phrases from text

Extracting key phrases from text may be useful if we want our application to know
key talking points. Using this, we can learn what people are discussing in articles,
discussions, or other such sources of text.

This call also uses the POST method, which requires a request body. As with
language detection, we need to specify documents. Each document will need
a unique ID, the text, and the language used. At the time of writing, English,
German, Spanish, and Japanese are the only languages that are supported.

To extract key phrases, we use the following code:

```
private async void DetectKeyPhrases(object obj)
{
    var queryString = HttpUtility.ParseQueryString("keyPhrases");
    TextRequests request = new TextRequests
    {
        documents = new List<TextDocumentRequest>
        {
            new TextDocumentRequest { id = "FirstId", text =
InputQuery, language = "en" }
        }
    };

    TextKeyPhrasesResponse response = await _webRequest.
MakeRequest<TextRequests, TextKeyPhrasesResponse>(HttpMethod.Post,
queryString.ToString(), request);
```

As you can see, it is quite similar to detecting languages. We create a `queryString`
using `keyPhrases` as the REST endpoint. We create a request object of
the `TextRequests` type. We add the documents list, creating one new
`TextDocumentRequest`. Again, we need the `id` and `text`, but we have also
added a `language` tag, as shown in the following code:

```
if (response.documents == null || response.documents?.Count == 0)
{
    Result = "No key phrases found.";
    return;
}

StringBuilder sb = new StringBuilder();

foreach (TextKeyPhrasesDocuments document in response.documents)
{
    sb.Append("Key phrases found:n");
    foreach (string phrase in document.keyPhrases)
    {
        sb.AppendFormat("{0}n", phrase);
    }
}

Result = sb.ToString();
```

If the response contains any key phrases then we loop through them and output them to the UI. A successful response will provide the following JSON:

```json
{
    "documents": [{
        "keyPhrases": [
        "string" ],
        "id": "string"
    }],
    "errors": [
    {
        "id": "string",
        "message": "string"
    } ]
}
```

Here we have an array of `documents`. Each document has a unique `id`, corresponding to the ID in the request. Each document also contains an array of strings, with `keyPhrases`.

As with language detection, any errors will be returned as well.

Learning whether a text is positive or negative

Using sentiment analysis, we can detect whether or not a text is positive. If you have a merchandise website where users can submit feedback, this feature can automatically analyze whether the feedback is generally positive or negative.

The sentiment scores are returned as a number between 0 and 1, where a high number indicates a positive sentiment.

As with the previous two analyses, this is a POST call, requiring a request body. Again, we need to specify the documents, and each document requires a unique ID, the text, and the language, as shown in the following code:

```csharp
private async void DetectSentiment(object obj)
{
    var queryString = HttpUtility.ParseQueryString("sentiment");
    TextRequests request = new TextRequests
    {
        documents = new List<TextDocumentRequest>
        {
            new TextDocumentRequest { id = "FirstId", text =
InputQuery, language = "en" }
```

```
            }
        };
```

```
        TextSentimentResponse response = await _webRequest.MakeRequest
    <TextRequests, TextSentimentResponse>(HttpMethod.Post, queryString.
    ToString(), request);
```

We create a `queryString` pointing to `sentiment` as the REST endpoint. The data contract is `TextRequests`, containing `documents`. The document we pass on has a unique `id`, the text, and the language:

A call to `MakeRequest` will require a request body of a `TextSentimentRequests` type, and we expect the result to be of a `TextSentimentResponse` type.

If the response contains any `documents`, we loop through them. For each document, we check the `score`, and output whether or not the text is positive or negative. This is then shown in the UI, as follows:

```
        if(response.documents == null || response.documents?.Count == 0)
        {
            Result = "No sentiments detected";
            return;
        }

        StringBuilder sb = new StringBuilder();

        foreach (TextSentimentDocuments document in response.documents)
        {
            sb.AppendFormat("Document ID: {0}n", document.id);

            if (document.score >= 0.5)
                sb.AppendFormat("Sentiment is positive, with a score of{0}
    n", document.score);
            else
                sb.AppendFormat("Sentiment is negative with a score of {0}
    n", document.score);
        }

        Result = sb.ToString();
```

A successful response will result in the following JSON:

```
        {
            "documents": [
            {
                "score": 0.0,
```

```
            "id": "string"
        }],
        "errors": [
        {
            "id": "string",
            "message": "string"
        }]
    }
```

This is an array of `documents`. Each document will have a corresponding `id` as the request and the sentiment `score`. If any `errors` have occurred, they will be entered as we saw in the language and key-phrase detection sections.

A successful test can look like the following:

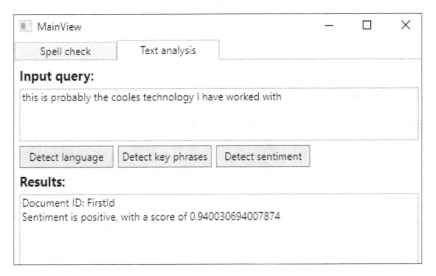

Translating text on the fly

Using the translator text API, you can easily add translations to your application. The API allows you to automatically detect the language. This can be used to serve localized content, or to quickly translate content. It also allows us to look up alternative translations that can be used to translate words into different contexts.

In addition, the translator text API can be used to build customized translation systems. This means that you can improve the existing models. This can be done by adding existing human translations related to expressions and vocabulary in your industry.

The translator text API is available as a REST API. We will cover the four endpoints that you can reach. To use the API, the following root URL should be used:

```
https://api.cognitive.microsofttranslator.com
```

Sign up for an API key at Microsoft Azure Portal.

Translating text

To translate text from one language to another, you should call the following URL path:

```
/translate
```

The following parameters must be specified:

```
To - Language to translate to. Must be specified as two-letter
language code.
```

This parameter can be specified multiple times.

The request body must contain the text that is to be translated.

A successful call will result in the following JSON output:

```
[
    {
        "detectedLanguage": {
            "language": "en",
            "score": 1.0
        },
        "translations": [
            "text": "Translated text",
            "to": "en"
        ]
    }
]
```

Converting text script

To translate text from one language script (such as Arabic) to another (such as Latin), you should call the following URL path:

```
/transliterate
```

The following parameters must be specified:

```
language - two-letter language code of language used in the language
script.
fromScript - four-letter code for script language you are translating
from.
toScript - four-letter code for script language you are translating
to.
```

The request body must contain the text that is to be translated.

A successful call will result in the following JSON output:

```
[
    {
        "text": "translated text"
        "script": "latin"
    }
]
```

Working with languages

There are two paths that you can use when working with languages. The first one is used to detect language in a specific text. The second one is used to get a list of languages supported by the other APIs.

Detecting the language

To detect the language that a certain text uses, you should call the following URL path:

```
/detect
```

The request body must contain the text that is to be translated. No parameters are needed.

A successful call will result in the following JSON output:

```
[
    {
        "language": "en",
        "score": 1.0,
        "isTranslationSupported": true,
        "isTransliterationSupported": false,
        "alternatives": [
```

```
        {
            "language": "pt",
            "score": 0.8,
            "isTranslationSupported": false
            "isTransliterationSupported": false
        },
        {

            "language": "latn",
            "score": 0.7,
            "isTranslationSupported": true
            "isTransliterationSupported": true
        }
    ]
    }
]
```

Getting supported languages

To get a list of supported languages, you should call the following URL path:

```
/languages
```

No parameters or body are required for this call.

A successful call will result in the following JSON output:

```
[
    "translation": {
        ...
        "en": {
            "name": "English",
            "nativeName": "English",
            "dir": "ltr"
        },
        ...
    },
    "transliteration": {
        "ar": {
            "name": "Latin",
            "nativeName": "",
            "scripts": [
                {
                    "code": "Arab",
                    "name": "Arabic",
                    "nativeName": "",
                    "dir": "rtl",
```

```
            "toScripts": [
                {
                    "code:" "Latn",
                    "name": "Latin",
                    "nativeName": "",
                    "dir": "ltr"
                }
            ]
        },
        {
            "code": "Latn",
            "name": "Latin",
            "nativeName": "",
            "dir": "ltr",
            "toScripts": [
                {
                    "code:" "Arab",
                    "name": "Arabic",
                    "nativeName": "",
                    "dir": "rtl"
                }
            ]
        }
    ]
},
...
},
"dictionary": {
    "af": {
        "name": "Afrikaans",
        "nativeName": "Afrikaans",
        "dir": "ltr",
        "translations": [
            {
                "name": "English",
                "nativeName": "English",
                "dir": "ltr",
                "code": "en"
            }
            ...
        ]
    }
    ...
}
]
```

As you can see, the two-letter country code is the key for each entry. You can also find the four-letter code for each transliterate language. This API path can be used as a basis for the other API paths.

Summary

In this chapter, we have focused on the language APIs. We started by creating the parts that are needed to execute the API calls to the different services. Following this, we looked at the Bing Spell Check API. We moved on to more analytical APIs, where we learned how to detect languages, key phrases, and sentiment. Finally, we looked into how we can use the translator text API.

The next chapter will take us from language APIs to knowledge APIs. In the following chapter, we will learn how to recognize and identify entities based on context. In addition, we will learn how to use the recommendations API.

7
Building Recommendation Systems for Businesses

"By leveraging Azure Machine Learning and the Recommendations API, we have launched a new Personalized Commerce Experience for retailers that grows shopper conversion and engagement on any channel."

– Frank Kouretas, Chief Product Officer at Orckestra

In the previous chapter, we covered the remaining language APIs. In this chapter, we will look at the Recommendations Solution template. This is a template for Microsoft Azure that contains the resources required to run Recommendations Solution. This is a solution well suited for e-commerce applications, where you can recommend different items based on different criteria. Recommending items in an online store is a process that can be very time-consuming if it is done by following a rule set. The Recommendations Solution allows us to utilize the power of machine learning to get good recommendations, potentially increasing the number of sales.

This chapter will cover the following topics:

- Deploying the Recommendations Solution template
- Training the recommendation model
- Consuming recommendations

Providing personalized recommendations

If you run an e-commerce site, a feature that is nice for your customers to have is recommendations. Using the Recommendation Solution, you can easily add this. Utilizing Microsoft Azure Machine Learning, the API can be trained to recognize items that should be recommended.

There are two common scenarios for recommendations, as follows:

- **Item-to-Item Recommendations (I2I)**: I2I is the scenario where certain items are often viewed after other items. Typically, this will be in the form of *people who visited this item also visited this other item.*

- **Customer-to-Item Recommendations (U2I)**: U2I is the scenario where you utilize a customer's previous actions to recommend items. If you sell movies, for example, then you can recommend other movies based on a customer's previous movie choices.

The general steps to use the Recommendation Solution are as follows:

1. Deploy the template in Azure
2. Import the catalog data (the items in your e-commerce site)
3. Import usage data
4. Train a recommendation model
5. Consume recommendations

If you have not already done so, you should sign up for an API key at `https://portal.azure.com`.

Deploying the Recommendation Solution template in Azure

To deploy the Recommendations Solution, you must have an active Microsoft Azure subscription.

Head over to `https://github.com/Microsoft/Product-Recommendations/tree/master/deploy` to start the deployment. Click on **Deploy to Azure**, as shown in the following screenshot:

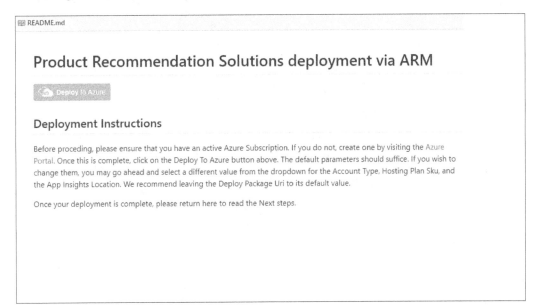

This will take you to the following page in Microsoft Azure:

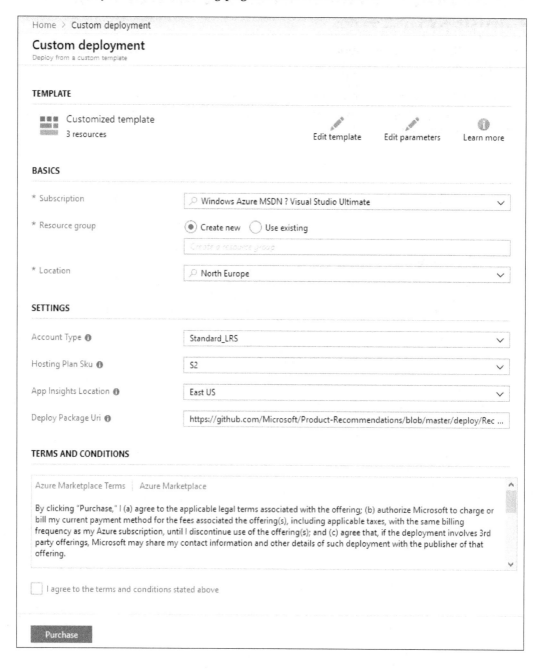

Enter the required information, accept the terms and conditions, and click on **Purchase**. This will start the process of deploying the required resources for the Recommendations Solution.

After a few minutes, the deployment is done. You are now ready to upload data to train a model.

Importing catalog data

With the solution deployed, we can add catalog data. This is where you would typically add items from your database. Items need to be uploaded as files. The files need to be in CSV format.

The following table describes the data that is required for each item in your catalog:

Name	Description
Item ID	A unique identifier for a given item
Item name	The name of the item
Item category	The category for the item, such as hardware, software, book genre, and so on

In addition, there are a few data fields that are optional. These are described in the following table:

Name	Description
Description	A description of the item
Feature list	A comma-separated feature list that can enhance recommendations

A file that has all the data included may have items that look like the following:

```
C9F00168, Kiruna Flip Cover, Accessories, Description of item,
compatibility = lumia, hardware type = mobile
```

It is typically better to add features as this improves the recommendations. Any new item that has little usage is unlikely to be recommended if no features exist.

Features should be categorical. This means that a feature can be a price range. A price alone would not serve as a good feature.

You can add up to 20 features per item. When a catalog containing features for items is uploaded, you need to perform a rank build. This will rank each feature, where features of a higher ranking will typically be better to use.

The code example for this chapter contains a sample catalog. We will use this for the following example. Alternatively, you can download some data from Microsoft from `http://aka.ms/RecoSampleData`. We want to use the data from `MsStoreData.zip`.

With the files downloaded, we can upload the catalog to our storage. This can be done by heading to your newly created storage account and creating a new blob container for the catalog, as shown in the following screenshot:

Click on **Upload**, browse to the sample files you downloaded, and choose the `catalog.csv` file. This will upload the catalog.

> Note that the catalog file is not required, but it is recommended that you upload it in order to supply it to the model.
>
> The maximum number of items in a catalog is 100,000. Any given catalog file cannot be larger than 200 MB. If your file is larger, and you still have more items, you can upload several files.

Importing usage data

The next step we need to make is to upload usage data. This is a file describing all the transactions from your customers in the past. The file contains rows, with transactions, where each transaction is a comma-separated line containing data.

The required data fields are as follows:

Name	Description
User ID	A unique identifier for each customer
Item ID	A unique identifier for items that correlate to the catalog
Time	The time of the transaction

In addition, it is possible to have a field called `Event`. This describes the type of transaction. The allowed values for this field are `Click`, `RecommendationClick`, `AddShopCart`, `RemoveShopCart`, and `Purchase`.

Given the preceding example from the catalog, a line in the usage file may look as follows:

```
00030000D16C4237, C9F00168, 2015/08/04 T 11:02:37, Purchase
```

The maximum file size for a usage file is 200 MB.

The quality of recommendations relies on the amount of usage data. Typically, you should have about 20 transactions registered per item. This means that if you have 100 items in the catalog, you should aim for 2,000 transactions in the usage file.

Note that the current maximum number of transactions that the API accepts is 5 million. If new transactions are added above this maximum, the oldest data will be deleted.

Again, you can find an example usage file at `http://aka.ms/RecoSampleData`. Create another blob container called `usage` and click on **Upload**. Upload all the usage files from the sample folder.

Training a model

With the catalog and usage data in place, it is time to train a model.

Starting to train

To start a training process, we need to make an API call to an endpoint on the newly created app service. This can be done using a tool, such as Postman, or through your own application. We will use Postman for the purposes of this book.

 To download Postman, please visit `https://www.getpostman.com/`.

The training process can be started by sending a POST request to the following URL:

```
https://<service_name>.azurewebsites.net/api/models
```

The request must include a header, `x-api-key`, with your API key. It must also include another header, `Content-Type`, which should be set to `application/json`.

In addition, the request must contain a body containing the following:

Property	Mandatory	Description
description	No	Textual description.
blobContainerName	Yes	Name of the blob container where the catalog and usage data are stored.
usageRelativePath	Yes	Relative path to either a virtual directory that contains the usage file(s) or a specific usage file to be used for training.
catalogFileRelativePath	No	Relative path to the catalog file.
evaluationUsageRelativePath	No	Relative path to either a virtual directory that contains the usage file(s) or to a specific usage file to be used for evaluation.
supportThreshold	No	How conservative the model is, measured in the number of cooccurrences of items to be considered for modeling.
cooccurrenceUnit	No	Indicates how to group usage events before counting cooccurrence.
similarityFunction	No	Defines the similarity function to be used. Can be Jaccard, Cooccurrence, or Lift.
enableColdItemPlacement	No	This will be either true or false. Indicates whether recommendations should push cold items via feature similarity.
enableColdToColdRecommendations	No	This will be either true or false. Indicates whether or not the similarity between pairs of cold items should be calculated.
enableUserAffinity	No	This will be either true or false. Defines whether the event type and time of event should be considered as inputs to the result.
enableBackfilling	No	This will be either true or false. This will backfill with popular items if not enough relevant items are returned.
allowSeedItemsInRecommendations	No	This will be either true or false. Determines whether input items can be returned as results.

Property	Mandatory	Description
`decayPeriodInDays`	No	The decay period in days. The longer the time since an event has occurred, the less weight the event will have.
`enableUserToItemRecommendations`	No	This will be either `true` or `false`. If `true`, the user ID will be taken into account when personalized recommendations are requested.

A successful call may yield the following result:

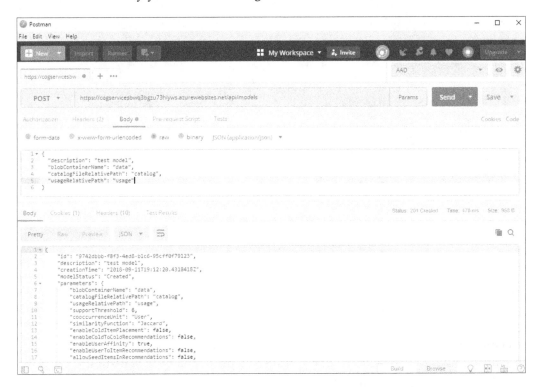

The `id` field returned can be used to check the training status.

Verifying the completion of training

Using the ID returned in the previous request, we can now run a GET request to the following endpoint:

```
https://<service_name>.azurewebsites.net/api/models/<model_id>
```

This request requires a header, x-api-key, containing your API key. A successful request may give the following response:

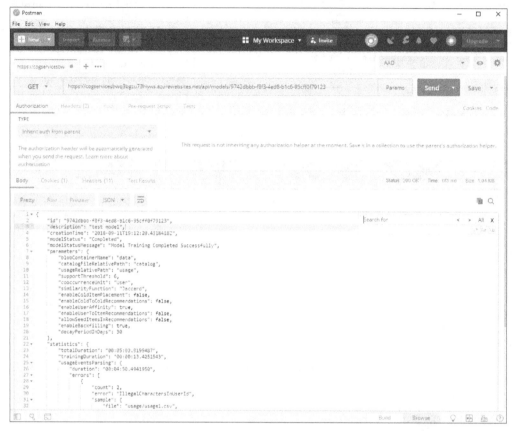

Response of GET request

As you can see, a modelStatus field is presented. Once this is Completed, the model is trained and ready to be used. You will also be presented with statistics, such as the duration of training, among other details.

If you prefer to use a user interface for the model training, you can visit https://<your_service>.azurewebsites.net/ui.

Consuming recommendations

To use the recommendation models we just created, we will create a new example application. Create this using the MVVM template we created previously.

At the time of writing, there is no client package for the recommendations API. This means that we need to rely on web requests, as we saw in *Chapter 6, Understanding Text*. To speed up the development time, copy the `WebRequest.cs` file from the example code in *Chapter 6, Understanding Text*. Paste this file into the `Model` folder, and make sure that you update the namespace.

 Remember to add references to System.Web and System.Runtime. Serialization.

As there is no need for much UI, we are going to add everything in the `MainView.xaml` file. We are going to need two `ComboBox` elements. These will list our recommendation models and catalog items. We also need a `Button` element to get the recommendations and a `TextBox` element to show the resultant recommendations.

The corresponding `ViewModel`, `MainViewModel.cs`, will need properties to correspond to the UI elements. Add an `ObservableCollection` of a `RecommendationModel` type to hold our models. We will look at the type in a bit. We need a property of a `RecommendationModel` type to hold the selected model. Add an `ObservableCollection` property of a `Product` type with a corresponding `Product` property for the available and selected properties. We will also need a `string` property for the results and an `ICommand` property for our button.

Add a `private` member of a `WebRequest` type so that we can call the API.

Add a new file called `Product` in the `Model` folder. To use the items from our catalog, we will load the catalog file into the application, creating a `Product` for each item. Ensure that `Product` looks as follows:

```csharp
public class Product {
    public string Id { get; set; }
    public string Name { get; set; }
    public string Category { get; set; }
    public Product(string id, string name, string category) {
        Id = id;
        Name = name;
        Category = category;
    }
}
```

We need the `Id` of an item, as well as the `Name` and the `Category`.

The constructor should create a `WebRequest` object, as shown in the following code:

```
public MainViewModel()
{
    _webRequest = new WebRequest ("https://<YOUR_WEB_SERVICE>.
azurewebsites.net/api/models/", "API_KEY_HERE");
    RecommendCommand = new DelegateCommand(RecommendBook,
CanRecommendBook);

    Initialize();
}
```

When we create the `WebRequest` object, we specify the recommendation endpoint and our API key. The RecommendCommand phrase is the `ICommand` object, as a `DelegateCommand`. We need to specify the action to be executed and the conditions under which we are allowed to execute the command. We should be allowed to execute the command if we have selected a recommendation model and a product.

The `Initialize` phrase will make sure that we fetch our recommendation models and products, as shown in the following code:

```
private async void Initialize() {
    await GetModels();
    GetProducts();
}
```

The `GetModels` method will make a call to the API, as shown in the following code:

```
private async Task GetModels()
{
    List<RecommandationModel> models = await _webRequest.
GetModels(HttpMethod.Get);
```

This call is a GET request, so we specify this in `GetModels`. A successful call should result in a JSON response that we then deserialize into a `RecommendationModel` object. This is a data contract, so add a file called `Models.cs` in a folder called `Contracts`.

A successful result will give the following output:

```
[
    {
        "id": "string",
        "description": "string",
        "creationTime": "string",
```

```
        "modelStatus": "string"
    }
    {...}
    {...}
]
```

We have an array of models. Each item in this array has an id, name, description, createdDateTime, activeBuildId, and catalogDisplayName. Make sure that the RecommendationModels class contains this data.

If the call succeeds, we add the models to the ObservableCollection of available models, as shown in the following code:

```
    foreach (RecommandationModel model in models) {
        AvailableModels.Add(model);
    }
    SelectedModel = AvailableModels.FirstOrDefault();
}
```

When all items are added, we set the SelectedModel to the first available option.

To add the items from our catalog, we need to read from the catalog file. In the example code provided with the book, this file is added to the project and copied to the output directory. The GetProducts method will look as follows:

```
private void GetProducts() {
    try {
        var reader = new StreamReader (File.OpenRead("catalog.
csv"));

        while(!reader.EndOfStream) {
            string line = reader.ReadLine();
            var productInfo = line.Split(',');

            AvailableProducts.Add(new Product(productInfo[0],
productInfo[1], productInfo[2]));
        }

        SelectedProduct = AvailableProducts.FirstOrDefault();
    }
    catch(Exception ex) {
        Debug.WriteLine(ex.Message);
    }
}
```

This is a basic file operation, reading in each line from the catalog. For each item, we get the required information, creating a `Product` for each item. This is then added to the `AvailableProducts` in the `ObservableCollection` property, and the `SelectedProduct` is the first available.

Now that we have our recommendation models and our products, we can execute the recommendation request, as shown in the following code:

```
private async void RecommendProduct(object obj)
{
    List<RecommendedItem> recommendations = await _
webRequest.RecommendItem(HttpMethod.Get, $"{SelectedModel.id}/
recommend?item={SelectedProduct.Id}");
```

The call to get the recommendations is a GET request. This requires us to add `itemIds`.

The `itemIds` parameter must be the ID of a selected product.

We call the `RecommendItem` method on the `_webRequest` object. This is a GET request, and we need to specify the ID of the `SelectedModel` in the query string. We also need to add a bit to the query string so that we reach the correct endpoint. A successful response will result in JSON output, which will look as follows:

```
[
    {
        "recommendedItemId": "string",
        "score": "float"
    },
    {...}
    {...}
]
```

The result consists of an array of objects. Each item will have a `recommendedItemId` and a `score`. The score gives an indication of how likely a customer is to want the given item.

This result should be deserialized into a list of data contracts of a `RecommandedItem` type, so make sure you add this in the `Contracts` folder.

When we have made a successful call, we want to display this in the UI, as follows:

```
if(recommendations.Count == 0) {
    Recommendations = "No recommendations found";
```

```
        return;
    }
    StringBuilder sb = new StringBuilder();
    sb.Append("Recommended items:\n\n");
```

First, we check to see whether we have any recommendations. If we do not have any, we will not move on. If we do have any items, we create a `StringBuilder` to format our output, as follows:

```
    foreach(RecommendedItem recommendedItem in recommendations)  {
        sb.AppendFormat("Score: {0}n", recommendedItem.score);
        sb.AppendFormat("Item ID: {0}\n", item.id);

        sb.Append("n");
    }
    Recommendations = sb.ToString();
}
```

We loop through all the `recommendedItems`. We output the `score` and the `id`. This will be printed in the UI.

A successful test run may give the following result:

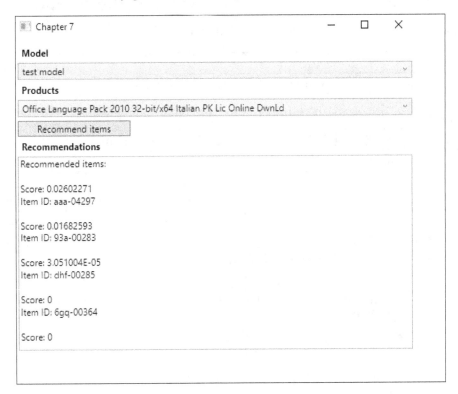

There are a few special cases to note:

- If the item list contains a single item that does not exist in the catalog, then an empty result is returned
- If the item list contains some items that are not in the catalog, then these are removed from the query
- If the item list contains only cold items (items that have no usage data connected to them), then the most popular recommendation is returned
- If the item list contains some cold items, then recommendations are returned for the other items

Recommending items based on prior activities

To make recommendations based on user activity, we need a list of users. As such a list would be too cumbersome to create just for an example, we will only look at the steps and parameters that are required to make this kind of recommendation.

The endpoint for this usage is a bit different, as it is another GET call. In code, it would look as follows:

```
$"{SelectedModel.id}/recommend/user?{queryString.ToString()}"
```

The parameters in the query string are as follows:

Parameter	Description
userId (required)	A unique identifier of a given user.
numberOfResults (required)	The number of recommendations returned.
itemsIds (optional)	A list or single ID of the selected item(s).
includeMetadata (optional)	If true, then the item's metadata will be included.
buildId (optional)	A number identifying the build we want to use. If none is specified, then the active build is used.

A successful call will result in the same JSON output as the other recommendation models. Recommended items will, of course, be based on users' past activities.

 Note that, to be able to use this, U2I must be set to true when creating a model build.

Summary

In this chapter, we dived into the recommendations API. We learned how to set up recommendation models using existing catalog and usage data. Using these models, we learned how to utilize these in a simple example application.

In the next chapter, we will start with the knowledge APIs. We will learn how to structure natural language queries and evaluate query expressions. In addition, we will learn how to add autocompletion to natural language queries.

8
Querying Structured Data in a Natural Way

In the previous chapter, we learned how we can use the current context to extend our knowledge on a certain topic. Throughout this chapter, we will continue discussing about the knowledge APIs. More specifically, we will learn how to explore relationships between academic papers and journals. We will see how we can interpret natural language queries, and retrieve query expressions. Using these expressions, we will learn how to find academic entities. We will then focus more on how to set up this kind of service on your own. At the end of this chapter, we will look at QnA Maker to see how we can create FAQ services from existing content.

This chapter will cover the following topics:

- Interpreting natural-language user queries using Project Academic Knowledge
- Assisting the user with queries using autocomplete features
- Using autocomplete queries to retrieve academic entities
- Calculating the distribution of academic entities from queries
- Hosting the Project Knowledge Exploration Service with your own schema
- Creating an FAQ service from existing content using QnA Maker

Tapping into academic content using the academic API

Microsoft Academic Graph (**MAG**) is a knowledge base for web-scale, heterogeneous entity graphs. Entities model scholarly activities, and contain information such as the field of study, author(s), institution, and more.

Data contained in MAG is indexed from the Bing web index. As this is continuously indexed, the data is always up to date.

Using the Project Academic Knowledge API, we can tap into this knowledge base. This API allows us to combine search suggestions, research paper graph search results, and histogram distributions. The API enables a knowledge-driven and interactive dialog.

When a user searches for research papers, the API can provide query completion. It may suggest queries based on the input. With a complete query, we can evaluate a query expression. This will retrieve a set of matching paper entities from the knowledge base.

Setting up an example project

To test Project Academic Knowledge, we will first want to create a new example project. We will create this from the MVVM template created in *Chapter 1, Getting Started with Microsoft Cognitive Services*.

Project Academic Knowledge does not have any client packages available. This means that we need to call the API ourselves. Copy the `WebRequest.cs` file from the `Model` folder in the smart house application and paste it into the `Model` folder of the newly created project. Make sure that you correct the namespace.

To be able to compile this, we will need to add references to `System.Web` and `System.Runtime.Serializable`. We will also be working with JSON, so go ahead and add the `Newtonsoft.Json` package through the NuGet package manager.

As this will be the only API tested in this sample project, we can add UI elements in the `MainView.xaml` file. Open this file now.

Our `View` should have a `TextBox` element for our input query. It should have a `ComboBox` element to list the suggested query expressions. We need three `Button` elements, one for `Interpret`, one for `Evaluate`, and one for `Histogram`, which are all functions we will be executing. Last but not least, we need a `TextBox` element to display our results.

In the `MainViewModel.cs` file, we will need to add corresponding properties. Add three `string` properties, one for the input query, one for the results, and one for the selected query expression. Add an `ObservableCollection` property of the `string` type for our available query expressions. We also need three `ICommand` properties, one for each of our buttons.

Add a private member for our `WebRequest` object. Make the constructor look like the following:

```
public MainViewModel()
{
    _webRequest = new WebRequest("https://api.labs.cognitive.
microsoft.com/academic/v1.0/",
        "API_KEY_HERE");

    InterpretCommand = new DelegateCommand(Interpret,
CanInterpret);
    EvaluateCommand = new DelegateCommand(Evaluate,
CanExecuteCommands);
    CalculateHistogramCommand = new DelegateCommand
(CalculateHistogram,
        CanExecuteCommands);
}
```

 If you have not already done so, sign up for an API key at `https://labs.cognitive.microsoft.com/en-us/project-academic-knowledge` and click the **Subscribe** button.

The `CanInterpret` parameter should return `true` if we have entered any text into the query textbox. The `CanExecuteCommands` parameter should return `true` if we have selected a query expression. We will cover `Interpret`, `Evaluate`, and the `CalculateHistogram` parameters in the upcoming sections.

Make sure that the application compiles and runs before continuing.

Interpreting natural language queries

The query expressions that the API uses to evaluate a query are not in a natural language format. To ensure that users can make queries in a natural way, we need to interpret their input.

When calling the `Interpret` feature of the API, it accepts a query string. This will be returned and formatted to reflect the user intent using academic grammar. In addition, this feature can be called as the user is writing, to provide an interactive experience.

The request is a GET request, as shown in the following code:

```
private async void Interpret(object obj)
{
    var queryString = HttpUtility.ParseQueryString(string.Empty);

    queryString["query"] = InputQuery;
    queryString["complete"] = "1";
    //queryString["count"] = "10";
    //queryString["offset"] = "0";
    //queryString["timeout"] = "1000";
    //queryString["model"] = "latest";
```

We start the call by creating a `queryString` variable. The parameters we can input are specified in the following table:

Parameter	Description
query (required)	The query from the user.
complete (optional)	If this is set to 1, then the service will return suggestions using the query as a prefix. A value of 0 means there will be no autocomplete.
count (optional)	The maximum number of interpretations to return.
offset (optional)	The index of the first interpretation. This is useful if a lot of results are expected and you need to add pagination.
timeout (optional)	The timeout specified in milliseconds. Only results found before this limit will be returned.
model (optional)	The name of the model you want to query. This defaults to the latest model.

We call the API to get interpretations, as shown in the following code:

```
InterpretResponse response = await _webRequest.MakeRequest<object,
    InterpretResponse>(HttpMethod.Get, $"interpret?{queryString.
ToString()}");

    if (response == null || response.interpretations.Length == 0)
        return;
```

As this is a `GET` request, we do not need to specify any request bodies. We do, however, expect a result to be serialized into an `InterpretResponse` object. This is a data contract, containing properties from the result.

A successful call to the API will result in a JSON response, which looks as follows:

```
{
    "query": "papers by jaime", "interpretations": [
    {
        "prob": 2.429e-006,
        "parse": "<rule id="#GetPapers"> papers by <attr
name="academic#AA.AuN">
        jaime teevan </attr></rule>",
        "rules": [
        {
            "name": "#GetPapers",
            "output": {
                "type": "query",
                "value": "Composite(AA.AuN=='jaime teevan')"
            }
        }]
    }]
}
```

The result contains the original `query`. It also contains an array with `interpretations`. Each item in this array consists of the data shown in the following table:

Data field	Description
`prob`	This is the probability of the current interpretation being correct. The scale goes from 0 to 1, where 1 is the highest.
`parse`	This is an XML string showing interpretations for each part of the string.
`rules`	This is an array with one or more rules defined. There will always be one rule for the academic API.
`rules[x].name`	This is the name of the current rule.
`rules[x].output`	This is the output of the current rule.
`rules[x].output.type`	This is the type of the rule output. This will always be `query` for the academic API.
`rules[x].output.value`	This is the output value for the rule. This will be a query expression string.

Create the `InterpretResponse` data contract based on the preceding JSON output. We are interested in the last data field, `rules[x].output.value`. This is the query expression string, which we will use to evaluate queries.

When the API call has succeeded, we want to update the `ObservableCollection` class as to the available query expressions, using the following code:

```
    ObservableCollection<string> tempList = new
ObservableCollection<string>();

    foreach (Interpretation interpretation in response.
interpretations)
    {
        foreach (Rule rule in interpretation.rules) {
            tempList.Add(rule.output.value);
        }
    }

    AvailableQueryExpressions = tempList;
    QueryExpression = AvailableQueryExpressions.FirstOrDefault();
```

We loop through all `interpretations`, adding the `outputvalue` from a rule to our `AvailableQueryExpressions`.

Finally, we set the selected `QueryExpression` as the first one available. This is just for our own convenience.

A successful test run can generate the following results:

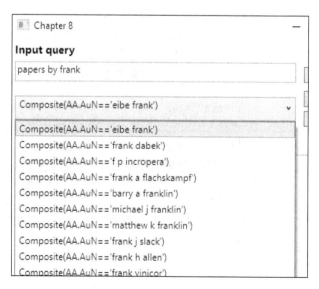

An unsuccessful call will produce an error response code. The response codes that can be generated are as follows:

Response code	Description
400	Bad argument; request parameter is missing
401	Invalid subscription key
403	The call volume quota has been exceeded
404	The requested resources are not found
500	Internal server error

Finding academic entities in query expressions

Now that we have a query expression available, we can retrieve a set of academic entities using the `Evaluate` endpoint. This is a GET request, where we need to specify the attributes we want returned for each entity. We will cover the available attributes later.

We start by creating a query string, as shown in the following code:

```
private async void Evaluate(object obj)
{
    string queryString = $"expr={QueryExpression} &
    attributes=Id,Ti,Y,D,CC,AA.AuN";

    //queryString += "&model=latest";
    //queryString += "&count=10";
    //queryString += "&offset=0";5
    //queryString += "&orderby=name:asc";
```

The parameters we can add are described in the following table:

Parameter	Description
expr (required)	This is the query expression found in the `Interpret` call.
attributes (optional)	This is a comma-separated list of attributes to be included in the response. Each attribute is case-sensitive.
model (optional)	This is the model you wish to use for a query. This defaults to the latest model.
count (optional)	This is the number of entities to return.
offset (optional)	This is the index of the first result to return; it can be useful for pagination purposes.

Parameter	Description
orderby (optional)	This specifies the order in which to sort the entities.

Note that, while the `attributes` parameter is optional, you should specify which attributes you want. If none are specified, only the entity ID is returned.

We call the API, as follows:

```
        EvaluateResponse response = await _webRequest.
    MakeRequest<object,
        EvaluateResponse>(HttpMethod.Get, $"evaluate?{queryString}");

    if (response == null || response.entities.Length == 0)
        return;
```

As this is a GET request, we do not need any request bodies. With a successful call, we expect an `EvaluateResponse` object in return. This is a data contract, which will be deserialized from the JSON response.

A successful response will give a JSON response like the following code (depending on the attributes specified):

```
    {
        "expr": "Composite(AA.AuN=='jaime teevan')",
        "entities": [
        {
            "prob": 2.266e-007,
            "Ti": "personalizing search via automated analysis of
    interests and
            activities",
            "Y": 2005,
            "CC": 372,
            "AA": [
            {
                "AuN": "jaime teevan",
                "AuId": 1968481722
            },
            {
```

```
            "AuN": "susan t dumais",
            "AuId": 676500258
        },
        {
            "AuN": "eric horvitz",
            "AuId": 1470530979
        }]
    }]
}
```

The response contains the query expression we used. It also contains an array of entities. Each item in this array will contain the probability of it being correct. It will also contain all the attributes that we specified, in the form of either string or numeric values. It can also be in the form of objects, which we will need to have data contracts for.

For our request, we specified some attributes. These were the entity ID, title, year and date of publication, citation count, and author name. Knowing these attributes, we can use the following code to output the result:

```
StringBuilder sb = new StringBuilder();
sb.AppendFormat("Expression {0} returned {1} entities\n\n",
response.expr,
    response.entities.Length);

    foreach (Entity entity in response.entities)
    {
        sb.AppendFormat("Paper title: {0}\n\tDate: {1}\n", entity.Ti,
entity.D);

        sb.Append("Authors:\n");
        foreach (AA author in entity.AA)
        {
            sb.AppendFormat("\t{0}\n", author.AuN);
        }

        sb.Append("\n");
    }
    Results = sb.ToString();
```

A successful call can give the following output:

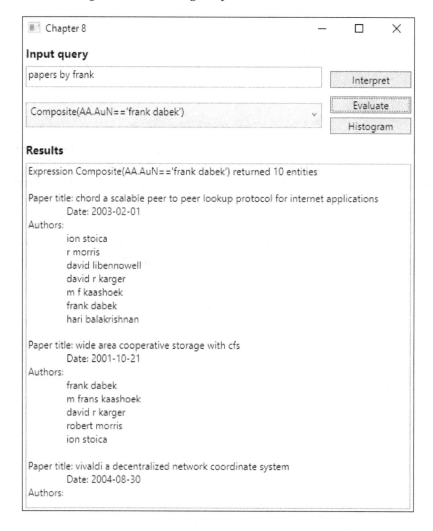

Any error responses will produce response codes, as described previously.

Calculating the distribution of attributes from academic entities

Another feature of the academic API is the ability to calculate the distribution of attribute values for a set of paper entities. This can be done by calling the `calchistogram` API endpoint.

This is a GET request, so we start by creating a query string, as follows:

```
string queryString = $"expr={QueryExpression}&attributes=Y,F.FN";

//queryString += "&model=latest";
//queryString += "&count=10";
//queryString += "&offset=0";
```

The parameters we can specify are the same as with Evaluate, except that we do not have the orderby parameter. For this call, we want to get the year of publication (Y) and the name of the field of study (F.FN).

We make the call to the API without specifying any request bodies, as shown in the following code:

```
HistogramResponse response = await _webRequest.MakeRequest<object,
HistogramResponse>(HttpMethod.Get, $"calchistogram?{queryStri
ng}");

if (response == null || response.histograms.Length == 0)
    return;
```

If the call succeeds, we expect a HistogramResponse object in return. This is a data contract, which should contain the data from the JSON response.

A successful request should give the following JSON response (depending on the requested attributes):

```
{
    "expr": "And(Composite(AA.AuN=='jaime teevan'),Y>2012)",
    "num_entities": 37,
    "histograms": [
    {
        "attribute": "Y",
        "distinct_values": 3,
        "total_count": 37,
        "histogram": [
        {
            "value": 2014,
            "prob": 1.275e-07,
            "count": 15
        },
        {
            "value": 2013,
            "prob": 1.184e-07,
            "count": 12
```

```
        },
        {
            "value": 2015,
            "prob": 8.279e-08,
            "count": 10
        }]
    },
    {

        "attribute": "F.FN",
        "distinct_values": 34,
        "total_count": 53,
        "histogram": [
        {
            "value": "crowdsourcing",
            "prob": 7.218e-08,
        "count": 9
    },
    {

        "value": "information retrieval",
        "prob": 4.082e-08,
        "count": 4
    },
    {

        "value": "personalization",
        "prob": 2.384e-08,
        "count": 3
    },
    {

        "value": "mobile search",
        "prob": 2.119e-08,
        "count": 2
        }]
    }]
}
```

The response contains the original query expression that we used. It will give us a count of the number of matching entities. An array of histograms will also be present. This will contain an item for each of the attributes we requested. The data for each item is described in the following table:

Data field	Description
attribute	This is the attribute name.
distinct_values	This is the number of distinct values that match the entities for this attribute.
total_count	This is the total number of value instances among the matching entities for this attribute.
histogram	This is an array containing the histogram data for this attribute.
histogram[x].value	This is the value for the current histogram.
histogram[x].prob	This is the probability that matching entities have this attribute value.
histogram[x].count	This is the number of matching entities that have this value.

With a successful response, we loop through the data, presenting it in the UI using the following code:

```
StringBuilder sb = new StringBuilder();

sb.AppendFormat("Totalt number of matching entities: {0}\n",
response.num_entities);

foreach (Histogram histogram in response.histograms)
{
    sb.AppendFormat("Attribute: {0}\n", histogram.attribute);
    foreach (HistogramY histogramY in histogram.histogram)
    {
        sb.AppendFormat("\tValue '{0}' was found {1} times\n",
histogramY.value,
        histogramY.count);
    }

    sb.Append("\n");
}
Results = sb.ToString();
```

A successful call gives us the following result:

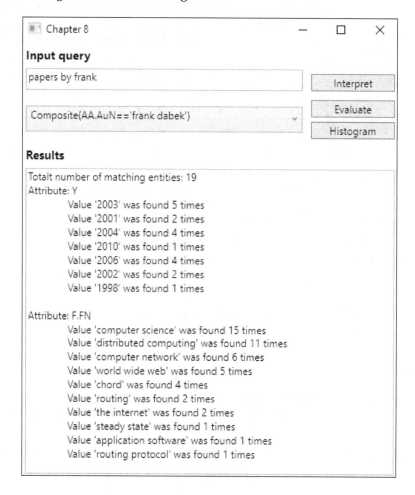

An unsuccessful API call will return an error, containing a response code. The potential response codes are the same as described in the previous section on the `Interpret` feature.

Entity attributes

A rather important element of this API is the usage of attributes. You will most definitely want to get some data from the query, but not all of the data.

We have previously seen how to specify attributes in each request. The following table describes all available attributes. Please make sure that all attributes specified in a request are correct per casing:

Attribute	Description
Id	Entity ID
Ti	Paper title
Y	Paper year
D	Paper date
CC	Citation count
ECC	Estimated citation count
AA.AuN	Author name
AA.AuId	Author ID
AA.AfN	Author affiliation name
AA.AfId	Author affiliation ID
F.FN	Name of field of study
F.Fid	Field of study ID
J.JN	Journal name
J.JId	Journal ID
C.CN	Conference series name
C.Cid	Conference series ID
Rid	Reference ID
W	Words from the paper title/abstract for full text search
E	Extended metadata

The extended metadata is described in the following table:

Attribute	Description
DN	Display name of the paper
D	Description
S	Sources (web sources of the paper, sorted by static rank)
S.Ty	Source type (HTML/text/PDF/DOC/PPT/XLS/PS)
S.U	Source URL
VFN	Venue full name - full name of journal or conference
VSN	Venue short name - short name of the journal or conference
V	Journal volume
I	Journal issue
FP	First page of paper
LP	Last page of paper
DOI	Digital object identifier

Creating the backend using the Knowledge Exploration Service

The **Knowledge Exploration Service (KES)** is, in some ways, the backend for the academic API. It allows us to build a compressed index from structured data, authoring grammar to interpret natural language.

To get started with the KES, we need to install the service locally.

 To download the KES installer, go to https://www.microsoft.com/en-us/download/details.aspx?id=51488.

With the installation comes some example data, which we will use.

The steps required to have a working service are as follows:

1. Define a schema
2. Generate data
3. Build the index
4. Author the grammar
5. Compile the grammar
6. Host the service

Defining attributes

The schema file defines the attribute structure in our domain. When we previously discussed the academic API, we saw a list of different entity attributes, which we could retrieve through the queries. This is defined in a schema.

If you open the Academic.schema file in the Example folder where the KES is installed, you will see the attributes defined. We have a title, year, and keyword, which are basic attribute types. In addition, we have a Composite attribute for the author. This attribute contains more attributes related to the author.

Each attribute will support all attribute operations. There may be cases where this is not desired. Explicitly defining the operations for a given attribute may reduce the index size. In the case of the author ID, we just want to be able to check whether it is equal to something, which we can achieve by adding the following:

```
{"name":"Author.Id", "type":"Int32", "operations":["equals"]}
```

Adding data

With a schema defined, we can add some data. The example contains a file, called `Academic.data`, which holds all the example data. Open the file to learn what the data can look like.

Each line in the data file specifies the attribute values for an object. It can also contain a `logprob` value, which will indicate the return order of matching objects.

Building the index

With the attribute schema and data file in place, we can build the compressed binary index. This will hold all our data objects.

Using our example files, we can build the index by running the following command:

```
kes.exe build_index Academic.schema Academic.data Academic.index
```

A successful execution should produce the `Academic.index` file, which we will use when we are hosting the service.

When running the command, the application will continuously output the status, which can look like the following:

```
00:00:00 Input Schema: \Programs\KES\Example\Academic.schema
00:00:00 Input Data: \Programs\KES\Example\Academic.data
00:00:00 Output Index: \Programs\KES\Example\Academic.index
00:00:00 Loading synonym file: Keyword.syn
00:00:00 Loaded 3700 synonyms (9.4 ms)
00:00:00 Pass 1 started
00:00:00 Total number of entities: 1000
00:00:00 Sorting entities
00:00:00 Pass 1 finished (14.5 ms)
00:00:00 Pass 2 started
00:00:00 Pass 2 finished (13.3 ms)
00:00:00 Processed attribute Title (20.0 ms)
00:00:00 Processed attribute Year (0.3 ms)
00:00:00 Processed attribute Author.Id (0.5 ms)
00:00:00 Processed attribute Author.Name (10.7 ms)
00:00:00 Processed attribute Author.Affiliation (2.3 ms)
00:00:00 Processed attribute Keyword (20.6 ms)
```

```
00:00:00 Pass 3 started
00:00:00 Pass 3 finished (15.5 ms, 73 page faults)
00:00:00 Post-processing started
00:00:00 Optimized attribute Title (0.1 ms)
00:00:00 Optimized attribute Year (0.0 ms)
00:00:00 Optimized attribute Author.Id (0.0 ms)
00:00:00 Optimized attribute Author.Name (0.5 ms)
00:00:00 Optimized attribute Author.Affiliation (0.2 ms)
00:00:00 Optimized attribute Keyword (0.6 ms)
00:00:00 Global optimization
00:00:00 Post-processing finished (17.2 ms)
00:00:00 Finalizing index
00:00:00 Total time: 157.6 ms
00:00:00 Peak memory usage: 23 MB (commit) + 0 MB (data file) = 23 MB
```

Understanding natural language

After we have built an index, we can start creating our grammar file. This specifies what natural language the service can understand, and how it can translate into semantic query expressions. Open the `academic.xml` file to see an example of how a grammar file can look.

The grammar is based on a **W3C** standard for speech recognition, called **SRGS**. The top-level element is the grammar element. This requires a `root` attribute to specify the root rule, which is the starting point of the grammar.

To allow attribute references, we add the `import` element. This needs to be a child of the `grammar` element, and should come before anything else. It contains two required attributes: the name of the schema file to import, and a name that elements can use for referencing the schema. Note that the schema file must be in the same folder as the grammar file.

Next in line is the `rule` element. This defines a structural unit, which specifies what query expressions the service can interpret. A `rule` element requires an `id` attribute. Optionally, you can add an `example` element, which is used to describe phrases that may be accepted by the `rule` element. In that case, this will be a child element of the rule.

A `rule` element also contains an `item` element. This groups a sequence of grammar constructs, and can be used to indicate repetitions of the sequence. Alternatively, it can be used to specify alternatives, together with one-of elements.

One-of elements specify expansions among one of the item elements. The item by may be defined as a one-of element, with written by and authored *by* as expansions.

Using the `ruleref` element allows us to create more complex expressions by using simpler rules. It simply references other rules by adding a URI attribute.

The `attrref` element references an `index` attribute, which allows us to match against attributes in the index. The attribute URI is required, which must specify the index schema and attribute name to reference. This must match a schema that is imported through the `import` element.

The `tag` element defines the path through the grammar. This element allows you to assign variables or execute functions to help the flow of the grammar.

Once the grammar file is completed, we can compile it into binary grammar. This is done by running the following command:

```
kes.exe build_grammar Academic.xml Academic.grammar
```

Running this command will produce output similar to the following:

```
Input XML: \Programs\KES\Example\Academic.xml
Output Grammar: \Programs\KES\Example\Academic.grammar
```

Local hosting and testing

With the index and grammar in place, we can go on to test the service locally. Locally testing the service allows for rapid prototyping, which allows us to define the scheme and grammar quickly.

When we are testing locally, the KES only supports up to 10,000 objects and 10 requests per second. It also terminates after a total of 1,000 requests have been executed. We will learn how to bypass these restrictions in a bit.

To host the KES locally, run the following command:

```
Kes.exe host_service Academic.grammar Academic.index -port 8080
```

This will start up the service, running on port `8080`. To verify that it is working as intended, open your browser and go to `http://localhost:8080`.

Doing so should present you with the following screen:

Running the KES as a local service also allows us to use the academic API for testing. We are going to make some modifications to our example application—created for the academic API—in order to support this.

First, we are going to modify the `WebRequest.cs` file. We need to make sure that we can change the endpoint, so add the following function to the class:

```
public void SetEndpoint(string uri) {
    _endpoint = uri;
}
```

Next, we need to add a new `TextBox` element to the `MainView.xaml` file. This will allow us to enter a URL. This needs a corresponding string property in the `MainViewModel.cs` file. When changing this property, we need to call `SetEndpoint` on the `_webRequest` object. This can look as follows:

```
private string _endpoint;
public string Endpoint {
    get { return _endpoint; }
    set {
        _endpoint = value;
        RaisePropertyChangedEvent("Endpoint");
        _webRequest?.SetEndpoint(value);
    }
}
```

Finally, we need to update the constructor of our `ViewModel`. Change the first line to the following:

```
Endpoint = "https://api.projectoxford.ai/academic/v1.0/";
_webRequest = new WebRequest(Endpoint, "API_KEY_HERE");
```

This will let the default endpoint be the original API address, but allows us to use the application to test the KES locally.

By testing the application with the local endpoint, the following result can be produced:

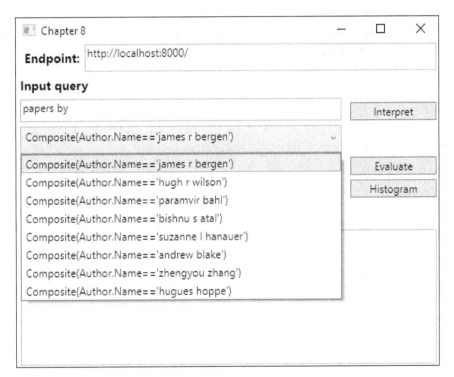

 Note that `evaluate` and `calchistogram` will need to update the attributes in the request of the test application for it to work with the local KES.

Going for scale

While it is nice to be able to create local prototypes, the limitations ensure that we need to deploy the service elsewhere for production. In this case, this means deploying the KES to Microsoft Azure.

We will now look at the steps required to deploy the KES to Microsoft Azure.

Hooking into Microsoft Azure

The first step is to download the **Azure publish settings** file. This needs to be saved as `AzurePublishSettings.xml` and stored in the directory in which `kes.exe` runs.

 You can find the Azure publish settings file at `https://manage.windowsazure.com/publishsettings/`.

There are two ways to build and host the KES without restrictions. The first way is to boot up a **Windows virtual machine** in Azure. On this VM, you should follow the same steps that we took locally. This allows for rapid prototyping, but without any restrictions.

The second way is to run `kes.exe` locally, but adding `--remote` as a parameter. This will create a temporary Azure VM, build the index, and upload the index to a specified target blob storage. An example command could look as follows:

```
kes.exe build_index

http://<account>.blob.core.windows.net/<container>/Academic.schema
http://<account>.blob.core.windows.net/<container>/Academic.full.data
http://<account>.blob.core.windows.net/<container>/Academic.full.index

--remote Large
```

This process can take up to 10 minutes, so ideally, prototyping should be done locally, or through an Azure VM.

Deploying the service

With the grammar and index in place and prototyping done, we can deploy the service to a Microsoft Azure cloud service.

 To learn how to create a Microsoft Azure cloud service, head over to `https://azure.microsoft.com/en-us/documentation/articles/cloud-services-how-to-create-deploy/`.

To deploy the service to a staging slot, run the following command:

```
kes.exe deploy_service
http://<account>.blob.core.windows.net/<container>/Academic.grammar
http://<account>.blob.core.windows.net/<container>/Academic.index
<serviceName> large --slot Staging
```

This will allow us to perform basic tests before deploying the service to a production slot. When the testing is done, we can deploy it to production by running the same command again, specifying `Production` as the last parameter.

When the service is deployed, we can test it by visiting `http://<serviceName>.cloudapp.net in a browser.`

Answering FAQs using QnA Maker

QnA Maker allows us to use existing **frequently asked questions (FAQs)** to create a bot that answers these questions. We can generate a knowledge base from existing FAQs, and train a model from it.

To get started, head over to `https://qnamaker.ai`. Log on or register by clicking Sign in, in the upper-right corner. This will present you with the following screen:

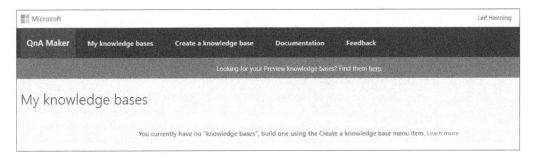

Creating a knowledge base from frequently asked questions

If no services have been created, we can create one by clicking on the Create a knowledge base tab. This will present us with the following screen, as shown in the following two screenshots:

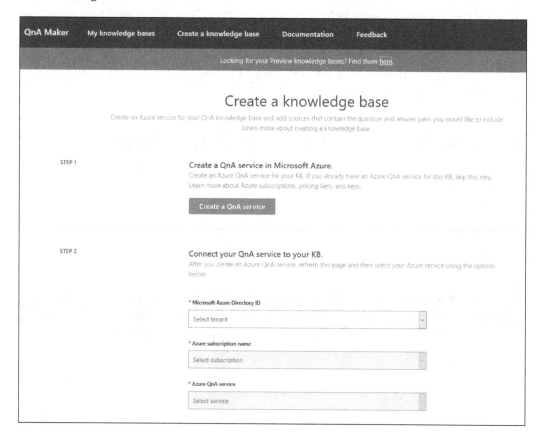

STEP 3

Name your KB.

The knowledge base name is for your reference and you can change it at anytime.

* Name

Name your service

STEP 4

Populate your KB.

Extract question-and-answer pairs from an online FAQ, product manuals, or other files. Supported formats are .tsv, .pdf, .doc, .docx, .xlsx, containing questions and answers in sequence. Learn more about knowledge base sources. Skip this step to add questions and answers manually after creation. The number of sources and file size you can add depends on the QnA service SKU you choose. Learn more about QnA Maker SKUs.

URL

http://

+ Add URL

File name

+ Add file

STEP 5

Create your KB

The tool will look through your documents and create a knowledge base for your service. If you are not using an existing document, the tool will create an empty knowledge base table which you can edit.

Create your KB

1. Create a QnA service in Microsoft Azure by clicking the blue button in **STEP 1** in the screenshot.

2. Connect the QnA service to the knowledge base.

3. Enter a name for the service.

4. Enter the baseline FAQs to use. This can either be in the form of one or more URLs, or a file containing question-and-answer pairs. For our example, we will be generating a knowledge base from the URL.

5. Let the rest of the settings be default.

6. Click **Create your KB**.

If you do not have any FAQs to use, you can use `https://www.microsoft.com/en-us/software-download/faq` from Microsoft.

Once the knowledge base has been created, you will be taken to a page with all the question-and-answer pairs. This is shown in the following screenshot:

On this page, we can look through all question-and-answer pairs, from all our FAQ sources. We can also add new pairs by clicking **Add QnA** pair.

Training the model

Every time we make changes to the knowledge base, it is wise to click **Save** and **Train**. This will ensure that our model is up to date, with the most current question-and-answer pairs.

Once we have trained the model, we can test it. This can be done by clicking the **Test** button on the right-hand side. This will present us with the following chat window:

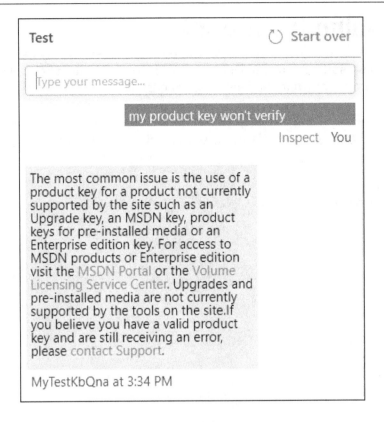

From this chat dialog, we can test some or all of our questions to verify that we get the correct answers. We can also improve the model by asking questions in different ways. In some cases, this will present us with the wrong answer.

If we have been presented with the wrong answer, we can change this by selecting the correct one. With any given question, the possible answers will be listed by clicking the Inspect button beneath the question, ordered by probability. Selecting the correct answer and retraining the model will ensure a correct answer when asking the same question later.

Publishing the model

Once we are done with training, it is time to publish the service. We can do so by clicking Publish in the top menu. Doing so will present us with a basic HTTP request that we can try, as shown in the following screenshot:

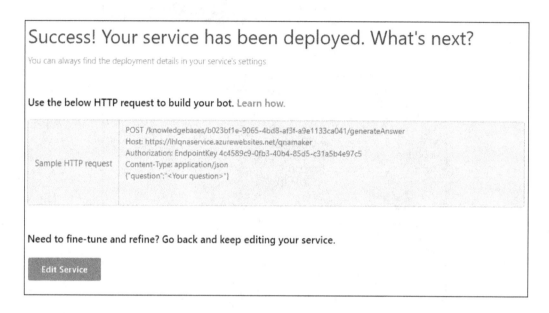

Success! Your service has been deployed. What's next?

You can always find the deployment details in your service's settings

Use the below HTTP request to build your bot. Learn how.

Sample HTTP request	POST /knowledgebases/b023bf1e-9065-4bd8-af3f-a9e1133ca041/generateAnswer Host: https://lhlqnaservice.azurewebsites.net/qnamaker Authorization: EndpointKey 4c4589c9-0fb3-40b4-85d5-c31a5b4e97c5 Content-Type: application/json {"question":"<Your question>"}

Need to fine-tune and refine? Go back and keep editing your service.

Edit Service

In the preceding screenshot, we can see the endpoint to use, the required application ID, the subscription key, and a sample question in the request body. All those parameters are required to get a successful response.

A successful call to the service will provide us with a JSON response as follows:

```
{ "Answer": "Sample response", "Score": "0" }
```

If we have an application that uses this, we can decide not to use the answer if the score has fallen below a certain threshold.

Typically, we would be using bots of different kinds to use this service. We can, for example, add this to a Skype bot or Slackbot, or simply integrate it with a chatbot on a customer support site.

Summary

Throughout this chapter, we have learned about the Project Academic Knowledge API and Project Knowledge Exploration Service. We looked at how to interpret natural language queries to get query expressions for evaluation. Through this evaluation, we have retrieved academic papers from the Microsoft Academic Graph knowledge base. From there, we learned how to set up the Knowledge Exploration Service itself, going from defining the schemas all the way to deploying it to a Microsoft Azure cloud service. In the end, we learned how to set up a simple QnA Maker service.

In the next chapter, we will move on to looking at search APIs, learning how to utilize the different search APIs offered by Bing.

Adding Specialized Searches

9

The previous chapter explored the relationship between academic papers and journals, and we learned how to search for academic papers. This chapter moves on to the last of the top-level APIs, Search. In this chapter, we will learn how to search for web content. We will see how we can search for the latest news with certain keywords or categories. Further on, we will search for images and videos, and learn how to automatically suggest search queries for the end user. By the end of this chapter, we will be introduced to Bing Visual Search and find out how to create customized search experiences by using Bing Custom Search.

In this chapter, we will learn about the following topics:

- How to search for web pages and documents
- How to search for news articles
- How to search for images and videos
- How to add autosuggestions in applications
- How to filter search results based on safe search policies

Searching the web using the smart-house application

The Bing Web Search API provides us with a search experience similar to what we find at `http://bing.com/search`. It returns results that are relevant to any queries.

A response for any request to this API will contain web pages, images, videos, and news articles. In a typical scenario, this is the API you would use for any of these searches.

Note that, in a real-life scenario, all requests should be made from a server-side application, not from a client, as we do in this example.

 If you have not already done so, sign up for the Bing Web Search API at https://portal.azure.com. You can read more on the API at https://azure.microsoft.com/en-us/services/cognitive-services/bing-web-search-api/.

Preparing the application for web searches

Before diving into the required technicalities for web searches, we are going to prepare our smart-house application.

Add a new View in the Views folder called BingSearchView.xaml. At the very least, this should contain two Combobox elements, one for the search type and one for the search filter. We need one TextBox element for our search query, as well as one Button element to execute the search. Finally, we need a TextBox element to display the search result.

To accompany the search types and search filter, we need to add a new file, called BingSearchTypes.cs, in the Model folder. Add the following two enums:

```
public enum BingSearchType {
    Web, News, NewsCategory
}

public enum SafeSearch {
    Strict, Moderate, Off
}
```

Adding this allows us to use both the Bing Web Search and Bing News Search APIs. The latter will be discussed later. The second enum, SafeSearch, will also be discussed in more detail later.

We need a new ViewModel. Add a new file called BingSearchViewModel. cs, to the ViewModels folder. In this, we need to add two string properties for our search query and the search results. We will also need one property of type BingSearchType to represent the selected search type. Also needed is a property of type SafeSearch to represent the selected safe-search filter. An ICommand property is needed for our button.

In addition, we need to be able to display the values from the previously created
`SafeSearch` enums. This can be achieved by adding the following properties:

```
public IEnumerable<BingSearchType> AvailableSearchTypes  {
    get {
        return Enum.GetValues (typeof(BingSearchType)).
Cast<BingSearchType>();
    }
}

public IEnumerable<SafeSearch> SafeSearchFilter {
    get {
        return Enum.GetValues(typeof(SafeSearch)).Cast<SafeSearch>();
    }
}
```

We get all the values from each `enum`, and return them as an `IEnumerable`.

At the time of writing, none of the search APIs have any NuGet client packages, so
we need to make the web requests ourselves. Copy the `WebRequest.cs` file we used
in earlier chapters into the `Model` folder. Rename the file `BingWebRequest.cs` and
the class `BingWebRequest`.

As all API calls are GET requests, we can simplify this class a bit. Remove the URL
parameter from the constructor, and remove the `_endpoint` member completely.
Doing so allows us to simplify the `MakeRequest` function, as follows:

```
public async Task<TResponse> MakeRequest<TResponse>(string url) {
    try {
        var request = new HttpRequestMessage(HttpMethod.Get, url);

        HttpResponseMessage response = await _httpClient.
SendAsync(request);

        if (response.IsSuccessStatusCode) {
            string responseContent = null;

            if (response.Content != null)
                responseContent = await response.Content.
ReadAsStringAsync();

            if (!string.IsNullOrWhiteSpace(responseContent))
                return JsonConvert.DeserializeObject<TResponse>
(responseContent, _settings);

            return default(TResponse);
        }
```

We do not need a request body, and have removed the TRequest and corresponding code. We have also hardcoded the HTTP method, and said that we will specify the complete URL endpoint when calling the function. The rest of the function should stay the same.

 Remember to add references to System.Web and System.Runtime. Serialization.

With that in place, we can move on. Make sure that the code compiles and executes before continuing.

Searching the web

To be able to use Bing Web Search, we need to create a new class. Add a new file called BingSearch.cs, to the Model folder.

We need to add a member of type BingWebRequest, which we will create in the constructor:

```
private BingWebRequest _webRequest;

public BingSearch() {
    _webRequest = new BingWebRequest("API_KEY_HERE");
}
```

Create a new function called SearchWeb. This should accept two parameters, a string for the search query and a SafeSearch parameter. The function should be marked as async and return a Task<WebSearchResponse>. WebSearchResponse is a data contract we will learn more about presently:

```
public async Task<WebSearchResponse> SearchWeb(string query,
SafeSearch safeSearch)
{
    string endpoint = string.Format("{0}{1}&safeSearch={2}
&count=5&mkt=en-US",
        "https://api.cognitive.microsoft.com/bing/v7.0/search?q=", query,
safeSearch.ToString());
```

First, we construct our endpoint, which points us to the web search service. We make sure that we specify the query, q, the safeSearch selection, and the market, mkt. The latter two will be discussed presently in this chapter.

The only required parameter is the query string. This should not exceed a length of 1,500 characters. Other optional parameters are described in the following table:

Parameter	Description
responseFilter	A **comma-delimited** list of the result types to include in the response. If not specified, results will contain all types. Legal values include Computation, Images, News, RelatedSearches, SpellSuggestions, TimeZone, Videos, and WebPages.
setLang	A two-letter language code to specify the language for user interface strings.
textDecorations	Specifies whether or not the query term is highlighted in the results. Defaults to false.
textFormat	The type of formatting to apply to display strings. Can be either raw or HTML, with raw being the default.

There are a few more parameters apart from these ones. They are, however, common to all searches and will be discussed at the end of this chapter.

With the endpoint in place, we can move on:

```
try {
    WebSearchResponse response = await _webRequest.MakeRequest<Web
SearchResponse>(endpoint);

    return response;
}
catch (Exception ex) {
    Debug.WriteLine(ex.Message);
}

return null;
```

With the newly constructed endpoint, we call MakeRequest on the _webRequest object. We specify the API key and endpoint as parameters to this call, and we expect a WebSearchResponse object as a response.

WebSearchResponse is a data contract, which we get by deserializing the JSON response from the API service. The top-level object will contain objects with the different result types. Look in the code samples provided in the file called BingSearchResponse.cs for a complete data contract.

For a complete list of response objects from Bing Web Search, visit https://msdn.microsoft.com/en-us/library/dn760794.aspx#searchresponse.

Heading back to the `BingSearchViewModel.cs` file, we can add `BingSearch` as a member. The constructor should look as follows:

```
public BingSearchViewModel() {
    _bingSearch = new BingSearch();
    SearchCommand = new DelegateCommand(Search, CanSearch);
}
```

The `CanSearch` parameter should return true if we have any text entered into the search query text field. `Search` should, for now, look as follows:

```
private async void Search(object obj) {
    switch (SelectedSearchType) {
        case BingSearchType.Web:
            var webResponse = await _bingSearch.
SearchWeb(SearchQuery, SelectedSafeSearchFilter);
            ParseWebSearchResponse(webResponse as
WebSearchResponse);
            break;
        default:
            break;
    }
}
```

We call the `SearchWeb` function on the `_bingSearch` object, passing on the `SearchQuery` and `SelectedSafeSearchFilter` properties as parameters. With a successful response, we send the response to a new function, `ParseWebSearch`:

```
private void ParseWebSearchResponse(WebSearchResponse
webSearchResponse) {
    StringBuilder sb = new StringBuilder();

    Webpages webPages = webSearchResponse.webPages;

    foreach (WebValue website in webPages.value)
    {
        sb.AppendFormat("{0}\n", website.name);
        sb.AppendFormat("URL: {0}\n", website.displayUrl);
        sb.AppendFormat("About: {0}\n\n", website.snippet);
    }

    SearchResults = sb.ToString();
}
```

When we interpret the results from a web search, we are interested in the resulting `webPages`. For each web page, we want to output the name, the display URL, and a descriptive snippet.

A successful test run with the web search should present us with the following result:

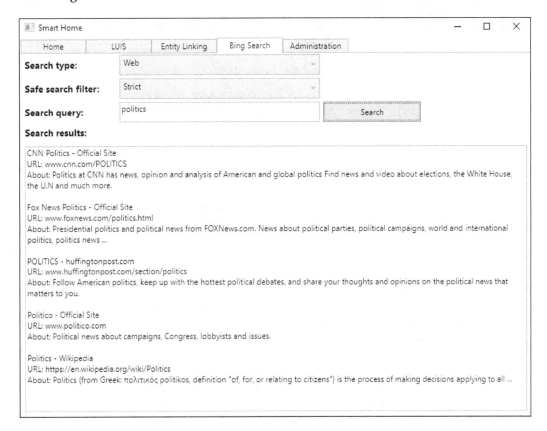

Result objects from a web search contain a `RankingResponse` object. This will identify how the results will typically be displayed on a search website, ordered in a mainline and sidebar. In a production system, you should always aim to display results in the order specified by `RankingResponse`.

This can be done in two ways. One is to use the specified ID field to rank all of the results. The other way is a bit more complex. It involves splitting the results based on answer types and the result index.

Apart from the queries we have seen up to now, we can also query for computations (for instance, 2 + 2), time zone calculations, and related searches. These queries will result in JSON responses, which is a bit different from a regular web search.

Getting the news

Using the Bing News Search API, we can search for news in several ways. There are three endpoints we can use for this API:

- `/news`: Get top news articles, based on category
- `/news/search`: Get news articles based on a search query
- `/news/trendingtopics`: Get top trending news topics

In our smart-house application, we will add the first two, while we will only cover the last one theoretically.

 If you have not already done so, sign up for the Bing News Search API at `https://portal.azure.com`.

News from queries

A lot of the groundwork for query-based news searches has already been done in the web search sample. To search for news based on given queries, we need to add a new function in the `BingSearch` class.

Open the `BingSearch.cs` file and add a new function called `SearchNews`. This should accept a `string` and a `SafeSearch` parameter. The function should be marked as `async`, and return a `Task<BingNewsResponse>` object:

```
public async Task<BingNewsResponse> SearchNews(string query,
SafeSearch safeSearch)
{
    string endpoint = string.Format("{0}
{1}&safeSearch={2}&count=5&mkt=en-US",
    "https://api.cognitive.microsoft.com/bing/v7.0/news/search?q=",
query,
    safeSearch.ToString());
```

We will construct an endpoint consisting of the URL, the search query, and the `safeSearch` parameter. Notice how we specify the market, `mkt`, while limiting the `count` to 5. Both of these parameters will be described presently in this chapter.

The only required parameter is the query string, q. Apart from parameters described for web searches (setLang, textDecorations, and textFormat), we can also specify a parameter called originalImg. This is a Boolean value, which, if set to true, will provide a URL to the original image (for any image in the article). If that is set to false, which is the default, a URL for the thumbnail is provided.

With an endpoint in place, we can call the API:

```
try {
    BingNewsResponse response = await _webRequest.MakeRequest<Bing
NewsResponse>(endpoint);

    return response;
}

catch (Exception ex) {
    Debug.WriteLine(ex.Message);
}

return null;
```

We call MakeRequest, on the _webRequest object, passing on the endpoint as a parameter.

A successful call will result in a JSON response, which we deserialize into a BingNewsResponse object. This object needs to be created as a data contract.

The BingNewsResponse object will contain an array of news articles. Each item in this array will contain the article name, URL, image, description, publishing date, and more.

For full details of each item in the news article array, visit
https://msdn.microsoft.com/en-us/library/dn760793.
aspx#newsarticle.

With that in place, we can head back into the BingSearchViewModel.cs file and modify the Search function. We do so by adding a case for BingSearchType.News inside the switch statement:

```
case BingSearchType.News:
    var newsResponse = await _bingSearch.SearchNews(SearchQuery,
SelectedSafeSearchFilter);
    ParseNewsResponse(newsResponse as BingNewsResponse);
    break;
```

A successful response will be parsed and displayed in the UI:

```
private void ParseNewsResponse(BingNewsResponse bingNewsResponse) {
    StringBuilder sb = new StringBuilder();

    foreach(Value news in bingNewsResponse.value) {
        sb.AppendFormat("{0}\n", news.name);
        sb.AppendFormat("Published: {0}\n", news.datePublished);
        sb.AppendFormat("{0}\n\n", news.description);
    }

    SearchResults = sb.ToString();
}
```

We are mostly interested in the news article name, the date it is published, and a description.

A good test run of this should present us with the following result:

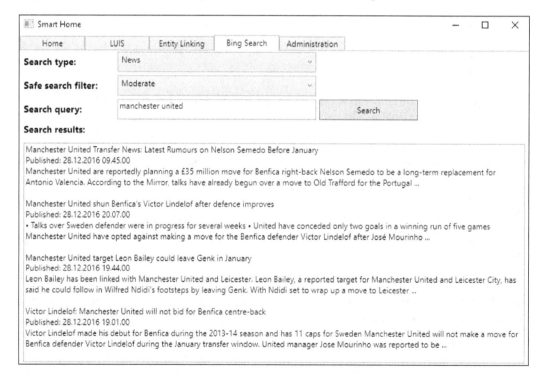

News from categories

When we want to get the top articles for certain categories, we go through a similar procedure as we did for regular news queries. The difference lies in the endpoint we construct.

Let's create a new function, `SearchNewsCategory`, in the `BingSearch` class:

```
public async Task<BingNewsResponse> SearchNewsCategory(string query)
{
    string endpoint = string.Format("{0}{1}&mkt=en-US", "https://api.
cognitive.microsoft.com/bing/v5.0/news?category=", query);
```

Here, we have a category parameter, with the topic we wish to search for. This is an optional parameter. If it is empty, we will get the top news article for all categories.

For this search, we can specify two different markets, `en-GB` and `en-US`. Each of these comes with a list of pre-defined categories that are currently supported:

 For a complete list of supported categories, visit `https://msdn.microsoft.com/en-us/library/dn760793.aspx#categoriesbymarket`.

```
try {
    BingNewsResponse response = await _webRequest.MakeRequest<Bing
NewsResponse>(endpoint);

    return response;
}

catch (Exception ex) {
    Debug.WriteLine(ex.Message);
}

return null;
```

With the newly constructed endpoint, we call `MakeRequest` on the `_webRequest` object. This should result in the same response object as for regular news queries. In our ViewModel, we add a `case` for this search type in the `Search` function. With the response, we utilize the already created `ParseNewsResponse` to get the data we want.

Trending news

The search for trending news is only available for the en-US and zh-CN markets. To execute this search, make a request to the following URL: `https://api.cognitive.microsoft.com/bing/v7.0/news/trendingtopics`.

No parameters are required by this call, but you can add filters, such as the common filters we will discuss later. The only exception is the `freshness` filter, which will not work for this request.

A successful call to this endpoint will result in a `TrendingTopicAnswer` object that will contain an array of trending topics. Each item in this array will contain the following data:

Data field	Description
`image`	A link to a related image
`isBreakingNews`	A Boolean indicating whether this topic is considered breaking news
`name`	The title of the topic
`query`	A query string that will return this topic
`webSearchUrl`	A URL to the Bing search results for this topic
`webSearchUrlPingSuffix`	A query string fragment to identify the `webSearchUrl`

Searching for images and videos

The Bing Image Search API and Bing Video Search API allow us to search directly for images or videos. These APIs should be used only if you need image or video content. There is a possibility that calling these APIs will affect performance and relevance negatively, and as such, one should aim to use the Bing Web Search API.

 If you have not already done so, sign up for the Bing Image Search API and the Bing Video Search API at `https://portal.azure.com`.

Using a common user interface

As we do not need image or video search in our smart-house application, we will go on to create a new project. Create this project using the MVVM template that we created in *Chapter 1, Getting Started with Microsoft Cognitive Services*.

These APIs do not come with any client packages. Like we did previously, we should really make these calls from the server-side application not the client application. In any case, we need to copy the `BingWebRequest.cs` file from the smart-house application to the `Model` folder. Make sure to change the namespace.

 Remember to add references to `System.Web` and `System.Runtime.Serialization`.

We will need to install the `Newtonsoft.Json` NuGet package for our deserialization to work. Do so through the NuGet package manager.

As we will output some of the results as text, we can get away with one common user interface.

Open the `MainView.xaml` file. Add two `TextBox` elements, one for the search query and one for the result. We need a `ComboBox` element to select between search types. Finally, we need to add a `Button` element for our search command.

In the `MainViewModel.xaml` file, we need to add an `enum` with the search types. Add the following at the bottom of the file, beneath the class:

```
public enum SearchType {
    ImageSearch,
    VideoSearch,
}
```

We are only interested in image and video searches with queries. In addition to these search forms, both APIs can search for trending images and videos. The Bing Video Search API also allows us to get more detail on any given video we have already searched for.

In the `MainViewModel` class, we need to add two `string` properties corresponding to our `TextBox` elements. We will also need a property of type `SearchType` to indicate the selected search type. To indicate what search types we have available, we add an `IEnumerable` property, as follows:

```
public IEnumerable<SearchType> SearchTypes {
    get {
        return Enum.GetValues(typeof(SearchType)).Cast<SearchType>();
    }
}
```

The last property we need to add to our ViewModel is the `ICommand` property, which will be bound to our `Button` element.

Now, we need to create a new class, so create a new file called `BingSearch.cs`, in the `Model` folder. This will be responsible for constructing the correct endpoints and executing both search types.

We will need to add a member of type `BingWebRequest`. This should be created in the constructor:

```
private BingWebRequest _webRequest;

public BingSearch() {
    _webRequest = new BingWebRequest("API_KEY_HERE");
}
```

That is all we need to do here for now.

Back in the ViewModel, we need to add a member of type `BingSearch`. With that in place, we can create our constructor:

```
public MainViewModel() {
    _bingSearch = new BingSearch();

    SearchCommand = new DelegateCommand(Search);

    SelectedSearchType = SearchTypes.FirstOrDefault();
}
```

With the ViewModel in place, we can do some searches.

Searching for images

For our example, we will only be executing the image search based on user queries. To allow for this, we will need to add a function in the `BingSearch` class. Call the function `SearchImages` and let it accept a string as a parameter. The function should return `Task<ImageSearchResponse>` and be marked as `async`. `ImageSearchResponse` will, in this case, be a data contract object, with data deserialized from our response:

```
public async Task<ImageSearchResponse> SearchImages(string query)
{
    string endpoint = string.Format("{0}{1}",
    "https://api.cognitive.microsoft.com/bing/v5.0/images/search?q=",
query);
```

We will start by constructing our endpoint. In this case, we only specify the query parameter, `q`. This is a required parameter.

Apart from the common query parameters, which we will see presently, we can also add the following parameters:

Parameter	Description
cab	Bottom coordinate of the region to crop, in a value from 0.0 to 1.0. Measured from the top-left corner.
cal	The left coordinate of the region to crop, in a value from 0.0 to 1.0.
car	The right coordinate of the region to crop, in a value from 0.0 to 1.0.
cat	The top coordinate of the region to crop, in a value from 0.0 to 1.0.
ct	The crop type to use. Currently, the only legal value is 0 - Rectangular.

In addition, we can specify the following parameters as filters:

Filter name	Description
aspect	Filter images by aspect ratio. Legal values are Square, Wide, Tall, and All.
color	Filter images by specific colors.
imageContent	Filter images by image content. Legal values are Face and Portrait.
imageType	Filter images by image types. Legal values are AnimatedGif, Clipart, Line, Photo, and Shopping.
license	Filter images by license that apply to the image. Legal values are Public, Share, ShareCommercially, Modify, ModifyCommercially, and All.
size	Filter images by size. Legal values are Small (< 200 x 200 pixels), Medium (200 x 200 to 500 x 500 pixels), Large (>500 x 500 pixels), Wallpaper, and All.
height	Only get results with a specific height.
width	Only get results with a specific width.

With the endpoint in place, we can execute the request:

```
    try {
        ImageSearchResponse response = await _webRequest.MakeRequest<Im
    ageSearchResponse>(endpoint);

        return response;
    }
    catch (Exception ex) {
        Debug.WriteLine(ex.Message);
    }

    return null;
```

We will call `MakeRequest` on the `_webRequest` object, passing on the endpoint as a parameter. A successful call will result in an `ImageSearchResponse`, which is the deserialized data contract object from the JSON response.

The resulting object will contain a lot of data. Among that data is an array that contains information about images. Each item in that array contains data, such as an image name, date published, URL, and image ID.

 For a complete list of the data available in a response, visit `https://msdn.microsoft.com/en-us/library/dn760791.aspx#images`.

Heading over to `MainViewModel.cs`, we can now create the `Search` function:

```
private async void Search(object obj) {
    SearchResult = string.Empty;

    switch(SelectedSearchType) {
        case SearchType.ImageSearch:
            var imageResponse = await _bingSearch.
SearchImages(SearchQuery);
            ParseImageResponse(imageResponse);
            break;
        default:
            break;
    }
}
```

With a successful response, we parse the `imageResponse`. Normally, this would mean displaying images in a list or similar, but we will take the easier option by outputting textual information:

```
private void ParseImageResponse(ImageSearchResponse imageResponse)
{
    StringBuilder sb = new StringBuilder();
    sb.Append("Image search results:\n\n");
    sb.AppendFormat("# of results: {0}\n\n", imageResponse.
totalEstimatedMatches);

    foreach (Value image in imageResponse.value) {
```

```
        sb.AppendFormat("\tImage name: {0}\n\tImage size: {1}\n\tImage
host: {2}\n\tImage URL:
        {3}\t\n\n", image.name, image.contentSize, image.
hostPageDisplayUrl, image.contentUrl);
    }

    SearchResult = sb.ToString();
}
```

We will print out the number of matches in the search. Then, we will loop through the image array, printing the name, size, host, and URL of each image.

A successful test run should present us with the following screen:

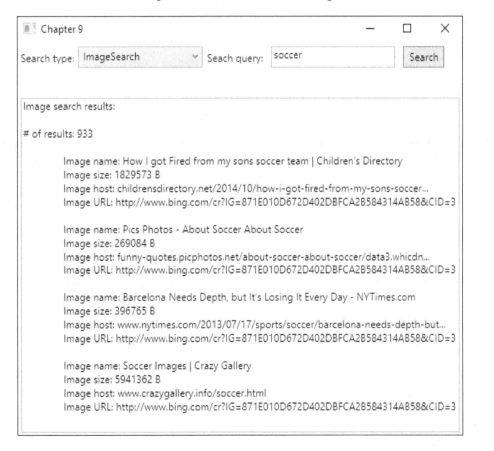

In addition to the query-based image search, we can also search for trending images. To do so, you will have to call the following endpoint: `https://api.cognitive.` `microsoft.com/bing/v7.0/images/trending`.

Currently, this is only available for the following markets: `en-US`, `en-CA`, and `en-AU`. A successful call to this endpoint will result in an array of categories. Each item in this array will contain an array of trending images, as well as the title of the category.

Searching for videos

Searching for videos is nearly the same process as for images. The only real difference is how we construct the endpoint and the response we get.

We are going to add a new function in the `BingSearch` class to accompany a video search:

```
public async Task<VideoSearchResponse> SearchVideos(string query)
{
    string endpoint = string.Format("{0}{1}", "https://api.cognitive.
microsoft.com/bing/v7.0/videos/search?q=", query);
```

As you can see, there is only one required parameter: the query string, `q`. We can also specify a few optional parameters that are common to all the search APIs, which will be described later.

Aside from common filters, video can also filter results based on the following filters:

Filter	Description
`pricing`	Filter videos by price. Legal values are Free, Paid, and All.
`resolution`	Filter by resolution. Legal values are 480p, 720p, 1080p, and All.
`videoLength`	Filter videos by length. Legal values is `Short` (< 5 minutes), `Medium` (5 to 20 minutes), `Long` (> 20 minutes), and `All`.

With the endpoint in place, we call the API:

```
try {
    VideoSearchResponse response = await _webRequest.MakeRequest<VideoS
earchResponse>(endpoint);

    return response;
}

catch (Exception ex) {
```

```
        Debug.WriteLine(ex.Message);
    }


    return null;
```

We will call `MakeRequest` on the `_webRequest` object, passing on the endpoint as a parameter. A successful call will result in a `VideoSearchResponse` object. This is a data contract, deserialized from the JSON response.

Among other data, it will contain an array of videos. Each item in this array contains a video name, description, publisher, duration, URL, and more.

 For a complete list of data available in the search response, visit `https://msdn.microsoft.com/en-US/library/dn760795.` `aspx#videos`.

To be able to search for videos, we add a new case in the `Search` function, in `MainViewModel`:

```
case SearchType.VideoSearch:
    var videoResponse = await _bingSearch.SearchVideos(SearchQuery);
    ParseVideoResponse(videoResponse);
    break;
```

We call the newly created `SearchVideos`, passing on the search query as a parameter. If the call succeeds, we go on to parse the video:

```
private void ParseVideoResponse(VideoSearchResponse videoResponse)
{
    StringBuilder sb = new StringBuilder();
    sb.Append("Video search results:\n\n");
    sb.AppendFormat("# of results: {0}\n\n",
    videoResponse.totalEstimatedMatches);

    foreach (VideoValue video in videoResponse.value) {
        sb.AppendFormat("\tVideo name: {0}\n\tVideo duration: {1}\n\
tVideo URL: {2}\t\n",
        video.name, video.duration, video.contentUrl);

        foreach(Publisher publisher in video.publisher) {
            sb.AppendFormat("\tPublisher: {0}\n", publisher.name);
        }
```

```
        sb.Append("\n");
    }
    SearchResult = sb.ToString();
}
```

As for images, we just show video information textually. In our example, we choose to show the video name, duration, URL, and all publishers of a video.

A successful video search should give the following result:

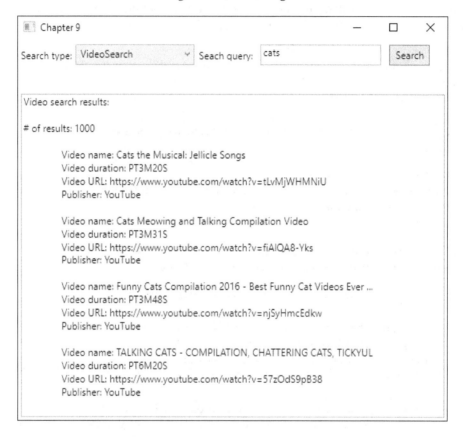

In addition to the query-based video search, we can also search for trending videos. To do so, you would have to call the following endpoint: `https://api.cognitive.microsoft.com/bing/v7.0/videos/trending`.

Currently, this is only available for the following markets: `en-US`, `en-CA`, and `en-AU`. A successful call to this endpoint will result in an array of categories and tiles. Each item in the category array will contain a title and an array of subcategories. Each subcategory will contain an array of tiles and the title. Each item in a tile array will contain the video thumbnail and a query to use to get the specific video.

If we want to get more information about any video, we can query the following endpoint: `https://api.cognitive.microsoft.com/bing/v7.0/videos/details`.

This requires us to specify an `id` so that we can identify a video. We can also specify the `modulesRequested`. This is a comma-separated list of the details we want. Currently, the legal values are `All`, `RelatedVideos`, and `VideoResult`.

> For a complete list of data available in the response from a details query, visit `https://msdn.microsoft.com/en-US/library/dn760795.aspx#video`.

Helping the user with autosuggestions

Autosuggestions are a great way to enhance user experience. The typical use case is where, whenever a user enters some text into a text field, a list of suggested words is displayed.

> If you have not already done so, sign up for the Bing Autosuggest API at `https://portal.azure.com`.

Adding autosuggest to the user interface

As textboxes in WPF do not contain any autosuggestion features, we need to add some on our own. We are going to use a third-party package, so install the `WPFTextBoxAutoComplete` package through the NuGet package manager, in our example project.

In the `MainView.xaml` file, add the following attribute to the starting `Window` tag:

```
xmlns:behaviors="clr-namespace: WPFTextBoxAutoComplete;assembly=WPFTextBoxAutoComplete"
```

We will also need to make sure that the `TextBox` binding for our search query updates whenever the user enters data. This can be done by making sure that the `Text` attribute looks as follows:

```
Text="{Binding SearchQuery, UpdateSourceTrigger=PropertyChanged}"
```

In the same `TextBox` element, add the following:

```
behaviors:AutoCompleteBehavior.AutoCompleteItemsSource = "{Binding Suggestions}"
```

In the ViewModel, in the `MainViewModel.cs` file, we need the corresponding property. This should be an `IEnumerable<string>` object. This will be updated with the result from the autosuggest query we will perform presently.

Suggesting queries

To get autosuggestions, we first add a new class. Add a new file called `BingAutoSuggest.cs`, to the `Model` folder. The `BingAutoSuggest` class should have a member of type `BingWebRequest`, which should be created in the constructor.

Create a new function called `Suggest`. This should accept a `string` as a parameter, returning a `Task<List<string>>` object. Mark the function as `async`.

We will start by constructing an endpoint, where we specify the query string, `q`. This field is required. We also specify the market, `mkt`, although this is not required. We do not need any other parameters. Before we execute the API call, we will create a list of suggestions, which we will return to the caller:

```
public async Task<List<string>> Suggest(string query) {
    string endpoint = string.Format("{0}{1}&mkt=en-US", "https://api.
cognitive.microsoft.com/bing/v7.0/suggestions/?q=", query);

    List<string> suggestionResult = new List<string>();
```

We will make a call to `MakeRequest` on the `_webRequest` object, passing on the endpoint as a parameter. If the call succeeds, we expect the JSON response to deserialize into a `BingAutoSuggestResponse` object. This object will contain an array of `suggestionGroups`, where each item contains an array of `SearchSuggestions`.

Each item of `SearchSuggestion` contains a URL, display text, a query string, and a search kind. We are interested in the display text, which we add to the `suggestionResult` list. This list is returned to the caller:

```
try {
    BingAutoSuggestResponse response = await _webRequest.MakeRequest<B
ingAutoSuggestResponse>(endpoint);

    if (response == null || response.suggestionGroups.Length == 0)
        return suggestionResult;

    foreach(Suggestiongroup suggestionGroup in response.
suggestionGroups) {

        foreach(Searchsuggestion suggestion in suggestionGroup.
searchSuggestions) {
```

```
                    suggestionResult.Add(suggestion.displayText);
                }
            }
        }

    catch(Exception ex) {
        Debug.WriteLine(ex.Message);
    }

    return suggestionResult;
```

 For a complete description of response data, go to https://msdn.
microsoft.com/en-us/library/mt711395.aspx#suggestions.

In the MainViewModel.cs file, we want to get suggestions as we type. We will create a new function, as follows:

```
private async void GetAutosuggestions() {

    var results = await _autoSuggest.Suggest(SearchQuery);

    if (results == null || results.Count == 0) return;

    Suggestions = results;
}
```

This will call the newly created Suggest function, with the current value of the SearchQuery. If any results are returned, we assign them to the SuggestionsIEnumerable that we created earlier. Make sure to call this function when we set the value in the SearchQuery property.

In the UI, this will have the first suggestion automatically populated in the search-query field. This is not ideal for users, but it will do for our test example.

Search commonalities

For all the APIs we have covered, there are a few similarities. We will cover these now.

Languages

It is highly recommended to specify which market you want results for. Searches will typically return results for the local market and language of the user, based on the current location. As you can imagine, this is not always what the user wants. By specifying the market, you can tailor the search results for the user.

How you choose to solve this technically is dependent on the requirements of your application. For a smart-house application, you would probably allow the user to set the market in the settings. For a web application created only for French users in France, you would probably not allow the user to change the market.

Specifying the market is done by adding the `mkt` parameter to the `GET` request. This should then specify the market code, for example, `en-US` for English in the United States.

 While any API may support a specific market, some features may not support a given market.

A subset of the languages supported is English, Spanish, German, Dutch, French, Portuguese, Traditional Chinese, Italian, Russian, and Arabic.

In addition, we can specify a `cc` parameter to the `GET` request. This specifies a country (typically, the country the user is in). This parameter should be in the form of a two-letter country code, for instance, GB for United Kingdom.

A wide variety of countries can be specified, and the list is continuously subject to change.

Pagination

Some searches may yield a large number of results. In these cases, you may want to perform pagination. This can be achieved by specifying the `count` and `offset` parameters in the GET request.

If you want 10 results per page, you would start by setting the count to 10, and the offset to 0 for the first page. When the user navigates to the next page, you would keep the `count` at 10, but increase the `offset` to 10. For the next page, you would increase the `offset` to 20, and so on.

The maximum number of results returned in each query (the count parameter) varies for each API. See the following table for the current maximum count per API:

API	Maximum search results	Default search results
Bing News Search	100	10
Bing Web Search	50	10
Bing Image Search	150	35
Bing Video Search	105	35

Filters

We have seen some filters for individual APIs. In addition to these, there are a couple of filters which can be applied to all searches.

Safe search

The safe search filter can be used to filter search results for adult content. This parameter is added in the request URL.

The `safeSearch` parameter can be one of the following values:

- **Off**: All result items will be returned
- **Moderate**: Result items can contain adult text, but no adult images or videos will be included
- **Strict**: No adult text, images, or videos are included in the result items

Note that, if the IP address of the user indicates a location that requires the Strict safe search, this setting will be ignored. Bing will, in this case, default to the Strict policy.

If the parameter has not been set, it defaults to moderate.

Freshness

By adding the `freshness` parameter to a request, you can filter search results based on the age of result items. The values that can be specified are as follows:

- **Day**: Results from the last 24 hours
- **Week**: Results from the last 7 days
- **Month**: Results from the last 30 days

Errors

Among all the APIs we have covered, there are a few possible response codes that you may receive for each request. The following table describes all of the possible response codes:

Code	Description
200	Successful request.
400	One or more required query parameters are missing, or one of the parameters is invalid. More details are described in the `ErrorResponse` field.
401	The provided subscription key is invalid or missing.
403	Typically returned if the monthly quota is exceeded. Can also be used if the caller does not have permission to access the requested resource.
410	The HTTP protocol has been used instead of HTTPS, which is the only supported protocol.
429	The quota per second has been exceeded.

Searching for visual content using Bing Visual Search

Using the **Bing Visual Search** API, one can interpret images. This API allows us to gain insights about images. This includes finding visually similar images, searches, and shopping sources. It can also identify people, places, and objects, as well as text.

Sending a request

You will typically upload an image to the API to retrieve insights on it. In addition, you can pass on an URL to an image.

 The endpoint you should use to query the Bing Visual Search API is `https://api.cognitive.microsoft.com/bing/v7.0/images/visualsearch`.

In either scenario, the following query parameters can be added:

- **cc**: The two-letter language code of the country where the results should come from.
- **mkt**: The market where the results come from. This should always be specified.
- **safeSearch**: The filter used to filter adult content. Can be *Off*, *Moderate*, or *Strict*.
- **setLang**: The language to use for user interface strings, that is, a two-letter language code.

In addition, two content headers must be specified. These are `Content-Type` and `Ocp-Apim-Subscription-Key`. The first one must be set to `multipart/form-data;boundary={BOUNDARY}`. The latter must specify the API key.

 For more information on content headers, please visit `https://docs.microsoft.com/en-us/azure/cognitive-services/bing-visual-search/overview#content-form-types`.

Receiving a response

Once the request has gone through, a JSON object will be returned as a response.

This object will contain two objects: an array of `tags` and an `image` string. The image string is simply the insights token for the image. The list of `tags` contains a `tag` name and a list of `actions` (insights). A tag, in this context, means category. For instance, if an actor is recognized in the image, the tag for this might be *Actor*.

Each action, or insight, describes something of the image. It might describe text in the image or different products discovered in the image. Each action includes a whole variety of data.

 To see a full list of default insights, please visit `https://docs.microsoft.com/en-us/azure/cognitive-services/bing-visual-search/default-insights-tag`.

Adding a custom search

Bing Custom Search gives you the opportunity to add a powerful, tailored search experience to your own applications. It allows you to search specifically for topics you care about.

By using the portal at `https://www.customsearch.ai/`, you can create a custom view of the web.

Typical workflow

If you want to build a custom search web page, the following steps describe the typical workflow.

1. **Create a custom search instance**: This can be done at the portal linked in the previous section.
2. **Add active entries**: This is a list of sites that should be included in the search results.
3. **Add blocked entries**: This is a list of sites that should be excluded from the search results.
4. **Add pinned entries**: If any search term should have websites pinned to the top of the search result, it should be specified in the pinned entries section.
5. **Configure hosted UI**: Set the layout, color theme, and other options for the hosted UI.
6. **Publish the search instance**: Publish the custom search instance.

Consuming the search instance

There are three ways to consume the custom search instance.

The first, and easiest option, is to integrate a JavaScript snippet. Once you have published the search instance, you will be provided with a pre-configured JavaScript snippet, rendering the hosted UI. This can be pasted into your existing web page. This will render the search form on your website.

Another option is to link to the custom HTML site directly. This is the link used in a JavaScript snippet, but it is only used directly.

The last option is to use the REST API directly from your own code. We will not go into deeper details on this in this book.

Summary

In this chapter, we have looked at the different Bing Search APIs. We started by looking at how we can use the Bing Web Search API to search for all kinds of content. Next, we found the latest news, based on query strings and categories. From there, we moved on to image and video searches. In addition, we looked at how to enhance the user experience by adding autosuggestions. We did this by using the Bing Autosuggestion API. Finally, we briefly introduced you to Bing Visual Search and Bing Custom Search.

In the next and final chapter, we will wrap things up. We will complete our smart-house application by connecting the pieces. We will also take a look at the road ahead.

10

Connecting the Pieces

The previous chapter focused on the last API umbrella, covering Bing Search APIs. Throughout this chapter, we will connect the pieces. Our smart-house application can currently utilize several APIs, but mostly individually. We will see how to connect LUIS, image analysis, Bing News Search, and Bing Speech APIs. We will also look at the next steps that you can take after completing this book.

In this chapter, we will learn about the following topics:

- Making an application smarter, by connecting several APIs
- Real-life applications utilizing Microsoft Cognitive Services
- Next steps

Completing our smart-house application

Until now, we have seen all the different APIs, mostly as individual APIs. The whole idea behind the smart-house application is to utilize several APIs at the same time.

Throughout this chapter, we will add a new intent in LUIS. This intent is for getting the latest news for different topics.

Next, we want to actually search for news, using the Bing News API. We will do so by allowing the end user to speak a command, converting spoken audio to text, with the Bing Speech API.

When we find a news article, we want to get the headline, publishing date, and description. If there is a corresponding image to the article, we want to get a description of the image. We will do this by adding the Computer Vision API.

With all the news article information in place, we want to get that read back to us. We will do this by converting text to spoken audio.

Creating an intent

Let us start by adding our new intent. Head over to `https://www.luis.ai`, and log on with the credentials created in *Chapter 4, Letting Applications Understand Commands*. From the front page, go into your smart-house application.

Before we start creating the intent, we need to add a new entity. As we want the possibility to get updates on news within certain topics, we will add a `NewsCategory` entity, as shown in the following screenshot:

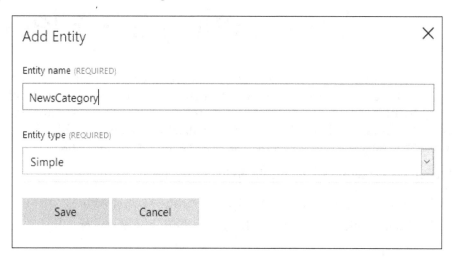

As this entity will work on its own, we do not need any children.

Now we can add a new intent. Go to **Intents** on the left-hand side and click **Add intent**. This will open the intent creation dialog. Enter a fitting name for the intent, such as `GetNews`:

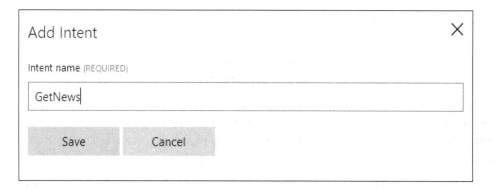

We also need to add an example command:

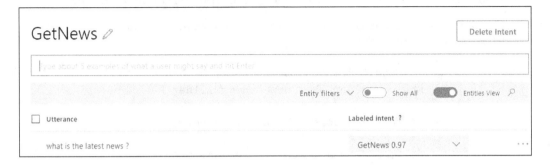

Add five or six more examples of how you would utter this intent. Make sure you train the model before continuing.

You can verify the model for testing by going to **Test** in the right-hand side.

Updating the code

With the new intent, we can start to update the smart-house application.

Executing actions from intents

The first step we need to do is to add an `enum` variable containing the intents. Create a new file called `LuisActions.cs`, in the `Model` folder, and add the following content to it:

```
public enum LuisActions {
    None, GetRoomTemperature, SetRoomTemperature, GetNews
}
```

If you have any other intents defined, add them as well.

This `enum` will be used later, to see which action to execute when triggered. For instance, if we ask to get the latest sports news, `GetNews` will be triggered, which will go on to retrieve news.

To make things a bit easier for ourselves, we are going to use the existing LUIS example for the rest of the chapter. An alternative would be to add this to the `HomeView`, where we could continuously listen to spoken commands from the users.

In order to trigger an action, we need to open the `LuisViewModel.cs` file. Find the `OnLuisUtteranceResultUpdated` function. Let us update it to the following:

```
private void OnLuisUtteranceResultUpdated(object sender,
LuisUtteranceResultEventArgs e)
    {
        Application.Current.Dispatcher.Invoke(async () => {
            StringBuilder sb = new StringBuilder(ResultText);

            _requiresResponse = e.RequiresReply;

            sb.AppendFormat("Status: {0}\n", e.Status);
            sb.AppendFormat("Summary: {0}\n\n", e.Message);
```

At this time, we have not added anything new. We have removed the output of entities, as we do not need this anymore.

If we find that any actions have been triggered, we want to do something. We call a new function, `TriggerActionExecution`, passing on the name of the intent as a parameter:

```
if (!string.IsNullOrEmpty(e.IntentName))
    await TriggerActionExectution(e.IntentName, e.EntityName);
```

We will get back to this function shortly.

Complete `OnLuisUtteranceResultUpdated` by adding the following code:

```
            ResultText = sb.ToString();
        });
    }
```

Again, you should see that there are no new features. We have, however, removed the last `else` clause. We do not want to have the application speak the summary to us anymore.

Create the new `TriggerActionExecution` function. Let it accept a `string` as the parameter, and have it return a `Task`. Mark the function as `async`:

```
private async Task TriggerActionExectution(string intentName) {
    LuisActions action;
    if (!Enum.TryParse(intentName, true, out action))
        return;
```

Here, we parse the `actionName` (intent name). If we have not defined the action, we will not do anything else.

With an action defined, we go into a `switch` statement to decide what to do. As we are only interested in the `GetNews` case, we break out from the other options:

```
switch(action) {
    case LuisActions.GetRoomTemperature:
    case LuisActions.SetRoomTemperature:
    case LuisActions.None:
    default:
        break;
    case LuisActions.GetNews:
  break;
}
}
```

Make sure that the code compiles before continuing.

Searching news on command

Next, we will need to modify the `Luis.cs` file. As we have defined an entity for the news topic, we want to ensure that we get this value from the LUIS response.

Add a new property to `LuisUtteranceResultEventArgs`:

```
public string EntityName { get; set; }
```

This will allow us to add the news topic value, if received.

We need to add this value. Locate `ProcessResult` in the `Luis` class. Modify the `if` check to look like the following:

```
if (!string.IsNullOrEmpty(result.TopScoringIntent.Name)) {
    var intentName = result.TopScoringIntent.Name;
    args.IntentName = intentName;
}

else {
    args.IntentName = string.Empty;
}

if(result.Entities.Count > 0) {
var entity = result.Entities.First().Value;

if(entity.Count > 0)  {
    var entityName = entity.First().Value;
    args.EntityName = entityName;
}
}
```

We make sure that the intent name, of the top-scoring intent, is set, and pass it on as an argument to the event. We also check if there is any entities set, and if so, pass on the first one. In a real-life application, you would probably check other entities as well.

Back into the `LuisViewModel.cs` file, we can now account for this new property. Let the `TriggerActionExecution` method accept a second `string` parameter. When calling the function, we can add the following parameter:

```
await TriggerActionExectution(e.IntentName, e.EntityName);
```

To be able to search for news, we need to add a new member of the `BingSearch` type. This is the class we created in the previous chapter:

```
private BingSearch _bingSearch;
```

Create the object in the constructor.

Now we can create a new function, called `GetLatestNews`. This should accept a `string` as the parameter, and return `Task`. Mark the function as `async`:

```
private async Task GetLatestNews(string queryString)
{
    BingNewsResponse news = await _bingSearch.SearchNews (queryString,
SafeSearch.Moderate);

    if (news.value == null || news.value.Length == 0)
        return;
```

When this function is called, we `SearchNews` on the newly created `_bingSearch` object. We pass on the `queryString`, which will be the action parameter, as the parameter. We also set the safe search to `Moderate`.

A successful API call will result in a `BingNewsResponse` object, which will contain an array of news articles. We are not going into more details on this class, as we covered it in *Chapter 9, Adding Specialized Searches*.

If no news is found, we simply return from the function. If we do find news, we do the following:

```
await ParseNews(news.value[0]);
```

We call a function, `ParseNews`, which we will get back to in a bit. We pass on the first news article, which will be parsed. Ideally, we would go through all the results, but for our case, this is enough to illustrate the point.

The `ParseNews` method should be marked as `async`. It should have the return type `Task`, and accept a parameter of type `Value`:

```
private async Task ParseNews(Value newsArticle)  {
    string articleDescription = $"{newsArticle.name}, published
{newsArticle.datePublished}. Description:
    {newsArticle.description}. ";

    await _ttsClient.SpeakAsync(articleDescription, CancellationToken.
None);
}
```

We create a string containing the headline, the publishing date, and the news description. Using this, we call `SpeakAsync` on the `_ttsClient` to have the application read the information back to us.

With this function in place, we can execute the action. In `TriggerActionExecuted`, call `GetLatestNews` from the `GetNews` case. Make sure to await the call.

With the application compiling, we can go for a test run:

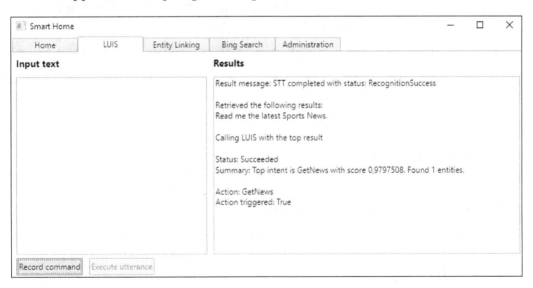

Naturally, the effects are not as good in an image as in real life. With a microphone and speakers or headset connected, we can ask for the latest news, using audio, and get the news read back to us with audio.

Describing news images

News articles often come with corresponding images as well. As an addition to what we already have, we can add image analysis.

The first step we need to do is to add a new NuGet package. Search for the `Microsoft.ProjectOxford.Vision` package, and install this using **NuGet Package Manager**.

In the `LuisViewModel.cs` file, add the following new member:

```
private IVisionServiceClient _visionClient;
```

This can be created in the constructor:

```
_visionClient = new VisionServiceClient("FACE_API_KEY", "ROOT_URI");
```

This member will be our access point to the Computer Vision API.

We want to get a string describing the image in the `ParseNews` function. We can achieve this by adding a new function, called `GetImageDescription`. This should accept a `string` parameter, which will be the image URL. The function should have return type `Task<string>` and be marked as `async`:

```
private async Task<string> GetImageDescription(string contentUrl)
{
    try {
        AnalysisResult imageAnalysisResult = await _visionClient.
AnalyzeImageAsync(contentUrl, new List<VisualFeature>() {
VisualFeature.Description });
```

In this function, we call `AnalyzeImageAsync` on the `_visionClient`. We want the image description, so we specify this in a list of `VisualFeature`. If the call succeeds, we expect an object of type `AnalysisResult`. This should contain image descriptions, ordered by probability of correctness.

If we do not get any descriptions, we return `none`. If we do have any descriptions, we return the text of the first one:

```
    if (imageAnalysisResult == null || imageAnalysisResult.
Description?.Captions?.Length == 0)
        return "none";
    return imageAnalysisResult.Description.Captions.First().Text;
}
```

If any exceptions occur, we print the exception message to the debug console. We also return none to the caller:

```
catch(Exception ex) {
    Debug.WriteLine(ex.Message);
    return "none";
}
}
```

In ParseNews, we can get the image description by adding the following at the top of the function:

```
string imageDescription = await GetImageDescription (newsArticle.
image.thumbnail.contentUrl);
```

With an image description, we can modify the articleDescription string to the following:

```
string articleDescription = $"{newsArticle.name}, published
        {newsArticle.datePublished}. Description:
        {newsArticle.description}. Corresponding image is

        {imageDescription}";
```

Running the application and asking for news will now also describe any images. That concludes our smart-house application.

Real-life applications using Microsoft Cognitive Services

There are some examples of applications that currently utilize Microsoft Cognitive Services. We will look at some of them here.

Uber

Uber is an app that was created to match drivers with people looking for rides. People can open the app, and request a ride. Drivers (registered Uber drivers, that is) located nearby can then pick up the person requesting a ride. After a ride, the driver is paid through the app.

To ensure a more secure experience, a photo of the driver is sent to the passenger. This way, passengers can feel safe that the driver is who they say they are. This may cause problems, as drivers may not always look like their photo. They may have grown a beard, or shaved off a beard, or similar changes may have occurred.

To account for this, Uber decided to add a new feature. Each driver needs to sign in when they are using the app. Doing so will periodically request them to take a selfie. This image is then sent to the Face API for verification. If the verification fails, due to glare from glasses, or something similar, the driver is requested to remove such items.

According to Uber, they spent around 3 weeks implementing the Face API into their systems.

DutchCrafters

DutchCrafters is an American company that sells handmade furniture. They do have a physical store, but more importantly, they have an e-commerce website. This site contains more than 10,000 products, where each product can be customized.

They had a low conversion rate on their site, and as an attempt to improve this, they used manual recommendations. Manually adding recommended products on each product is rather time-consuming. Looking into their options, they discovered the Recommendations API from Microsoft Cognitive Services.

They were already relying on REST APIs, and as such implementing the Recommendations API was quick. `DutchCrafters` have stated that they spent 5 days in total implementing the functionality needed.

As their site was already built with ASP.NET and running on IIS, they decided to move everything to the cloud. Doing so has improved their site, and with the addition of the Recommendations API, their foundation has improved.

At the time of writing, they are utilizing the *You might like this* feature, recommending 10 items per product. They are also looking into adding real-time recommendations, based on users' history, which we have seen is possible using the Recommendations API.

A direct result of implementing the Recommendations API is an improvement of the conversion rate. They have seen a three times increase in the conversion rate, with about 15% of the sales coming from recommended products.

CelebsLike.me

CelebsLike.me is a web application from Microsoft. It was primarily created to show off some of the features of Microsoft Cognitive Services.

The purpose of the application is to find your celebrity doppelganger. You can upload a photo, or use one found online, and the app will match faces found with similar celebrities.

The app takes advantage of the Bing Image Search API, the Computer Vision API, and the Face API. It recognizes celebrity faces in web images. When someone uploads a photo of themselves, facial features will be used to find matching celebrities.

Pivothead

Pivothead is a company working with wearable technology. They have combined eyeglasses with high-quality cameras, providing still images and videos. These glasses allow people to capture vivid point-of-view content of what they see. Pivothead currently has customers in the consumer market, but also in the business market.

Over time, Pivothead had seen growing success, but could not seem to create a device to help visually impaired and/or blind people. They struggled with the technology, as machine learning itself can be quite complex. When they learned of Microsoft Cognitive Services, they were able to reach a breakthrough.

If a person is wearing the glasses, they can slide a finger along an earpiece. This will capture an image of what is in front of the person. The glasses utilize five APIs from Microsoft Cognitive Services. These are Computer Vision, Emotion, Face, Speech, and LUIS.

With the image of whatever is in front of a person, the image is analyzed. The person wearing the glasses will then get the image described through an earpiece. If a person is detected, the gender, how they look, what they are doing, their age, and their emotion is detected and described. If text is detected, it will be read back to the person.

According to Pivothead, they spent around three months months developing prototypes of these glasses. They also stated that they could have done it in three weeks, had they been working with it full-time.

Zero Keyboard

The **Zero Keyboard** app was created by a Finnish company called **Blucup**. The company had discovered a common problem for salespeople. They wanted a way for salespeople to capture customer data and generate leads while on the go.

They started developing an app for iOS, Android, and Windows Phone to help solve this problem. The idea behind the app is to record customer information, which is then automatically stored in the **Customer Relationship Management** (**CRM**) system.

At the time of development, Microsoft Cognitive Services emerged, and Blucup decided to give it a go. Earlier, they had tried a few types of open source speech recognition software and image analysis software. None provided the quality and features needed.

Using the Computer Vision API, the app can take pictures of business cards or identification badges, and identify text. This data is directly uploaded to their CRM system. By using the Speech API, sales representatives can also record voice memos for each contact.

Blucup states that Microsoft Cognitive Services delivers very accurate data. In addition, they have been able to implement the needed APIs rapidly, as the APIs are a good match from a developer standpoint.

The common theme

As you can see from all these examples, Microsoft Cognitive Services provides good quality. It is also quick to implement, which is important when considering new APIs.

Another great thing about the APIs is that you do not need to be a data scientist to use them. Even though the technology powering the APIs is complex, we, as developers, do not need to think about it. We can focus on what we do best.

Where to go from here

By now, you should know the basics of Microsoft Cognitive Services, enough to get started with building your own applications.

A natural way forward is to play around with the different APIs. The APIs are continuously improved and worked upon. It is worth going through the API documentation, to keep up with changes and to learn more. In addition, Microsoft keeps adding new APIs to the services. Through the writing process of this book, I have seen three new APIs added. Those might be interesting to look into.

Another possibility is to build upon the smart-house application that we have started on. We have put down some groundwork, but there are still a lot of opportunities. Perhaps you can work on improving what we have already got. Maybe you can see some opportunities to mix in other APIs, which we have covered.

Reading through this book might have given you some ideas of your own. A great way forward would be to implement them.

As we have seen, there are many possible areas to use the APIs for. Only the imagination limits the usage.

Perhaps this book has triggered a deeper interest in machine learning. Everything we have seen so far is machine learning. Even though it is more complex than just using APIs, it is certainly worth exploring further.

Summary

With this chapter, we have completed our journey. We created a new intent for news retrieval. We learned how to deal with an action, triggered from this intent. Based on voice commands, we managed to fetch the latest news, for one topic, and have the smart-house application read it back to us. Next, we went on to see what kind of real-life applications are utilizing Microsoft Cognitive Services today. Finally, we concluded this chapter by looking at some natural next steps that you can take after completing this book.

LUIS Entities

In this appendix, we will list the prebuilt entities in LUIS.

LUIS prebuilt entities

The following list shows all the available entities that can be added to your application:

- DatetimeV2
- Datetime
- Number
- Ordinal
- Percentage
- Temperature
- Dimension
- Money
- Age
- Geography
- Encyclopedia
- URL
- Email
- Phone Number

A complete and updated list of prebuilt entities can be found at https://docs.microsoft.com/en-us/azure/cognitive-services/LUIS/pre-builtentities.

B
License Information

This appendix contains several third-party libraries, which have different licenses. All libraries, along with the applicable licenses, are covered in the next few pages.

Video Frame Analyzer

Copyright (c) Microsoft. All rights reserved.

Licensed under the MIT license.

Microsoft Cognitive Services: `http://www.microsoft.com/cognitive`

Microsoft Cognitive Services GitHub: `https://github.com/Microsoft/Cognitive`

Copyright (c) Microsoft Corporation

All rights reserved.

MIT License:

Permission is hereby granted, free of charge, to any person obtaining a copy of this software and associated documentation files (the "Software"), to deal in the Software without restriction, including without limitation the rights to use, copy, modify, merge, publish, distribute, sublicense, and/or sell copies of the Software, and to permit persons to whom the Software is furnished to do so, subject to the following conditions:

The above copyright notice and this permission notice shall be included in all copies or substantial portions of the Software.

THE SOFTWARE IS PROVIDED ""AS IS"", WITHOUT WARRANTY OF ANY KIND, EXPRESS OR IMPLIED, INCLUDING BUT NOT LIMITED TO THE WARRANTIES OF MERCHANTABILITY, FITNESS FOR A PARTICULAR PURPOSE AND NONINFRINGEMENT. IN NO EVENT SHALL THE AUTHORS OR COPYRIGHT HOLDERS BE LIABLE FOR ANY CLAIM, DAMAGES OR OTHER LIABILITY, WHETHER IN AN ACTION OF CONTRACT, TORT OR OTHERWISE, ARISING FROM, OUT OF OR IN CONNECTION WITH THE SOFTWARE OR THE USE OR OTHER DEALINGS IN THE SOFTWARE.

OpenCvSharp3

This license has also been called the **New BSD License** or **Modified BSD License**. See also the **2-clause BSD License**.

Redistribution and use in source and binary forms, with or without modification, are permitted provided that the following conditions are met:

1. Redistributions of source code must retain the above copyright notice, this list of conditions and the following disclaimer.

2. Redistributions in binary form must reproduce the above copyright notice, this list of conditions and the following disclaimer in the documentation and/or other materials provided with the distribution.

3. Neither the name of the copyright holder nor the names of its contributors may be used to endorse or promote products derived from this software without specific prior written permission.

THIS SOFTWARE IS PROVIDED BY THE COPYRIGHT HOLDERS AND CONTRIBUTORS "AS IS" AND ANY EXPRESS OR IMPLIED WARRANTIES, INCLUDING, BUT NOT LIMITED TO, THE IMPLIED WARRANTIES OF MERCHANTABILITY AND FITNESS FOR A PARTICULAR PURPOSE ARE DISCLAIMED. IN NO EVENT SHALL THE COPYRIGHT HOLDER OR CONTRIBUTORS BE LIABLE FOR ANY DIRECT, INDIRECT, INCIDENTAL, SPECIAL, EXEMPLARY, OR CONSEQUENTIAL DAMAGES (INCLUDING, BUT NOT LIMITED TO, PROCUREMENT OF SUBSTITUTE GOODS OR SERVICES; LOSS OF USE, DATA, OR PROFITS; OR BUSINESS INTERRUPTION) HOWEVER CAUSED AND ON ANY THEORY OF LIABILITY, WHETHER IN CONTRACT, STRICT LIABILITY, OR TORT (INCLUDING NEGLIGENCE OR OTHERWISE) ARISING IN ANY WAY OUT OF THE USE OF THIS SOFTWARE, EVEN IF ADVISED OF THE POSSIBILITY OF SUCH DAMAGE.

Newtonsoft.Json

The MIT License (MIT)

Copyright (c) 2007 James Newton-King

Permission is hereby granted, free of charge, to any person obtaining a copy of this software and associated documentation files (the "Software"), to deal in the Software without restriction, including without limitation the rights to use, copy, modify, merge, publish, distribute, sublicense, and/or sell copies of the Software, and to permit persons to whom the Software is furnished to do so, subject to the following conditions:

The above copyright notice and this permission notice shall be included in all copies or substantial portions of the Software.

THE SOFTWARE IS PROVIDED "AS IS", WITHOUT WARRANTY OF ANY KIND, EXPRESS OR IMPLIED, INCLUDING BUT NOT LIMITED TO THE WARRANTIES OF MERCHANTABILITY, FITNESS FOR A PARTICULAR PURPOSE AND NONINFRINGEMENT. IN NO EVENT SHALL THE AUTHORS OR COPYRIGHT HOLDERS BE LIABLE FOR ANY CLAIM, DAMAGES OR OTHER LIABILITY, WHETHER IN AN ACTION OF CONTRACT, TORT OR OTHERWISE, ARISING FROM, OUT OF OR IN CONNECTION WITH THE SOFTWARE OR THE USE OR OTHER DEALINGS IN THE SOFTWARE.

NAudio

Microsoft Public License (Ms-PL)

This license governs use of the accompanying software. If you use the software, you accept this license. If you do not accept the license, do not use the software.

Definitions

The terms **reproduce, reproduction, derivative works**, and **distribution** have the same meaning here as under U.S. copyright law.

A *contribution* is the original software, or any additions or changes to the software.

A *contributor* is any person that distributes its contribution under this license.

Licensed patents are a contributor's patent claims that read directly on its contribution.

Grant of Rights

(A) Copyright Grant - Subject to the terms of this license, including the license conditions and limitations in section 3, each contributor grants you a non-exclusive, worldwide, royalty-free copyright license to reproduce its contribution, prepare derivative works of its contribution, and distribute its contribution or any derivative works that you create.

(B) Patent Grant - Subject to the terms of this license, including the license conditions and limitations in section 3, each contributor grants you a non-exclusive, worldwide, royalty-free license under its licensed patents to make, have made, use, sell, offer for sale, import, and/or otherwise dispose of its contribution in the software or derivative works of the contribution in the software.

Conditions and Limitations

(A) **No Trademark License**: This license does not grant you rights to use any contributor's name, logo, or trademarks.

(B) If you bring a patent claim against any contributor over patents that you claim are infringed by the software, your patent license from such contributor to the software ends automatically.

(C) If you distribute any portion of the software, you must retain all copyright, patent, trademark, and attribution notices that are present in the software.

(D) If you distribute any portion of the software in source code form, you may do so only under this license by including a complete copy of this license with your distribution. If you distribute any portion of the software in compiled or object code form, you may only do so under a license that complies with this license.

(E) The software is licensed **as-is**. You bear the risk of using it. The contributors give no express warranties, guarantees or conditions. You may have additional consumer rights under your local laws which this license cannot change. To the extent permitted under your local laws, the contributors exclude the implied warranties of merchantability, fitness for a particular purpose and non-infringement.

Another Book You May Enjoy

If you enjoyed this book, you may be interested in another book by Packt:

Learning Azure Cosmos DB

Shahid Shaikh

ISBN: 978-1-78847-617-1

- ▶ Build highly responsive and mission-critical applications
- ▶ Understand how distributed databases are important for global scale and low latency
- ▶ Understand how to write globally distributed applications the right way
- ▶ Implement comprehensive SLAs for throughput, latency, consistency, and availability
- ▶ Implement multiple data models and popular APIs for accessing and querying data
- ▶ Implement best practices covering data security in order to detect, prevent and respond to database breaches

Azure for Architects

Ritesh Modi

ISBN: 978-1-78839-739-1

- ▸ Familiarize yourself with the components of the Azure Cloud platform
- ▸ Understand the cloud design patterns
- ▸ Use enterprise security guidelines for your Azure deployment
- ▸ Design and implement Serverless solutions
- ▸ See Cloud architecture and the deployment pipeline
- ▸ Understand cost management for Azure solutions

Leave a review – let other readers know what you think

Please share your thoughts on this book with others by leaving a review on the site that you bought it from. If you purchased the book from Amazon, please leave us an honest review on this book's Amazon page. This is vital so that other potential readers can see and use your unbiased opinion to make purchasing decisions, we can understand what our customers think about our products, and our authors can see your feedback on the title that they have worked with Packt to create. It will only take a few minutes of your time, but is valuable to other potential customers, our authors, and Packt. Thank you!

Index

image moderation API
about 86
using 86
images
searching 244-250
searching, with common user interface 245
image thumbnails
generating 51, 52
index
building 219
intents
about 108
creating 264, 265
used, for recognizing user wants 108, 109
items
recommending, based on prior
activities 200
Item-to-Item Recommendations (I2I) 186

K

KES installer
download link 218
knowledge APIs
about 22
knowledge exploration API 22, 23
Project Academic Knowledge API 22
Project Custom Decision Service 23
QnA Maker 23
recommendations solution API 23
knowledge base
creating, from frequently asked
questions 226, 227
model, publishing 230
model, training 228, 229
knowledge exploration API 22
Knowledge Exploration Service (KES)
backend, creating for academic API 218
deploying, to Microsoft Azure 224

L

language domain, APIs
about 21
Bing Spell Check API 21
LUIS API 21
text analytics API 22
translator text API 22

languages
detecting 181
supported languages, obtaining 182-184
working with 181
Language Understanding Intelligent
Service (LUIS)
about 20, 21, 103,
prebuilt entities 277
reference 104
URL, for prebuilt entities 277
language-understanding models
application, creating 104, 105
connecting, to smart house
application 116-120
creating 103
development, simplifying
with prebuilt models 109
intents, using 108, 109
key data, recognizing with entities 105-108
prebuilt domains, using 111, 112
publishing 113-116
training 113-116
language-understanding models,
improvement
active learning 124, 125
performance problems, resolving 122
performance, visualizing 121, 122
through active usage 121
language-understanding models,
performance problems
incorrect utterance labels, searching 123
labeled utterances, adding 123
model features, adding 123
resolving 122
schema, modifying 123
Licensed patents 281
list entity 107
List manager API 89
local hosting 221, 222

M

Microsoft Academic Graph (MAG) 204
Microsoft Azure
Knowledge Exploration Service (KES),
deploying to 224

review tool
about 87
URL 87
using 87, 88

S

Search APIs
Bing Autosuggest 24
Bing Custom Search API 25
Bing Entity Search 25
Bing Image Search API 24
Bing News Search 24
Bing Video Search 24
Bing Visual Search API 25
Bing Web Search 24
search commonalities
about 255
errors 258
filters 257
languages 256
pagination 256
service
testing 221, 222
shimat 78
smart-house application
actions, executing from intents 265, 266
additional functionality 74
code, updating 265
completing 263
creating 66
emotions, recognizing from images 78
faces, associating with person 72
identification, adding 66
intent, creating 264
language-understanding models,
    connecting to 116-120
mood identifying, from image 81-85
new persons, adding 70
news images, describing 270
news, searching on command 267-269
people to be identified, adding 66
person groups, adding 68, 69
person group, training 72, 73
person, identifying 74-76

used, for searching web 233
view, creating 66-68
Speaker Recognition API
about 21
reference 139
using 139-141
speakers
identifying 139-141, 149-152
profiles, adding 141-146
profiles, enrolling 146-149
Speech APIs
about 20
Bing Speech API 20
speaker recognition API 21
translator speech API 21
speech recognition
custom acoustic model, creating 159
customizing 159
custom language model, creating 160
Speech Synthesis Markup Language
    (SSML) template 29
spelling errors
correcting 168-171
supported languages
reference 161

T

text
script, converting 180
translating 179, 180
text analytics API 22
text moderation API 86
text to audio conversion 127, 128
textual analysis API
information, extracting through 172
key phrases, extracting from text 175-177
language, detecting 173-175
negative text, detecting 177, 178
positive text, detecting 177, 178
Translator Speech API
about 21
reference 161
using 161
translator text API 22
trending news 244

CPSIA information can be obtained
at www.ICGtesting.com
Printed in the USA
LVHW102350010519
616359LV00003B/85/P

9 781789 800616